WITHDRAWN

A HISTORY OF THE WHALE FISHERIES

THE SPITZBERGEN FISHERY (DE JONG, 1791).

A HISTORY OF THE WHALE FISHERIES

FROM THE BASQUE FISHERIES OF THE TENTH CENTURY TO THE HUNTING OF THE FINNER WHALE AT THE PRESENT DATE

BY

J. T. JENKINS, D.Sc., Ph.D.

WITH REPRODUCTIONS FROM PHOTOGRAPHS, AND OLD ENGRAVINGS

KENNIKAT PRESS
Port Washington, N. Y./London

A HISTORY OF THE WHALE FISHERIES

First published in 1921
Reissued in 1971 by Kennikat Press
Library of Congress Catalog Card No: 72-115321
ISBN 0-8046-1112-2

Manufactured by Taylor Publishing Company   Dallas, Texas

PREFACE

It is difficult to give within brief compass a detailed history of the whale fisheries, and hitherto no attempt has been made to do so in the English language. Since whaling falls into four or five well-defined, and more or less independent, phases it is possible to give a brief, and, allowing for the disconnection of the periods, consecutive account of the main aspects of this important fishery.

There is no authoritative account of British whaling which can be compared with Müller's " Geschiednis der Noordsche Compagnie " for the Dutch fishery; Brinner's " Die deutsche Grönlandfahrt " for the German whalers, or Tower's " History of the American Whale Fishery "; each of which gives a fairly complete account of special periods of whaling. It is to be hoped that further research may be directed to certain aspects of whaling which have hitherto received inadequate attention. There is material for several theses which might reasonably be proposed for research degrees by postgraduate students at our Universities. Further references to the subject are given under the heading " Bibliography " (p. 315).

Necessarily some of the subject-matter is only of interest to the specialist, but whaling is so unique in many respects—in the romance of the life of the whalers, and in the natural history of one of the most remarkable groups of living creatures—that even detailed studies of the subject are not without interest.

The romance of the whalers' life can only be realised by a perusal of the original writings of the whalers. In this book the main facts of the progress of the whaling trade have been marshalled. In many, if not in most cases, these facts speak for themselves. If within the next few decades whaling is not become entirely extinct, owing to the practical disappearance from the seas of the globe of the animals whose presence is necessary to its continued existence, it is imperative that further steps should be taken to regulate the industry by international action. Otherwise a most interesting group of marine animals will be hunted to the verge of extinction, and a great natural asset rendered worthless to enrich a small group of speculators and capitalists. This book has been written in the hope that, before it is too late, steps will be taken to control this ruthless destruction.

J. T. J.

CONTENTS

	PAGE
PREFACE	5

CHAPTER I

WHALES AND THEIR CLASSIFICATION

The migrations of whales—The Greenland Right Whale—The Biscayan Whale or Nordcaper—The Californian Grey Whale—The Humpback—The Finners . . . 11

CHAPTER II

THE ECONOMICS OF WHALING

The regulations for the protection of whales 39

CHAPTER III

THE EARLY HISTORY OF WHALING (TO 1623)

The Basque whalers—The discovery of " Greenland " (Spitsbergen)—The first British whalers—The Spitsbergen fishery—The whales found there—The disputes between the English and the Dutch—Edge's description of the fishery 59

CHAPTER IV

THE DUTCH WHALERS PREDOMINANT (1623-1750)

The methods of the Dutch whalers at Spitsbergen—Smeerenburg—The French at Spitsbergen—The English Muscovy Company—Anderson and Gray's description of the fishery—The German whalers—The pre-eminence of the Dutch 119

CONTENTS

CHAPTER V

THE BOUNTY SYSTEM

The whalers apply for State assistance—The South Sea Company and the Whale Fisheries—Development of the British whaling industry as a result of the bounty stimulus—Description of Arctic whaling voyages . . 177

CHAPTER VI

THE SOUTHERN FISHERY

The capture of the Sperm Whale—Commencement of a southern fishery—The voyages of Colnett, Beale, and Bennett 207

CHAPTER VII

THE AMERICAN WHALE FISHERIES

Importance of whales to the early colonists—Gradual extension of the fishery—Firmly established in 1775—Setback caused by the Revolution—Gradual recovery—Checked again by the war of 1812—Subsequent rapid expansion—Mid-nineteenth century American whaling fleet the largest ever known—Gradual decline of the industry, and the reasons for it 223

CHAPTER VIII

THE LAST PHASE OF WHALING

The introduction of steam—The harpoon gun and the capture of Rorquals—The disappearance of the old right whalers—The Norwegian whalers—Gradual extension of their operations—The Scottish and Irish whaling stations—Antarctic whaling 256

APPENDICES 301

BIBLIOGRAPHY 315

INDEX 333

LIST OF ILLUSTRATIONS

	PAGE
THE SPITSBERGEN FISHERY (DE JONG, 1791) *Frontispiece*	
EDGE'S MAP OF "GREENLAND" (SPITSBERGEN) *Facing*	58
EDGE'S DESCRIPTION OF THE SPITSBERGEN FISHERY. I. . . . . . . „	64
EDGE'S DESCRIPTION OF THE SPITSBERGEN FISHERY. II. . . . . . . „	80
EARLY TYPE OF DUTCH WHALER, WITH WHALING IMPLEMENTS (VAN OELEN) . . . „	128
THE NORTHERN FISHERY, SECOND PHASE, THE ICE FISHERY (ZORGDRAGER) . . . „	160
THE AMERICAN WHALER. A SHIP ON THE NORTH-WEST COAST CUTTING-IN HER LAST RIGHT WHALE . . . . . „	224
THE "ARCTIC" WITH BOATS FAST TO A FISH (1875) . . . . „	256
PLANS OF A WHALING STEAMER OF MODERN TYPE . . . . „	264
MODERN WHALING GUN, LOADED WITH HARPOON, AND READY TO FIRE . . „	272
MODERN WHALING STEAMER. IN THE FOREGROUND TWO FINNER WHALES ARE BEING TOWED TO THE FACTORY SLIP . . . „	280
MODERN WHALING—THE CHASE . . . „	288

A HISTORY OF THE WHALE FISHERIES

CHAPTER I

WHALES AND THEIR CLASSIFICATION

The migrations of whales—The Greenland Right Whale—The Biscayan Whale or Nordcaper—The Californian Grey Whale—The Humpback—The Finners.

" WHALES are in many respects the most interesting and wonderful of all creatures; there is much in their structure and habits well worthy of study, much that is difficult to understand, and much that leads to great generalisations and throws light upon far-reaching philosophical speculations."

It is not proposed to enter into the anatomy or classification of the order Cetacea; to which whales, porpoises and dolphins belong; save in so far as such knowledge is required to understand the probable effects of whaling on the future existence of many species of this order of animals. A brief account, suitable for the general reader, may be obtained from such a work as " An introduction to the study of Mammals " by Flower and Lydekker, from which the above quotation is taken. But since zoological knowledge is not so generally distributed as zoological specialists imagine, it may be well, even at the risk of being thought platitudinous, to recapitulate some of the leading characteristics of the order Cetacea.

Whales, porpoises and dolphins are mammals or, in the popular acceptation of the term, animals and not fish, that is to say they belong to that class of the animal kingdom which is characterised (among other things) by being warm-blooded, by having a prolonged organic connection between the mother and the unborn young, by the suckling of the young after birth, by the possession of hair and by a high brain development.

Among mammals, whales are further distinguished by their fish-like body, the absence of a distinct neck, by the reduction of the fore-limbs to the form of paddles or flukes, by the absence of externally visible hind limbs, by the presence of a thick layer of fat (blubber) immediately beneath the skin serving to retain the heat of the body, by the opening of the nostrils near the vertex of the head instead of at the tip of the snout. In nearly all Cetacea there is a median dorsal tegumentary fin. The eyes are small and there is no external ear. The bones are spongy, the cavities filled with oil. The brain-case is nearly spherical; teeth are generally present, but in one group in the fœtal condition only.

The larynx is of peculiar shape, being elongated

WHALES AND THEIR CLASSIFICATION 13

to meet the posterior nares, forming a continuous canal down which air passes from nostrils to lungs. Cetaceans must rise to the surface to breathe, but the expiration occurs at longer intervals than in land mammals.

The water vapour expelled along with the air from the lungs condenses into the cloud visible when the whale " spouts " or " blows," which is nothing more than the ordinary act of respiration.

The testes are abdominal and there are no seminal vesicles. The *mammæ* are two in number, the nipples being placed in depressions on each side of the vulva. The principal ducts of the mammary gland are, during the period of lactation, much dilated, forming large reservoirs in which the milk collects. From these reservoirs it is ejected by the action of a compressor muscle into the mouth of the young, and by this means the process of suckling in and under water is facilitated.

Usually one young is born at a time, rarely two and never more than two.

The sexes are easily distinguished. Details of the reproductive organs and " pairing " have been published for porpoises by Meek.[1] Off the east coast of England porpoises pair in July and August, and they are frequently taken at this time by the salmon net fishermen of Cullercoats. The summer inshore migration of these creatures is doubtless for the birth of the young and pairing.

[1] " The Reproductive Organs of Cetacea," by A. Meek, *Journal of Anatomy*, Vol. lii., p. 186.

The period of gestation is not known with any certainty, but is generally supposed to be from ten months to over a year.

For the common Fin-whale (*Balænoptera musculus*, L.) it is supposed to be about eleven months; for the Blue Whale (*B. sibbaldi*, Gray) from eighteen to twenty months.

Cetacea are generally gregarious, swimming in "schools," formerly many thousands being met together. They are timid, inoffensive animals, affectionate in their disposition, especially the mother towards the young.

All are predaceous, living on animal food. One form alone, the Killer Whale or Grampus (*Orca gladiator*), eats other warm-blooded forms, such as seals. Some feed on fish, such as herring, others on the plankton or drifting organisms of the surface layers of sea water, such as small crustacea, while still others live on deep-sea cephalopods. In size there is great variation, some of the smaller dolphins scarcely exceeding four feet in length. The question of size has an important bearing on the future of the species, since whalers in the waters of the British Islands find it does not pay to kill Cetacea under forty feet in length.

Cetacea formerly abounded in all known seas, some species being also found in the larger rivers of South America and Asia.

Considerable information as to the species found in British seas and their relative abundance has recently been obtained from the Annual Reports of

WHALES AND THEIR CLASSIFICATION 15

the whaling stations in Scotland and Ireland and from a return of stranded Cetacea published annually by the British Museum.[1]

The Cetacea are divided into two sub-orders: the Mystacoceti the Whalebone or True Whales; and the Odontoceti the Toothed Whales. (We are not concerned with extinct forms).

The Mystacoceti are distinguished by the absence of teeth, the presence of baleen or " whalebone," the form and size of the mouth, a symmetrical skull, a distinctly developed olfactory organ, and other pecularities which may be ascertained in any work on comparative anatomy. The essential characteristic is that the palate carries two longitudinal series of transverse horny plates, with their free edges frayed out into a hair-like fringe, forming a uniform mat-like surface during life.

Lydekker enumerates five genera and nine species of Whalebone Whales, and of these seven species are (or were) sufficiently abundant to be the objects of commercial exploitation.

For practical purposes *Neobalæna marginata*, a small whale of Australian and New Zealand waters, and *Rhachianectes glaucus*, the Grey Whale of the North Pacific, may be ignored, the former from its small size (under twenty feet), the latter from its rarity.[2]

[1] British Museum (Natural History), " Report on Cetacea stranded on the British Coasts," by S. F. Harmer. Seven parts issued up to 1921, i.e., for years 1914-20.
[2] But see " Present Condition of the Californian Grey Whale Fishery," by C. H. Townsend, *U.S. Fish. Comm. Bull.*, Vol. vi., for 1886-87. (See also p. 253.)

The three remaining genera, the Right Whales (*Balæna*), the Humpback Whales (*Megaptera*) and the Rorquals or Finners (*Balænoptera*) are all pursued by commercial whalers. Some representatives of all three genera are found in waters surrounding the British Isles, the Finners or Rorquals being the commonest.

Lydekker recognises two species of Right Whale, the Greenland or Arctic Right Whale (*Balæna mysticetus*) and the Southern Right Whale (*Balæna australis*). The Southern Right Whale is subdivided into so-called species or varieties according to their geographical distribution, e.g., the *B. biscayensis* of the North Atlantic, *B. japonica* of the North Pacific, *B. australis* of the South Atlantic, and *B. antipodarum* and *B. novæ-zealandiæ* of the South Pacific.

The variety known to the whalers as the Nordcaper (*B. biscayensis*) is the only Right Whale taken in the seas off the British Islands. It is by no means uncommon off the Hebrides, twenty being taken there in 1908, twenty-one in 1909, and five in 1910. In this year the Nordcaper was taken for the first time on the Shetland grounds, four specimens being captured. In 1911 there were no Right Whales taken anywhere in Scottish waters, eleven in 1912, one in 1913, and five in 1914. There was no whaling in the five following years on account of the war.

The species of Balæna or Right Whale are most readily distinguished from the other whales by their

WHALES AND THEIR CLASSIFICATION 17

smooth throat and the absence of a dorsal fin. In the Humpback and Finners or Rorquals the skin of the throat is plicated. The Right Whales were probably the first to be the subject of chase by man, and the Atlantic Right Whale (*B. biscayensis*) was pursued by Basque fishermen from the earliest times of which we have any record of whaling (from the tenth to the sixteenth centuries).

The Greenland or Arctic Right Whale is probably the same species as the " Bowhead " of the Okhotsk Sea and Behring Strait, and is therefore circumpolar in range. It attains a length of from forty-five to fifty feet, and although a truly ice whale, has for centuries been the object of an extensive fishery. It has never been reported in the waters off the British Islands.

The Southern Right Whale, which is distinguished from the former species by possessing a smaller head in proportion to its body, had also been extensively hunted by whalemen. If we admit, with Lydekker, that all the varieties are really only one species, then it is seen that this whale is very widely distributed in the temperate seas of both northern and southern hemispheres.

The Humpback (*Megaptera boops*), which grows to about fifty feet, resembles the Rorquals in having throat-grooves and a dorsal fin, but differs in its very long flipper (pectoral fins), from ten to fourteen feet in length, having the outer surface white and the front edge scalloped. The whalebone is black.

This species is relatively abundant in British seas, fifty-nine being captured in Scottish waters in the eleven years 1904-14. In 1863 a young female humpbacked whale was stranded on a sandbank in the Mersey opposite Speke (not in the Dee, as stated by Lydekker). This species probably derives its name from the low hump-like character of the dorsal fin.

The Rorquals, Fin-whales, Fin-backs, Finners or Razorbacks are species of the genus Balænoptera. They form the mainstay of the whale fisheries in British waters, where four species occur.

Rorquals are of extremely wide distribution, being found in all seas except in extreme Arctic and Antarctic regions. The name Rorqual is derived from the Norse Rorq-val, signifying a whale with pleats or folds in the skin. Compared with the Humpback, the Rorquals are long and slender, the furrows of the throat are more numerous and closer set, the pectoral fin is comparatively small, and the tail much compressed before it is expanded into flukes.

Owing to their great activity these whales were not much pursued until the introduction of the small modern steam whalers with gun and explosive harpoon.

Of the four British species the smaller or lesser Fin-whale or Rorqual (*Balænoptera rostrata*) rarely exceeds thirty feet, and is exempt on that account from the attention of the whalers.

Of the other three, the Blue Whale (Sibbald's

WHALES AND THEIR CLASSIFICATION

Whale—*Balænoptera sibbaldi*) is the largest of all living creatures. It attains a length of eighty or even eighty-five feet. It spends, like the other species of the Rorqual, the winter in the open sea, approaching the land at the end of April or beginning of May.

The Common Rorqual or Finner (*Balænoptera musculus*) grows to seventy feet, and is the commonest of all the large whales on the British coasts. It feeds on fish, and is frequently seen among the herring shoals.

Rudolphi's Rorqual or the Sei Whale (*Balænoptera borealis*) is a smaller edition to the common Finner, attaining a length of from thirty-eight to fifty feet. Until recently it was considered the rarest of European whales, but in 1906 no less than three hundred and twenty-six specimens of this species were taken by the whalers in Scottish waters.

Hundreds of Rorquals are annually captured in British waters (see Appendix V), and every year specimens are stranded on our coasts.

The sub-order of the Odontoceti comprises the toothed whales, in which calcified teeth are always present after birth. These teeth are generally numerous, though in some cases only a few are present. There is no baleen or whale "bone." The upper surface of the skull is more or less asymmetrical. The olfactory organ is rudimentary or absent. For details of the anatomical differences between this and the preceding sub-order of the Mystacoceti a textbook on Comparative Anatomy, such as Flower and Lyddeker, should be consulted.

The Odontoceti are represented by three living and one extinct families, of these one family only, the Sperm Whale (*Physeteridæ*), is of any considerable economic importance.

Two Physeterids have been the object of a considerable fishery, the Sperm Whale or Cachalot (*Physeter macrocephalus*) and the Bottlenose (*Hyperoodon rostratus*).

The Sperm Whale is one of the largest of animals equalling, if not exceeding, in bulk the Greenland Right Whale, which it further resembles in having been from the early days of whaling the object of an important fishery. The Sperm Whale is very widely distributed, being found (until it became scarcer through over-fishing) in " schools " in all tropical and sub-tropical seas, but only accidentally in arctic or sub-arctic water. Occasionally stragglers appear in the waters of the British Islands, and are caught by the commercial whalers working these waters, or even washed ashore. In the ten years 1904-13 no less than sixty-six Sperm Whales were captured by the whalers in Scottish waters; in Irish waters in the years 1909-13 the number was forty-four. On 23rd May, 1917, a Sperm Whale was stranded at Latheron, Caithness.

Details of the Sperm Whale fishery are given below. The so-called " Southern " fishery of the British, the Pacific fisheries of British and American whalers were mainly for this species. Although not extinct, this species has been so much hunted and harassed that it no longer serves as the sole object

WHALES AND THEIR CLASSIFICATION

of a fishery, though, as already stated, it is still not infrequently captured with other species, even in the waters surrounding the British Isles.

Of the other Physeterids the only one of economic importance is the " Bottlenose " (*Hyperoodon rostratus*), a regular inhabitant of the North Atlantic, where it passes the summer in Spitsbergen waters, going farther south in winter. Captain Gray[1] says: " These whales are occasionally met with immediately after leaving the Shetlands in March and north across the ocean till the ice is reached." They are met with from the entrance to Hudson Strait and up Davis Strait as far as 70° N., and down the east side round Cape Farewell, all round Iceland, north along the Greenland Ice to 77° N., also along the west coast of Spitsbergen, and east to Bear Island. In the period 1905-13 twenty-four Bottlenose Whales were captured in Scottish waters.

The second family of Odontoceti, the Platanistidæ, are small Cetacea, inhabiting the rivers and estuaries of certain rivers in the tropics. They are of no commercial importance.

The third and last family, the Delphinidæ, comprise the porpoises and dolphins of our waters as well as the Narwhal of Arctic seas. None of the members of this family is the object of a regular fishery, except the Pilot Whale, Ca'ing Whale or Grindhval of the Faroes and the Shetlands, which at times is the object of a regular fiord fishery well described by Müller.[2]

[1] Proceedings Zoological Society, 1882.
[2] " Whale Fishing in the Faroe Isles," by Sysselmand H. C.

This statement is, however, not strictly correct, since the White Whale or Beluga (*Delphinapterus leucas*) was fished for by the early English whalers at Spitsbergen, but not by the Dutch.[1]

It was described under the name of " Sewria " by Thomas Edge in 1609. The White Whales were captured in the bays by nets or driven ashore by the same means. In 1670 there is a record of a Greenland ship arriving in Yarmouth Roads with " about twenty-four tons of oil made from white-fish."[2] The Russian trappers, who frequented Spitsbergen in the nineteenth century, were provided with long nets which they used in such places as Cross Road and Green Harbour, for the capture of White Whales in the event of a school approaching their station in the open season of the year.[3]

In the first place, are whales to be considered as coastal or deep-sea animals? According to Vanhöffen[4] whales are generally seen in coastal or bank areas and rarely in the open ocean or deep sea; the reason being that they find more abundant food in the former localities. Recent information as to the distribution of plankton (the floating organisms which form the food of the Whalebone Whales) shows that it is found much more abundantly over the continental shelf and shallow banks than over

Müller, " Fish and Fisheries," Prize Essays, International Fisheries Exhibition, Edinburgh, 1883.
[1] Zorgdrager. *Bloyende Opkomst.*, 1st edition, p. 162.
[2] *State Papers, Domestic*, 1660-70, p. 433.
[3] Conway, " No Man's Land," p. 255.
[4] *Anat. Anz.*, Bd. xxii., 1899, p. 396.

deep water. This plankton, even when it does not serve as the direct food of certain species of whales, nevertheless forms the basis of the food supply of the cephalopods and fish on which these whales feed.

Guldberg[1] agrees with this theory provided that too narrow an interpretation is not placed on the word " coastal." Unquestionably the food problem is the one which mainly governs the movements of whales, and therefore they are most often met with in localities where such food is most abundant. The coastal areas and banks are naturally very extensive, and not susceptible of being closed (either partially or wholly) to whaling operations by the governments of the countries off whose shores they lie. For instance, the Kodiac ground in the Pacific Ocean is a very extensive area covering hundreds of square miles. There is, however, one whale which is unquestionably not to be regarded as coastal in its habitat, and that is the Cachalot or Sperm Whale. When a whale is found to live mainly or exclusively on a given species of plankton the distribution of the whale corresponds with the distribution of that species. The second factor in the distribution of the whale is reproduction. The female whale seeks out a quiet area for the birth of her young and for the first few months of its life. Pairing also, for the most part, takes place in quiet weather, although there are very few authentic observations of this. A third factor is the water temperature.

[1] *Biol. Centralblatt.*, xxiii. and xxiv., 1903-4.

One of the most important whales to the earliest northern whalers was the Polar or Greenland, or Right Whale, the Bowhead of the Americans (*Balæna mysticetus*). This whale appears to make regular seasonal migrations. In summer it is found in the farthest northern waters, e.g., in 75° to 78° N. Latitude in Baffin Bay. In winter it migrates farther south, being found as low as 65° N. Latitude on the east side of Greenland, or even in 58° N. on the west side. It frequents the water between the ice-floes where abundant Pteropoda (*Clio borealis*) and Entomostraca are met with. Although it is found in more open water in summer it never moves far from the ice.

In former times, as will be seen from the sequel (Chapter III) this whale was very abundant off Spitsbergen. According to Martens, it was found in spring in the west near Jan Mayen and Greenland, but in summer in open water east of Spitsbergen.

It is doubtful whether the Greenland Right Whale was found off the northern Norwegian coast in earlier historical times. At any rate the earliest whalers, who probably fished in these waters, distinguished between this whale and the "Nordcaper." The Greenland Right Whale is not found now in Scandinavian waters, though the balance of evidence is that it was so found in the seventeenth century, at any rate in severe winters.

A true migration of the Greenland Right Whale is mentioned by Brown (1875) who describes hundreds as moving together from Paul's Bay

WHALES AND THEIR CLASSIFICATION 25

(Baffin Land) to Lancaster Sound. Scammon gives the ground of the Bowhead, as the American whalers call this whale, in winter at 55° N. or in Okhotsk Sea 54° or 53° N. Latitude, while in summer it keeps to the edge of the ice.

Off Northern Asia, from Nova Zembla eastward, the Greenland Right Whale is not met with.

In the seventeenth, eighteenth, and nineteenth centuries, from 1611 onwards, there was a regular fishery in Arctic waters between Spitsbergen and Greenland for this whale, but it has now practically disappeared in these waters. This is unquestionably due to over "fishing" on the part of the whalers. First of all the bay fishery at Spitsbergen was exhausted (about 1623), then the open water between Spitsbergen and the ice off Greenland, then Davis Strait and Baffin Bay were in turn exploited. In 1896 the Scottish whaling fleet of nine ships obtained only eleven species of this whale. In 1901 six Scottish whaling steamers caught fourteen Greenland Whales. The history of the whale fisheries shows clearly that in the Arctic region between Northern America and Europe this species of whale has almost become extinct. In the American-Arctic regions this same whale (Bowhead) still holds its own to some extent, since whaling only commenced here two hundred years after the Spitsbergen fishery. Moreover, the whaling season north of Behring Strait is a much shorter one. There were then originally three chief areas in which this whale was found:

(1) The eastern—Spitsbergen-Greenland area.

(2) A western—Greenland - Arctic - North - American area.

(3) The American-Asiatic area. (Behring Sea.)

The first area has now been fished to death, the second has only a few whales still left, whereas in the third the whale holds its own fairly well. No census of this whale is possible; we have no accurate idea of its former abundance. The recovery of a species of whale of the dimensions of the Greenland Right Whale from the effects of over-fishing is extremely slow. The females carry the young for probably at least a year; then there is a period of helplessness and dependence on the mother during the time of suckling. Possibly the mother only bears one young every second year. There are many factors, most of which cannot be estimated, but on the whole the evidence is in favour of a very slow recovery.

The second important whale to the old whalers was the Nordcaper (*Balæna biscayensis*)[1] which formerly frequented the European and American coasts of the North Atlantic. This whale was probably hunted by the Biscayans in the eleventh and twelfth centuries, although their principal fishery seems to have been in the fifteenth and sixteenth centuries. The chase went more and more to the

[1] Or according to some authorities a variety of *Balæna australis*.

north as the whales became scarce and shy through excessive hunting, until ultimately the chief whaling grounds were off Iceland and the North Cape of Norway. The Biscayans, who called this whale " Sarda " (the Norwegian names were Nordcaper or Slettibakka) hunted it from October to February. In the summer it went farther north where it was, like the Greenland Right Whale, hunted by the Dutch and other early Spitsbergen whalers. In these waters it is now extremely rare. Stranded Nordcapers have been found in the Mediterranean at Taranto and Algiers. The Norwegian whaling records from 1884 to 1891 show that this whale is still found in summer in Icelandic waters. Its range is from the Azores and Bermudas in the south to Bear Island in the north. The whalers distinguished this species from the Polar or Greenland Right Whale as early as 1611, the latter being more valuable and also more easy to kill. The earliest American whalers caught the Nordcaper on the New England coasts in the early years of the seventeenth century. The season here lasted from early November to March or April.

Before America was colonised it is probable that occasional specimens of this whale were killed by the Indians. Certainly, the earliest colonists captured it off the coasts of New Hampshire, Massachusetts, Connecticut, and Rhode Island. The period of prosperity of this whaling ranged, in New England, from 1750 to 1784. The accidental discovery of a Sperm Whale off this coast and the developments it led to are described later (Chapter VII).

Probably there were two main groups of the Nordcaper (*B. biscayensis*); one on the American and the other on the European coasts of the North Atlantic. The European stock first became reduced. The history of nineteenth-century whaling shows that this whale, like its near relative, the Greenland Right Whale, has sadly diminished on its old feeding grounds. More recently it appears to have increased in numbers. It is certainly of migratory habits, being found in winter to the south, and in summer to the north.

In the northern half of the Pacific is found the Japan Whale or the Right Whale of the north-west coast, but whether this is a variety of the Nordcaper or is identical with the Southern Right Whale (*Balæna australis*) is doubtful. This whale ranges from the Aleutian Islands in the north to the coasts of Japan and Oregon. The Japanese and the American Pacific whalers both hunted this species. In Scammon's time (1874) it was very abundant off the Pacific coast of the United States. Its chief habitat was the celebrated " Kodiac Ground " from Vancouver Island north-west to the Aleutian chain, and from the west coast to 150° W. Longitude. There were large shoals also in the southern part of Behring Sea, off the coast of Kamschatka and in the Sea of Okhotsk.

Off the American north-west coast this whale was hunted by the American whalers in summer from

April to September inclusive; in spring from February to April south of 29° N. Latitude in the Bay of St Sebastian Viscaino and round the Cerres Islands.

The Southern Right Whale (*Balæna australis*) is regarded by some cetologists as the same species as the Nordcaper and the Japan Whale. A century and a half ago the southern waters were full of these whales. The American whalers alone caught 193,522 whales of this species in southern waters from 1804 to 1817. In spite of the fact that millions of dollars were made and thousands of whales killed, we have not sufficient information for a correct zoological differentiation of this species. This whale is also migratory, leaving and seeking colder and warmer water according to the season. It is, on the whole, a whale of temperate seas and possibly not found to any extent in Antarctic waters,[1] although other species are at present found there in great abundance, where they are the object of incessant slaughter by the Norwegian whalers; the last phase in the History of Whaling.

The California Grey Whale (*Rhachianectes glaucus*) is an inhabitant of the Pacific coasts of the North American continent. From November to May it is found off the coast of California, where the female enters the lagoons to give birth to the young, the male remaining outside off the coast. Later the male enters the lagoons (at the end of winter) and then the male, female, and young are seen migrating

---

[1] Racowitza. *Expedition Antarctique Belge*, 1903.

to the northward, swimming close inshore. The California Grey Whale is a true coastal species.

In the summer it frequents Behring Sea and Okhotsk Sea. In autumn it is again noticed, from October to November, off the coast of Oregon. It does not appear to migrate below 20° N. Latitude. This whale is also known to the Japanese under the name " Kokujira." It was also hunted by the Indians, on its migration, in the Straits of Fuca (Vancouver), and near Charlotte Island.

The Nordcaper and California Grey Whale are essentially plankton feeders.

According to Andrews[1] the annual migration of the California Grey Whale occurs as regularly as the seasons. On both sides of the Pacific the migrations take place almost at the same time. Along the Korean coast near the end of November single pregnant females appear, travelling steadily southwards; a little later both males and females are seen, finally males bring up the rear, all having passed by 25th January.

During the latter part of the nineteenth century the hunting of the whale by small steamers specially built to carry a harpoon gun, has led to an enormous destruction of Finner Whales or Rorquals (*Balænopteridæ*). Many thousands of these whales have been killed by the harpoon gun (see p. 272).

Of the Balænopteridæ the Humpback (*Megaptera boops*) is one of the most important. It was known

[1] " Whale hunting with gun and Camera," New York, 1916.

to the old Norwegians as " Skeljungr." It is of wide distribution, being found in the southern and northern parts of the Atlantic Ocean, in the Indian and Pacific Oceans, in the latter as far north as Behring Strait. Probably there is only one species of Humpback, though at different times several species have been described by cetologists.

The Humpback is found in August and September in high northerly latitudes. In November it migrates to the south, and after the winter is over, north again. In February it is abundant off the Bermudas, leaving there in May for Greenland, Baffin Bay, and the Finmark coast (Norway).

At the end of the summer, it leaves northern waters again and seeks the African coast or the West Indies. The Humpback crosses the Equator off the Peruvian coast. According to Scammon, individual Humpbacks are recognised by the whalers; off Greenland the same individuals are met with from year to year, and they even have their nicknames.

Hjort has recently collected important information on the migration of the Humpback,[1] which in the North Atlantic feeds on either a small crustacean or a small fish (*Osmerus arcticus*), preferring the former. Hjort analysed the whalers' catches for 1896 and 1898, and found that the Humpback approaches the Norwegian coast at two different seasons of the year, firstly in February and March,

[1] *Fiskeri og Hvalfangst i det Nordlige Norge*, Bergen, 1902.

and secondly in June and July. The Humpback swims quietly and slowly in summer, but otherwise in winter when it moves to the westward with the speed of a steamer, and approaches the coast as nearly as possible. Many whalers believe that it rubs itself on the stones of the coast to free itself of parasites. Certain it is that the whole Varanger Fiord in the month of March simply bubbles or boils with these whales.

On the Finmark coast the Humpbacks are noticed to have their stomachs empty in the migration period. The females are pregnant, being near the birth period.

At the beginning of April they are found feeding on fish. Where they go when they leave the Norwegian coast is not certain, possibly to the African coast, or the Cape Verde Islands or the Azores.

The spring migration of the Humpback from the Norwegian coast is concerned with its reproduction. The female probably carries her young for eleven months. Whether pairing takes place soon after the birth of the young, as in the seals, is not known. The Bear Island whalers have observed the young suckling when twenty feet long. The larger young ones follow their mother even in the subsequent year when they leave the Finmark coast. Where the northern Humpback goes in the season from autumn to the following January or Febuary is not known, because the whaling season finishes in September. The Humpback is also found off the Greenland

WHALES AND THEIR CLASSIFICATION 33

coast in summer in Davis Strait and Baffin Bay from 62° to 76° N. Latitude, leaving the open water at the end of summer.

Recently whaling has been tried off the Newfoundland coast. In 1902 there were two whaling steamers working in these waters, and from the 1st January to the 19th April they caught five Humpbacks; but from the 20th April to the end of August, over one hundred. They were most abundant in May and June. They probably pass through these waters on their way north.

The Humpback appears to be distributed into groups or races in the different seas of the world, each group possibly frequenting a more or less limited but still somewhat extensive area. There are two such groups in the Atlantic, one in the north, the other in the south. There may be one (or two) groups in the Indian and several in the Pacific Oceans. Each group has its own migration paths. The North Atlantic group is found between the old and the new world from June to late autumn (or possibly to the following February or March) in high latitudes off the coasts of Greenland, Iceland, Jan Mayen, and northern Norway. In autumn they probably scatter in shoals looking for the best feeding-places. The females are still accompanied by their young. The best feeding-places are probably in the " Florida Current " or Gulf Stream, off the Norwegian coast. Both in November and in February the favourite food of the Humpback, the small crustacea *Boreophausia* and *Nycti-*

phanes norwegicus are still abundant in $67\frac{1}{2}°$ N. Latitude.

There are only very few records of the appearance of the Humpback in winter. In April and May they are also absent from the Northern Whaling grounds.

There are few records of the Humpback in the South Atlantic. In the North Pacific it is well known to the coastal inhabitants. The chief hunting grounds of the Indians were the Bays of Magdalena, Balena, and Monterey. The visits of the Humpbacks here are regular, in autumn they all leave for the south, and in summer they move northward.

In Antarctic regions the Humpback appears to be the commonest whale. There are two main groups apparently, the South American, and the South Australian.

The most recent account of the migrations of the Humpback is that given by Risting[1] and Olsen,[2] the former dealing with northern seas, the latter with the conditions off the east and west coasts of South Africa.

Risting concludes that the Humpback's migrations, both north and south of the Equator, are divisible into a feeding migration towards the Polar Seas and a breeding migration into warmer regions. These migrations are so regular that once the

---

[1] *Hvalfangsten i* 1912. Bergen, 1913.
[2] Orjan Olsen. See a report in *Naturen 3-die Hefte*, 1912. Bergen.

WHALES AND THEIR CLASSIFICATION 35

whalers have found a station from which the Humpback can be hunted its extermination is easier than that of any other species. The percentage of Humpbacks, to total whales captured in the Antarctic waters of the Falkland Dependencies, sank from 96·8 in 1910-11 to 2·5 in 1917-18.

On its breeding migration the Humpback moves with great speed, keeping at the same time close to the land. The migration westward of the Humpback along the Finmark coast, already referred to as taking place in February and March, is that of individuals coming from the east sea, where they must have spent the winter. At this time the females are nearly ready to give birth to their young. The second appearance off the Finmark coast is from June to August. In the meanwhile they have been observed off the coast of North-West Africa in April and May, where they are accompanied by the newly-born young. In their return journey they pass the whaling stations off the Faroes and Hebrides. Comparatively small numbers of this species are killed by the whalers in Scottish (Appendix V) and Irish (p. 281) waters. In autumn, when the water becomes colder, the Humpback migrates northward into the eastern parts of the northern sea, where it passes the winter, and here its food consists partly of herring.

A similar migration appears to take place on the American side of the Atlantic, where the Humpback is abundant in Greenland waters during summer and early autumn. At its inception, whaling in

Antarctic waters was almost entirely dependent on the Humpback. Here the plankton on which this whale feeds begins to become abundant in November, and this food is carried by the currents towards the coast of the great South Polar Island groups. The Humpback now puts in an appearance, being at first in poor condition, but as the summer advances it rapidly gets fatter, being at its best from February to April. With the approach of the southern winter the Humpback moves north into warmer waters where the young are born and pairing takes place. The females captured off South Georgia and the South Shetlands in summer are nearly all pregnant. In its northern migration the Humpback approaches the coasts of the continents where it is found from the middle of May, or even earlier, off South America and Africa. The migration lasts till the end of July, the Humpback even going north of the Equator.

The large proportion of Humpbacks captured by whalers off the Natal coast is referred to below (p. 295). Towards the end of August the southward migration along these coasts begins, and this lasts until November; the females now being accompanied by their young. Similar migration takes place in the Pacific on both sides of the Equator. Off the African coast the birth of the young Humpbacks takes place in the warm Mozambique current. According to Olsen, the first Humpbacks arrive at the breeding-places off Portuguese West and East Africa at the beginning of

June, the majority arriving in mid-July. The females and young are seen moving south off Angola as early as the end of August, and the majority have left the African coast by October. A similar migration of Humpbacks takes place between New Zealand and the adjacent waters of the Antarctic.

Here again the northward migration is for breeding purposes.

In the genus Balænoptera (Finner Whales) are found the largest living creatures.

In the North Atlantic waters four species are distinguished (see above, p. 18).

The Blue Whale (*Balænoptera sibbaldi*) is the largest of all living animals. It lives mainly on small pelagic crustacea (*Boreophausia*), and is a true plankton whale. It can devour one thousand litres of crustacea at a meal. Many thousands of this whale have been taken off the Norwegian coasts since 1865. The Blue Whale is of migratory habits. It appears in the north in spring, in many years appearing in the Varanger Fiord on 8th May.

It also appears off Iceland in spring, and off Newfoundland in February. Where it goes in winter is not known. The Blue Whale is also found on the Japan grounds.

The Sei Whale (*Balænoptera borealis*) is also a true plankton whale, and is found from Biarritz to the North Cape. The majority of the whales captured off the Faroes belong to this species. The common Finner (*Balænoptera musculus* or *physalus*) is distributed over the whole Atlantic Ocean. The lesser Finner (*B. rostrata*) has a very wide distribution. Both these whales are fish-eaters. The common Finner follows the shoals of herring and " lodde " (*Osmerus*), and approaches the coasts at the same time that they do.

Reference is made below (p. 56) to the legislation affecting the hunting of whales in Norwegian waters. According to Guldberg, this prohibition of hunting the whales in Norwegian waters can only damage the local whalers, without protecting the whales, since they all migrate over large areas.

What of the future of these whales? An extinction of the Finners is perhaps hardly possible, although the number of individuals of these species is unquestionably diminishing rapidly. In the case of the Right Whales and Sperm Whales it is already a thing of the past for vessels to fit out solely for their capture. Only by international regulation can the future of the whales and the continued prosperity of whaling itself be secured.

The migrations of the toothed whales, the Cachalot (Chapter VI) and the Bottlenose (p. 269) are dealt with elsewhere.

CHAPTER II

THE ECONOMICS OF WHALING

The regulations for the protection of whales.

ORIGINALLY whales were hunted for their oil. Their bodies are covered, immediately under the skin, with a layer of fat or blubber, which in a large specimen is from twelve to eighteen inches thick. In young whales this blubber resembles hog's lard, in old ones it is of a reddish colour. This was formerly considered to be the valuable part of the whale, but, as will be seen, very little of the whale's carcass is now wasted. The blubber yields by expression and boiling nearly its own weight of a thick viscid oil (train oil). The word train has nothing to do with railways, but is derived from the Dutch " Traan," a tear, i.e., a drop. The oil was originally used in the old-fashioned offensive " whale oil " lamps as an illuminant. Early in the nineteenth century it became gradually displaced by other illuminants.

A full account of the uses of whale oil is given by Scoresby (1820). Up to that date it was largely used in the lighting of the streets of towns, and the interior of places of worship, houses, shops and factories. It was extensively employed in the manufacture of soft soap and in the preparation of leather and coarse woollen cloths, in the manufacture of coarse varnishes and paints, and as a lubricant for machinery. A gas was manufactured from whale oil in 1816 or 1817, and in 1819 Ipswich, Norwich and other towns in England lighted their streets with gas made from oil.

The discovery of petroleum in America in 1859 decided the fate of whale oil as an illuminant.

Modern methods of extraction of oil and its uses are dealt with below.

A superior kind of oil was found in the head of the Sperm Whale.

In this whale the valuable part was the spongy mass dug from the cavity of the head.

Spermaceti may be defined as a neutral, inodorous and nearly tasteless fatty substance extracted from the oily matter of the head of the Sperm Whale by filtration and treatment with potash-ley. It is white, brittle, soft to the touch with a specific gravity of 0·943 at 15°, melts from 38° to 47°.

Spermaceti was formerly used in the manufacture of candles, being mixed with beeswax to prevent granulation. It is also used in the manufacture of unguents and ointments.

At one period in the history of whaling whalebone was the most important product of the fishery. "Whalebone" is a substance of horny nature adhering in thin parallel laminæ to the upper jaw

THE ECONOMICS OF WHALING

of certain species of whales. It acts as a strainer in the whale's mouth, detaining its food. Some three hundred of these plates are found in the mouth of an adult whale, their length being in the Greenland Whale from ten to twelve feet. They are very flexible, strong, elastic and light.

The value of the "bone" lies in the fact that when softened with hot water or by heating before a fire, it retains any given shape, provided it is secured in that shape until cold.

Whalebone at one time commanded a very high price, since it served as a base for the rigid stays and expanded hoops of our great-grandmothers. The Dutch have at times obtained seven hundred pounds a ton for it, and it is said their export trade to England for this one article alone reached the annual sum of a hundred thousand pounds. In 1763 its price was five hundred pounds per ton. In the early part of the nineteenth century its price varied from sixty to three hundred pounds, seldom falling to the lowest rate and rarely exceeding a hundred and fifty pounds. Scoresby estimated the price for the five years ending 1818 at ninety pounds per ton, but in July, 1830, it was quoted at a hundred and sixty to a hundred and eighty pounds per ton.

Towards the end of the nineteenth century the American fishery depended almost exclusively on whalebone.[1]

[1] "Whalebone—Its Production and Utilisation," by Charles H. Stevenson, *U.S.A. Bureau of Fisheries Document*, No. 626, Washington Government Printing Office, 1907.

Ambergris, another product of the whale fishery, is now regarded as a secretion from the intestines of the Sperm Whale, a result of disease. It may be defined as a light, inflammable, fatty substance, opaque in lustre, ashy in colour, with variegations like marble, and giving forth a pleasant odour when heated. It is now used exclusively in the preparation of perfumes, having the property of adding to the strength of other perfumes.

Ambergris is comparatively rare, and is worth more than its weight in gold.

In a modern factory very little of the whale's body is wasted. Burfield[1] has described the *modus operandi* at a modern whaling factory.

In July, 1920, the author visited the whaling station at Bunaveneader (Hebrides), and from personal observation from information kindly supplied by Mr Herlofson, the manager there, and from Burfield, the following summary is compiled.

The chief products now are: Oil, whalebone, meat (both food for human beings and cattle), manure, bonemeal, salted meat, and spermaceti; with two subsidiary products ambergris and sperm teeth. Oil is still the most important product. To extract it every part of the animal, except the whalebone and sperm teeth, is boiled for twenty-four hours. The whale is towed to the factory from the place where it was killed, and anchored to a buoy until the factory is ready for it. A large chain

[1] Belmullet Whaling Station. *Report of the Committee of the British Association*, Section D, Dundee, 1912.

THE ECONOMICS OF WHALING

is then attached round the tail connected to a steel warp, and the whale is slowly hauled up the flensing-slip by means of a steam winch. The animal is drawn up on its side or back; owing to the distension of the abdomen by the accumulation of gases the whale floats in this position. The flensing plane has to be strongly built, since a sixty foot whale weighs from seventy to eighty tons.

The first process is the stripping off the blubber "blanket." This is done by the blubber-flensers, whose work consists exclusively in stripping off the blubber and taking out the baleen. The blubber is cut through along the mid-dorsal and ventral lines, two cuts being also made on each side. There are thus three strips taken off each side of the whale. A chain fastened to a steel-wire rope is attached to the head end of each of these strips, the blubber being taken off from the head end towards the tail by the assistance of a steam winch, the flensers using their knives to ensure the blubber coming off without the meat.

The blubber is now cut up into manageable blocks by labourers. The blocks are further divided by a revolving circular knife; and are thus transferred into fairly small pieces into the boilers as soon as removed from the whale.

After the blubber is removed a "meat-flenser" cuts off the whale's head, which is chopped up separately. The carcass, from which the intestines have been removed, is also dealt with by the meat-flenser, who strips the meat from the bones, the whole of the meat being taken off in four strips, two on each side. Finally he cuts up the backbone, and the whole of the meat and bones in manageable pieces is raised by elevators and tipped into boilers.

The blubber-boilers are open, but the meat and bone boilers are closed, the pressure of the steam in the latter helping to extract the less abundant oil. The blubber is given three successive boilings, the average duration of each being eight hours.

After each boiling the contents settle, the oil being run off into vats. At the third boiling the boiler is closed at the top, the steam pressing the contents to ensure complete extraction of the oil. Ultimately all the fat disappears, a dark mud remaining. All the oil, blood and scraps which accumulate when the whale is being cut up, are gathered together and boiled, and at one factory in 1911 no less than two hundred barrels of No. 4 oil were obtained in this way, the value being about six hundred pounds.

The oils are classified according to quality:

1. Spermaceti (from head of Sperm Whale).
2. Sperm blubber oil.
3. No. 1 oil (from blubber of Fin-whales).
4. No. 2. oil (from second boiling of blubber of Fin-whales).
5. No. 3 oil (from meat and blubber in closed boiler).
6. No. 4 oil (from bones, scraps, and sperm meat).

Most of the oil is used for soap-making, but during the war it was sold to manufacturers of explosives for extraction of glycerine. The lower grades are chiefly used for the manufacture of lubricating greases.

THE ECONOMICS OF WHALING 45

A rough average of the yield of the four commoner species of whale captured at British stations is:

		Barrels.
1. Rudolphis Rorqual or Seihval (*Balænoptera borealis*)	.	10
2. Common Fin-whale (*B. musculus*)	.	15-70
3. Blue Whale (*B. sibbaldi*)	.	50-70
4. Sperm Whale (*Physeter macrocephalus*)	. .	65-80

The whalebone plates are separated, scrubbed, and soaked in warm soda solution, washed in warm water and dried in the open. When dry they are packed in sacks. The baleen from the Fin-whales gives fourteen sacks to the ton. Most of the whalebone goes to Paris, where it is used in the form of fine threads woven into silken fabrics for stiffening purposes.

The residue from the meat and bones is dried in a large rotating cylinder. The dried products, which have a not unpleasant smell and look like coarsely ground coffee, are packed in sacks and exported to Norway, where it is used as cattle-food (the meat only). A mixture of meat (two parts) and bone (one part) is used as manure.

The meat of most of the Balænopteridæ, when fresh, can be eaten, and some factories specialise in canning this for sale as human food.[1]

The water formed by the condensation of the steam in the boilers was formerly discharged into the sea. This water is of a gluey nature, the glue

---

[1] Whales and Porpoises as Food. With thirty-two recipes. *U.S. Department of Commerce Bureau of Fisheries. Economic Circular*, No. 38. Issued 6th November, 1918.

being particularly abundant in the dark skin situated between the epidermis and the blubber.

This, in the form of the dark mud mentioned above, was formerly thrown away, but steps are now being taken to utilise it.

Before passing on to consider the regulations which have been, and which might be, made for the protection of the various species of whales, it is necessary briefly to summarise the effect of whaling on the abundance and distribution of those species which have been most persistently hunted.

In all cases where whales have been the object of a regular fishery the operations of the whalers have had one inevitable result, and the sequence of events in each case presents a remarkable similarity. In every case the commencement of whaling is marked by a great abundance of whales, and the industry has been for a time exceedingly prosperous. Sooner or later a decline has set in, and naturally, with improved methods of killing, the period of decline has set in earlier and proceeded more rapidly in the later phases of whaling. Contrast the lengthy period during which the fishery for the Greenland Whale persisted, with the remarkably rapid decline of the Humpback fishery in the Antarctic region to the south of the South American coasts. The Greenland Whale, though easier of capture than the Humpback, defied the primitive efforts of the whaler of Spitsbergen for a couple of centuries; the Humpback, a more agile species than the Greenland Whale, and consequently more

THE ECONOMICS OF WHALING

difficult of capture, could not defy the modern steam whaling methods of the Norwegians in the waters of the Falkland Island Dependencies for a decade.

Once the decline has set in, no ameliorative measures which have yet been tried have been efficacious in stopping it, with the inevitable result that there has followed a total cessation of whaling for that particular species, or for the particular area. Moreover, in no case has the cessation of whaling taken place sufficiently soon to render possible the recovery of the whales to any appreciable extent.

The successive phases in the history of whaling described in the succeeding chapters have been, for the most part, only possible because either a new species has been attacked, or a new haunt of a previously attacked species has been discovered. In the latter case, it is more than probable that a distinct variety of the original species has been the object of the fishery, though of this there is, unfortunately, no positive evidence. The Atlantic Right Whale, or Biscay Whale or Nordcaper, was the object of the first regular whale fishery, that of the Basques, which originated probably a thousand years ago in the Bay of Biscay. It is probable that early whaling voyages, of which all record is now lost, by the Basques, in pursuit of this whale, took place to the Norwegian coast on the one hand, and to Newfoundland on the other.

Most probably, the earliest voyages of the Bretons to the Newfoundland Banks for the cod fishery were preceded by voyages of the Basques to the same region for whales, and it seems likely that the former may have first heard of the resources of the Grand Banks from the Basques. At any rate, the Basques were essentially whalers, and the Bretons fishers of cod.

The Biscayan Whale was hunted to the verge of extinction when, fortunately for its persistence as a species, the Greenland Whale was discovered in Spitsbergen waters in the early years of the seventeenth century. The Biscayan Whale has never recovered from the effects of its early persecution.

Similarly the Southern Right Whale, of which the Biscayan Whale is regarded as a variety by many balænologists, has been hunted to the verge of extinction, and only a miserable remnant of the former enormous schools are now found in its old haunts in southern waters.

The second great whale fishery was for the Greenland Right Whale, and it originated in Spitsbergen waters. A detailed account of this fishery is given in a subsequent chapter. Originally a bay fishery in Spitsbergen waters, it soon became an open sea fishery, and even as early as the commencement of the eighteenth century the whalers were compelled to go as far as Davis Strait to make satisfactory captures. This second period, i.e., the real Greenland fishery (as distinguished from the first " Greenland," really a Spitsbergen fishery) lasted, like its predecessor, for nearly a century, and was followed by the third and last hunt for the Greenland Right Whale, that of the Americans in the

THE ECONOMICS OF WHALING

extreme North Pacific and adjacent parts of the Arctic Ocean. This industry declined in its turn, so that this fishery is practically extinct in all three of the regions where it formerly flourished. The Greenland Right Whale has made no substantial recovery even in those seas in which it has longest been unmolested.

The next whale to be attacked was the Sperm Whale. The great days of the Sperm or Cachalot whaling have long since passed away, and although the Sperm Whale is by no means extinct, since a few individuals are captured in Scottish waters every year, it cannot be said that, in spite of the long cessation of Sperm whaling, the species has made anything like a substantial recovery.

The Pacific Grey Whale was also formerly the object of a special fishery, which, however, did not last long.

Continual slaughter on the breeding-grounds soon produced a marked effect, and the species became so scarce that for a time it was thought to be extinct.

There is, however, a fishery in Japanese waters for the Pacific Grey Whale, but there are no records of its reappearance off the Californian coast, where it was formerly so abundant.

The White Whale (*Delphinapterus leucas*) was hunted in Spitsbergen, though only sporadically, from the earliest days of whaling. From 1869 to 1878 there was a regular fishery for it in Spitsbergen waters, with the result that it has practically disappeared there, though it is still fairly abundant to the north of Siberia.

In no case has it reappeared in the bays from which it has been driven by excessive hunting. The Rorquals and the Humpback, owing to their greater activity and smaller commercial value as individuals, were not hunted by the older whalers, though on rare occasions an individual is recorded as being killed with the old hand harpoon.

The extension of whaling to these whales was rendered possible by the invention of the gun harpoon. The decline of this fishery in all places, where it has been tried for even a few years, is remarkable.

In Newfoundland the first whaling station in which modern methods were adopted was established in 1897. In the first ten years, 1898-1907, the annual average slaughter of Rorquals was four hundred; but while in 1903 three steamers took an average of two hundred and eighty-six each, in 1905 fifteen steamers only averaged fifty-nine each. The smaller companies were ruined, and the fishery has steadily declined. Reference is made below to the hunting of the Rorquals in the waters of Finmark, and to the restrictive legislation enforced by the Norwegian Government, partly, it must be added, as a measure of protection for the herring fisheries.

The last and most striking instance is the rapid decline in the abundance of the Humpback in the waters of the Falkland Island Dependencies.

THE ECONOMICS OF WHALING

Here the percentage captured by the whalers was as follows:

1910-11	1911-12	1912-13	1913-14	1914-15	1915-16	1916-17	1917-18
96.8	90.9	53.8	18.6	15.6	22.9	9.3	2.5

Similarly the Fin-whale has recently shown a decline:

| 1.8 | 5.3 | 41.2 | 55.7 | 36.5 | 33.6 | 37.4 | 29.3 |

So that the Blue Whale has now become the most important:

| 1.4 | 4.7 | 5.1 | 25.6 | 47.8 | 43.5 | 53.3 | 68.2 |

The actual numbers of Humpbacks captured in the South Georgia whaling season from October to March has declined from 5,299 in 1910-11, to 335 in 1916-17; the Finner from 1,852 in 1915-16, to 1,345 in 1916-17; while the number of Blue Whales captured has increased from 76 in 1910-11 to 2,398 in 1915-16, and 1,920 in 1916-17. Not only was the Humpback hunted on its feeding migration to Antarctic waters, but it was also extensively captured by whalers off the African coast when engaged in reproduction.

It is convenient to consider here the various legislative enactments and orders which have been made by the maritime nations concerned to prevent undue destruction and the gradual extermination of whales. Most of the older enactments had for their object the regulation of the fishery in the interest of the seamen of the country making the enactment. For instance, the charters, resolutions, placards, and regulations relating to whaling in the Groot

Placaet-Boek and other collections of Dutch regulations for the years 1597 to 1857 number at least two hundred and fifty-two, but none has for its special object the protection of the whale. The earliest regulation refers to stranded whales, the whaling regulations proper commencing in 1613 with an order prohibiting whalers from engaging in foreign service.

The territorial waters are usually, though erroneously, considered to extend for three miles from low water mark. Even were they to extend for a considerable distance beyond this it is obvious, since whales frequent the high seas, that national legislation for the protection of whales will be of little effect, and international regulation is necessary.

Attempts have been made by various nations to prohibit whaling in wide areas of open sea, except to their own subjects; instances of this are given in the following chapters, both James I. of England and the Count Maurice of Holland asserting such rights to Spitsbergen waters.

The Danes also interfered in Spitsbergen waters in 1615, 1623, and 1693. In these earlier assertions of authority no specific limit of sea, assumed to be controlled, is defined.

The first definition was apparently in December, 1692, when Denmark issued an edict declaring that no one could, without royal authority, carry on whale fishing within ten Norwegian leagues or forty geographical miles of the coast. The

Russian Government issued an ukase in 1821, in which it was declared that the pursuit of commerce, whaling, and fishery, on the north-west coast of America from Behring Strait to 51° N. Latitude had been granted exclusively to Russian subjects, and all foreign vessels were forbidden to approach these coasts within less than a hundred Italian miles. The execution of this ukase was soon suspended, the Russian ships of war being instructed to confine their supervision to an extent of the sea within the range of cannon-shot from the shore.

After this, British and American whalers increased greatly in numbers in Behring Sea, and the Russian officials frequently urged their government to preserve the sea as a *mare clausum*, and to prohibit foreign whalers from approaching nearer the coast than forty Italian miles (1842). The Russian Government objected, pointing out that such extensive limits were contrary to conventions, and would lead to protests from other nations " since no clear and uniform agreement has yet been arrived at among nations in regard to the limit of jurisdiction at sea." In 1847, the Russian Government repeated their objections, but in 1852, as a result of repeated complaints by the Russian-American Company, instructions were issued to the Russian cruisers to prevent foreign whalers from entering bays or gulfs, or from coming " within three Italian miles of the shores " of Russian-America (north of 54° 41'), the peninsula of

Kamschatka, Siberia, the Kadjak archipelago, the Aleutian Islands, the Pribyloff, and Commander Islands, and the others in Behring Sea, and Sakhalin and others, and it was declared at the same time that while the Sea of Okhotsk, from its geographical position, was a Russian inland sea, foreigners were allowed to take whales there. Some of these claims were revived by the United States Government (which had in 1867 acquired Alaska by purchase from Russia) at the Behring Sea arbitration in 1891.

These attempts at regulating the whaling industry, though they had national interests in the forefront, and the protection of the whales in the background, are worth consideration, since they prove how difficult it is for one nation acting alone to protect an animal like the whale.

The Norwegian Government has made certain enactments, having for their object the restriction or prohibition of whaling in certain areas off the Norwegian coasts, and although these regulations were enacted more for the protection of the local sea fisheries, which it is alleged were detrimentally affected by whaling, than for the protection of the whale, some of the provisions may be noted here.

In the Norwegian whaling law of June, 1896, a close season for whaling was prescribed from the 1st January to the end of May, off the coast of the counties of Finmark and Tromsö. It was likewise forbidden to hunt the whale in such a manner as to leave it to chance whether the whale was recovered or not. This regulation is more

THE ECONOMICS OF WHALING 55

explicitly defined in the Canadian Act of 1902, Section 13 of which, reads:

> "It shall be unlawful to use, in the catching of whales, such methods by which it depends on chance alone that a whale can be traced and found, or to use any contrivance for the catching or killing of whales which does not include a harpoon with a whaling line attached thereto, and fixed or fastened to the boat or vessel from which the whale is captured or killed"; under penalty—(set forth).

A similar regulation prescribing, as the only method allowable, a harpoon with a line attached, fixed, or fastened to a steamer is inserted in the Whale Fisheries (Scotland) Act 1907, and the Whale Fisheries (Ireland) Act of 1908.

The Irish Act contains a further proviso whereby by-laws may be made prohibiting the use of any engine or implement in the pursuit, capture or towing of whales, or any method of whaling which in the opinion of that authority[1] is injurious to the fisheries. Close times are also provided in both the Scottish and Irish Acts, and these of two kinds. First, an absolute prohibition from the 1st November, to the 31st March next following, and a partial prohibition, within forty miles of the Scottish and within twenty miles of the Irish coast, during the local summer herring season, such period not to exceed five weeks.

Since it does not appear that any of the Norwegian companies working off the Scottish or Irish coast

[1] i.e., the Central Authority in Ireland.

prior to the passing of these Acts fished between the 1st November, and the 31st March, it follows that this section of the Act affords no additional protection to whales. Since the whaling companies working from Scottish or Irish soil had to obtain licences from the fishery authorities, the regulations in the Act were capable of being enforced. In both Acts there were prohibitions against any sort of whaling within the three mile limit, against the killing of the herring-hog (which is supposed to indicate to the herring fishermen the presence of herring shoals), and the killing of any whale accompanied by a calf.

The increase of whaling in Scottish and Irish waters by Norwegian subjects which led to the passing of these Acts was due in part at any rate to a Norwegian law of 1904 which forbade for the period of ten years the hunting of the whale within Norwegian territorial waters off the counties of Nordland, Finmark, and Tromsö and the landing of whales in these counties.

Further, a similar prohibition could by Royal Decree be extended to the remaining seaboard of the kingdom, or parts thereof.

A large expanse of sea in East Finmarken, the Varanger Fiord, was closed to whalers for a distance of one geographical mile outside a line drawn from Kibergsnæs on the north to Jacobs River on the south. This arm of the sea is thirty-two miles across at the entrance, extends inland for a distance of fifty miles, and comprises an area of six hundred

THE ECONOMICS OF WHALING

and thirty square miles. The Norwegian minister for Foreign Affairs stated that this fiord had always been regarded as part of the territorial waters of Norway.

There can be little doubt that in the future whaling all over the world should be the subject of suitable regulation, having for its main object the protection of the few remaining Cetacea. The Basque fishery of the Bay of Biscay and the " Greenland " fishery alike came to an end because of overfishing. The modern Arctic fishery is also on its last legs, and the great Cachalot fisheries are equally moribund. Only in the Antarctic regions do whales flourish, and even here they are now the object of ceaseless hunting and shooting.

The great objection to whaling as at present carried on is that so many pregnant females or females with suckling young are killed; while there is, theoretically, a prohibition against killing the latter in some areas, there is no effective means whereby the whaler can identify a gravid female while it is swimming in the water.

The whalers themselves say that long before the whales become extinct, whaling will cease to be profitable on account of the increasing scarcity of the more valuable species. At present it does not pay to kill whales under forty feet in length, and this, of course, protects the smaller species, and the young members of the larger kinds, but since young whales up to forty-five or even fifty feet in length have been seen accompanying the mother, in case of the larger species, it follows that this size limit it not very effective.

The whalers say that there is only a given number of whales present on their hunting grounds, of these they capture a certain percentage. To render whaling profitable a minimum number of whales per steamer must be captured each season; this varies from thirty in British waters to three times that number in the Antarctic, on account of the greater cost of transport, etc., in those latitudes.

Consequently when the number of whales captured per steamer on any given whaling ground falls below the minimum number required to yield a profit, the whaling will, *ipso facto*, be abandoned. The whalers' argument is that this is in itself a sufficient protection for the whales, and there is no fear of absolute extinction of any species.

Probably there is some truth in this contention, and for years to come there is no fear of the extinction of any cetacean. Nevertheless, all zoologists should be on the alert, and should endeavour, when opportunity occurs, to educate public opinion on this subject, since it is only through the pressure of public opinion on government that effective steps can be taken to prevent the exploitation of one of the most interesting groups of animals in the interests of a small section of capitalists.

EDGE'S MAP OF GREENLAND.
(*Really Spitzbergen, circa 1611.*)

CHAPTER III

THE EARLY HISTORY OF WHALING (TO 1623)

The Basque whalers—The discovery of "Greenland" (Spitsbergen)—The first British whalers—The Spitsbergen fishery—The whales found there—The disputes between the English and the Dutch—Edge's description of the fishery.

ALTHOUGH the general opinion is that the Basques were the earliest whalers, Noel de la Morinière[1] says that this is a misapprehension and that the Northmen were really the first in the field.

He quotes the voyage of Ochther,[2] who travelled towards the end of the ninth century beyond the North Cape to Perm, and afterwards described his journey to King Alfred. There was evidently a hunting of whales and walruses in northern waters at this time, but there is no evidence that it developed into a regular fishery such as that of the Basques.

The Norwegians are stated to have used a balista for the discharge of the harpoon with an attached rope, thus anticipating the harpoon gun of the English (1731). At the time of the Norman invasion of France there is evidence of whaling in

[1] *Histoire generale des Pêches*, 1815, Vol. i., p. 218.
[2] Schneider. *Sammlung vermischter Abhandlungen zur Aufklärung der Zoologie und der Handelsgeschichte*, Berlin, 1784.

the Channel. In a book entitled, "*de la translation et des miracles des Saint Waast*," A Life of Saint Arnould, Bishop of Soissons in the eleventh century, there is mention of a whale fishery by means of the harpoon on the coast of Flanders in 875.

According to Ducéré,[1] the history of the whale fisheries of the Basques has yet to be written. In this fishery the Bayonnais took part, and it is one of the most interesting features in the ancient records of the town of Bayonne. In early historical times it is fairly certain that the whale fisheries were carried on only off the north coast of Spain and the south-west coast of France, i.e., in the Bay of Biscay. Ducéré says that it is still possible to trace the remains of the watch towers and furnaces of the whalers along the shores of the Bay of Biscay, the former naturally being used for the lookout, the latter for boiling the blubber. There is documentary evidence of a fishery off Biarritz in the thirteenth century, and the seal of the town[2] contains a representation of a "chaloupe" harpooning a whale. In the Middle Ages the Basques seemed to have picked up a living on the coast, partly by different kinds of fishing and partly by pillaging their neighbours. They killed whales

---

[1] Dictionnaire Historique de Bayonne. *Commission des Archives Municipales Ville de Bayonne, par* Edouard Ducéré. Bayonne, 1911. 2 Vols.

[2] See "La Marina de Castilla," by Fernandez Duro. Madrid, 1892. The seals of Bermeo, Lequeitio, and Castrourdiales, which are reproduced on p. 218, show views of the old Basque Whale Fisheries.

EARLY HISTORY OF WHALING 61

when the latter approached the shore, towing the body to the land to extract the oil. Later they fitted out rowing boats and killed the whale on the open sea. Fischer[1] says the whaling was at its apogee in the twelfth and thirteenth centuries, as indicated by the number of documents relating to it. Up to this time it was entirely free. According to the judgments of Oleron, the fishermen of Cape Breton (near Bayonne), Plech, Biarritz, Guetary, Saint Jean de Luz, and of the Labourd country were exempt from all dues. They gave to the church the whales' tongues, but this was a voluntary gift. The first attempt to interfere with these fishermen was by the kings of England, who, as Dukes of Guyenne, usurped the seignorial rights.

In 1197 King John gave Vital de Biole and his heirs and successors the sum of fifty angevin livres, to be levied on the first two whales captured annually at Biarritz, in exchange for the rent of the fishery at Guernsey.

An act of the Abbey of Honce in 1261 announced that permission was granted to pay a tithe on the whales landed at Bayonne. This tithe was a conversion of the previous free gift of whales' tongues. In 1257 William Lavielle gave to the bishop and chapter of Bayonne a tithe of the whales captured on the ocean by the people of Biarritz, and this was apparently paid until 1498. Although there is

[1] "Cétacées du sud-ouest de la France," P. Fischer. *Actes de la Société Linnéenne de Bordeaux*, Vol. xxxiv., 1881, Bordeaux.

documentary evidence in the Archives of Bayonne and elsewhere as to the existence of a flourishing fishery as early as the twelfth and thirteenth centuries, a fishery which must have persisted until the seventeenth century, since the earliest harpooners engaged in Spitsbergen were Basques, there is but little evidence as to the manner in which the fishery was carried on. The term " Baleinier " occurs frequently in marine documents of Bayonne in the Middle Ages. It referred to a special type of vessel, very seaworthy, as ships went in those days, of eighty to one hundred tons burden, devised originally for the whalers, but extended in its use, firstly by the pirates, and secondly on the voyages of discovery of the fifteenth century.

Fischer gives a long list of references to whales and whaling, but these are mostly acknowledgments of the lordship of the coasts and the seas and the inhabitants thereof; or documents of a similar nature.

In the sixteenth century the flesh, and especially the tongue of the whale, was sold in the markets of Bayonne, Cibourre, and Biarritz. The blubber was salted and sold inland, in the east of France. The first detailed description of the Basque whaling is that by Ambroise Paré, who visited Bayonne when Charles IX. was there in 1564.

The whale is taken in several places in winter,[1]

---

[1] But Clayrac fixes the time of the appearance of the whales off the coasts of Guienne and Biarritz as the September equinox. See *Us et coutumes de la mer*, Rouen, 1671.

EARLY HISTORY OF WHALING 63

especially on the coast of Bayonne, near a little village called " Biarris," distant three leagues from that town. Near this village there is a rock upon which, for many years past, there has been a tower, on which a look-out is kept, by day and night, for whales. (There is now a lighthouse on this rock, overlooking the Chambre d'amour.) The whales are recognised by their spouting. As soon as one is observed, the look-out sounds a bell, upon which warning all the village run prepared with the necessary apparatus for the slaughter of the whale. There were several vessels and skiffs utilised for this. Apparently some were manned exclusively by those who killed or attempted to kill the whale on the high sea. Other boats specialised in the attempt to drive the whales ashore, where they were dispatched by the whole population of the village. Dead whales found floating in the sea were also towed ashore and utilised. After the whale was struck with harpoons it was killed with lances. Each harpooner was rewarded by the result of his efforts as determined by the number of his harpoons found in the whale's body. The females were considered easier prey than the males *pour ce qu'elles sont soigneuses de sauver leurs petits.*

The flesh is not esteemed, except the tongue. Originally the oil was extracted on land, the whales being towed ashore and then cut up and the blubber boiled down.

The discovery of the possibility of boiling down the oil at sea, " trying-out " as it is called, is

64   A HISTORY OF THE WHALE FISHERIES

due to a captain of Cibourre named François Sopite.

The whalebone is used for ladies' stays and knife handles, the skeletons to make enclosures for gardens, the vertebræ as chairs and seats in houses. In the seventeenth century and possibly even in the sixteenth, this Basque fishery had declined. Probably the whales were getting more shy and difficult to capture as the result of persistent fishing. Clayrac records them as passing Biarritz regularly towards the end of the seventeenth century (1671).

The Basques fished for whales before the invention or use of the mariner's compass. Nevertheless, they fished in the open sea to the west and are said to have attained in 1372 the banks of Newfoundland, where they encountered whales in abundance. This whale they called the Sarda, to distinguish it from the species commonly found in the Bay of Biscay. The word Sarda in the Basque language signifies a whale that keeps together in schools.

Continuing their voyages the Basques reached the Gulf of St Lawrence, where they discovered another different species of whale which they called the "Grand Bay Whale," a name used by Thomas Edge in his classification of Spitsbergen whales.

When the Gulf of St Lawrence became impoverished, the Basque whalers pushed on to the edge of the ice off Greenland, where they captured the Greenland Whale which appeared to them to be the same as that of the Gulf of St Lawrence.

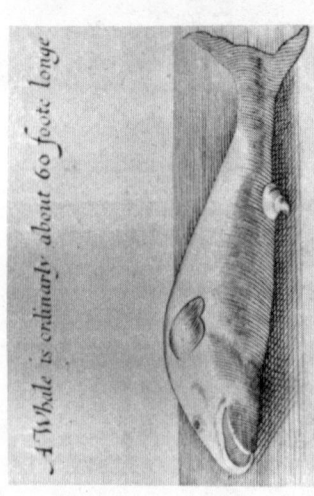

EDGE'S DESCRIPTION OF THE SPITZBERGEN FISHERY, I.

EARLY HISTORY OF WHALING 65

They noticed that the thickness of the large whale of the north was double that of the Sarda, its whalebone longer, and that its oil was clear, whereas that of the Sarda was always cloudy.

Thomas Edge, who took charge of the first English whaling expedition to Spitsbergen, received instructions as to the voyage in which two distinct species of whales are mentioned; one is unquestionably the Greenland Whale, and the other the Sarda. This Sarda is the Nordcaper of the Dutch, but is it the same as the Sarda of the Basques? Most probably it is, and the Basques were mistaken in thinking that the whales of the Bay of Biscay and the whales they met off the Grand Banks were two distinct species.

Prior to the first voyages of Columbus (1492) and John Cabot (1497) to America there was an extensive fishery for sea fish at Iceland, a fishery participated in by British, Bretons, and Basques, and probably not confined to Icelandic waters but extending both to Greenland and the Grand Banks of Newfoundland.

The traces of these fishermen's voyages, undertaken when the science of navigation was in its infancy, are scattered and fragmentary. The actual references to whaling are of the slightest, but are nevertheless sufficient to indicate that there was some whaling prior to the great Spitsbergen fishery.

In the will of John Sparks of Cromer (1483), there is mention of a "Bloberhouse";[1] in the Carta

---

[1] Rye. "Cromer, Past and Present," p. 51.

Marina of Olaus Magnus (1539) there is a representation of an English whaler.

Actual records of whaling voyages in the sixteenth century are rare, though a French Basque named Savalet told Lescarbot that he had made forty-two voyages, and Echevete the Spanish Basque had made twenty-eight voyages across the Atlantic to the Newfoundland coast, and as the Basques were predominantly whalers it is very probable that some, if not all, of these voyages were for whales.

The Basques, moreover, had the best ships at this period, and were therefore better able to hunt the whale. English vessels were small, their average size being less than fifty tons; the Bretons and Normans had also poor vessels, whereas a Basque ship of four hundred tons with a crew of forty men is recorded. Ordinary fishing vessels at this period had flush decks, three masts, the foremast being very far forward, the mizzen very far aft; the sails were three big lug sails, the ballast sand and the cook-room a solid structure of brick and mortar built on the ballast.

On the whole the available evidence tends to show that the Basque whalers regularly visited the Newfoundland bays toward the middle of the sixteenth century. According to Harrisse the presence of Basques at Newfoundland is not attested before 1528.[1]

The Spanish authorities in general agree with

[1] *Découverte et évolution cartographique de Terre-Neuve et des Pays Circonvoisins*, 1497, 1501, 1769, *par* Henry Harrisse, Paris, 1890.

this. The fishermen of Guipuzcoa frequented the banks of Newfoundland, but not certainly before 1530. Navarrete, who investigated the subject, fixes the first voyages at about 1541. Towards 1550, the evidence is more definite, and we have the name of a commander of a whaler Jean de Urdaire, who afterwards became admiral. There is good documentary evidence that from 1557 to the end of the seventeenth century Biarritz, Caberton, Pasajes, Renteria, Saint Jean de Luz, Saint Sebastian and Zubibura continually sent ships to Newfoundland both for whaling and cod fishing. At this time the Basque cod fishermen left the Cantabrian coast towards the end of March or beginning of April, returning from mid-September to October. The whalers left in mid-June, and returned in December or early January, their larger and better vessels enabling them to withstand the storms of winter.

Although there must have been a considerable trade in whale oil between the Basques and Great Britain in the fifteenth and sixteenth centuries, there is not much evidence of it.

Late in the sixteenth century there is positive evidence that the soap-makers used whale oil, and that there was trade with Bayonne and other ports for this product of the fisheries.

Guerau de Spes, writing on the 5th August, 1569, to the Spanish King, says, " Three ships of St Jean de Luz have put into Bristol loaded with Biscay iron, and are now leaving for their own country with a cargo of cloths, pewter and others things, all of which are destined to be taken into Spain. The want of oil here is so pressing that they are getting oil from rape-seed to dress their wool, and they say they can manage with it. There is little of the seed, however, yet, and no matter how active they may be in sowing it the out-turn of cloth by means of it will be small and poor. They are trying also to utilise the oil which they obtain from boiling sheep's feet. Their great hope is to get soap and oil from Spain through France and from the Easterlings, who I am told have already left for the purpose."[1]

In 1578 we have a further reference to the whale fisheries. Bernardino de Mendoza was ordered by the Spanish King to make inquiries into a voyage made by the English two years previously " to the country called Labrador, which joins Newfoundland, where the Biscay men go in search of whales."[2]

This same year there are numerous complaints about the soap-makers using fish oil and train oil in the manufacture of soap.[3]

These complaints led to the Privy Council forbidding the London soap-boilers to use in making soap, or even to have in their possession " any more blubber oyle, pumpe oyle, trane oyle, whale or other fishe oyle."

About this time there was a dispute between

---

[1] *State Papers, Spanish,* 1568-79, p. 186.
[2] *Ibid.,* p. 567.
[3] *State Papers, Domestic,* 1547-80, p. 605.

EARLY HISTORY OF WHALING 69

Laurence Mellows and the " sope-makers " of the City of London, which was referred by the Privy Council to the Controller of Her Majesty's Household and the two Chief Secretaries of State.[1] Mellows demanded eighteen pounds per ton for his seed oil, and the soap-makers would only offer thirteen pounds. The Council ordered the soap-makers to take from Mellows eighty tons of seed oil at sixteen pounds the ton, civil gage, and fifty-one tons of whale oil at sixteen pounds the ton, Biscay cask, and to pay ready money for the same. Upon doing this the soap-makers could at their liberty use both train and whale oil in making of soap for a period of eighteen months. On the 14th December, 1579, the Privy Council ordered the Lord Mayor to induce the soap-makers to buy one hundred tons of seed oil from Mellows, and to report on his success to the Council.

On 19th April, 1602, seven ships went from St Jean de Luz to Newfoundland for the whale fisheries, and many more for the fishing.[2] There is evidence scattered through the State Papers of this time of a considerable impressment of Biscayan whalers and mariners to strengthen the Spanish fleet.

Spitsbergen was known and spoken of up to the times of Scoresby (1820) as East Greenland. Consequently early references to the " Greenland " whale fishery must be taken to include references to

[1] *Acts of the Privy Council*, 1578-80, p. 50.
[2] *State Papers, Addenda, Domestic*, 1547-65, p. 178.

Spitsbergen, in fact the earliest references are exclusively to the latter.

The first attempts to establish a whale fishery in Spitsbergen were the occasion of considerable disputes between the English and the Dutch, both of whom claimed territorial jurisdiction over Spitsbergen and the adjacent seas by right of discovery. The Dutch claim was based on the discovery of Spitsbergen by Van Heemskerk in 1596, that of the British Muscovy Company on the discovery of the same land by Willoughby in 1553. The British claim was strongly supported by King James I., notwithstanding the statement supporting the other side which had been drawn up by Plancius. Sir Hugh Willoughby set out in 1553 to discover the north-east route to "Cathay," and perished at the river or haven called Arzina in Lapland. Richard Chancellor, pilot-major under Willoughby and captain of the *Edward Bonaventure*, one of Willoughby's fleet, had better luck and was the discoverer " of the kingdome of Moscovia by the North-east in the year 1553."

Early in the seventeenth century English whalers began to fish at Spitsbergen, where whales were found in enormous numbers. The voyagers of the Muscovy Company had reported this in the previous century. Anthonie Jenkinson, who made his first voyage to Russia in 1557, reported " thus proceeding and sailing forward, we fell in with an island called Zenam, being in the latitude of 70 degrees. About this island we saw many whales, very monstrous, about our ships, some by estimation of sixty feet long, and being the ingendring time they roared and cried terriblie."[1]

The Muscovy Company was the first of the great English Joint-stock Corporations of foreign trade. It was incorporated by a charter signed on the 6th February, 1555, under the name of " Merchants Adventurers of England for the Discovery of lands, territories, isles, dominions and seigniories, unknown and not before that late adventure or enterprise by sea or navigation commonly frequented."[2] Sebastian Cabot was made the life governor. " After his death the same fellowship shall in places convenient and honest assemble together to elect and choose one Governor or two and twenty-eight of the most sad, discreete and honest persons "; of whom four were to be Consuls, and the remaining twenty-four assistants to the " saide Governour."

The Company was afterwards re-incorporated by statute, and the corporate name shortened to " Fellowship of English Merchants for Discovery of New Trades " (12th February, 1576-7).[3]

The Company, as its popular name indicates, was mainly engaged in the trade to Russia by the northeast, and the whaling business was subsidiary to this. In the re-incorporation referred to the Queen granted a monopoly of the right to kill whales and make train oil for a period of twenty years to Sir

[1] Hakluyt, " Voyages," Dent's Everyman Edition, Vol. i., p. 410.
[2] *Ibid.*, p. 318.
[3] *Patent Rolls*, 19 Eliz., Part XII.

Roland Heyward and Sir Lionel Duckett. (See Appendix I., p. 303).

In Hakluyt's "Voyages" (1575) there is a request of an honest merchant to a friend of his to be advised and directed on the course of killing the whale. A number of questions relative to whaling are set forth and duly answered.

"The whaler should be of two hundred tons, with a crew of fifty-five men, and should set out in April for Wardhouse and be furnished with four kintals and a half of bread for every man, with two hundred and fifty hogshead to put the bread in. The further specification includes: One hundred and fifty hogsheads of cidar, six kintals of oile, eight kintals of bacon, six hogsheds of beefe, ten quarters of salt, a hundred and fifty pounds of candles, eight quarters of beans and pease, saltfish and herring a quantity convenient, four tunnes of wines, half a quarter of mustard seed and a querne, a grindstone, eight hundred empty shaken hogsheds, three hundred and fifty bundles of hoops, and six quintalines, eight hundred pairs of heds for the hogsheds, ten estachas called roxes for harping irons, ten pieces of arporieras, three pieces of baibens for the javelins small, two tackles to turn the whales, a halser of twenty-seven fadom long to turne ye whales, fifteen great javelins, eighteen small javelins, fifty harping irons, six machicos to cut the whale withall, two doozen of machetos to minch the whale, two great hookes to turne the whale, three pair of can hookes, six hookes for staves, three

EARLY HISTORY OF WHALING

dozen of staves for the harping irons, six pullies to turn the whale with, ten great baskets, ten lampes of iron to carry light, five kettles of a hundred and fifty li. the piece, and six ladles, a thousand of nailes for the pinnases, five hundred of nailes of carabelie for the houses and the wharfe, eighteen axes and hatches to cleave wood, twelve pieces of lines and six dozens of hookes, two beetles of rosemarie, four dozen of oares for the pinnases, six lanterns, five hundred of tesia. Item, gun powder and matches for harquebushes as shal be needfull. Item, there must be carried from hence five pinnases, five men to strike with harping irons, two cutters of whale, five coopers and a purser or two."

To this is added a note of certain other necessary things belonging to the whale fishing, received of Master Burrow, who was captain general of a fleet of thirteen vessels on a voyage to the Narve in Liefland in 1570.

" A sufficient number of pulleys for tackle for the whale. A dozen of great baskets. Four furnaces to melt the whale in. Six ladles of copper. A thousand of nailes to mend the pinases. Five hundred great nails of spikes to make their house. Three pair of boots great and strong, for them that shall cut the whale. Eight calve skins to make aprons or barbecans."[1]

It is evident that prior to the Spitsbergen whale fishery, whales were killed and captured off the

---

[1] Hakluyt's, " Voyages," Dent's Everyman Edition, Vol. ii., p. 162.

Norwegian coast at Vardohuus, in addition to an important fishery at Newfoundland, of which nearly all trace has been lost.

Anthony Parkhurst, a merchant of Bristol, writing to Hakluyt on the 13th November, 1578, says:

"He had made four voyages to Newfoundland, and had searched the harbours, creeks and lands more than any other Englishman. That there were generally more than one hundred sail of Spaniards taking cod, and from twenty to thirty killing whales; fifty sail of Portuguese; one hundred and fifty sail of French and Bretons, mostly very small; but of English only fifty sail."

Sir Richard Whitbourne, who first visited Newfoundland in 1583, says:

"We were bound to the Grand Bay (which lieth on the north side of that land) purporting there to trade then with the savage people (for whom we carried sundry commodities), and to kill whales and to make trayne oil as the Biscaines do there yearly in great abundance. But then our intended voyage was overthrown by the indiscretion of our captain and faintheartednesse of some gentlemen of our company, whereupon we set saile from thence and bare with Trinity Harbour in Newfoundland, where we killed great store of fish, deere, beares, beavers, seales, otters, and such like, with abundance of seafowle, and so returning to England we arrived safe at Southampton."

There are frequent references to the abundance of whales off the Newfoundland coast at this time.

In the account of the voyage of the *Marigold* of M. Hill of Redrife unto Cape Briton and beyond to the latitude of 44 degrees and a half, in 1593, written by Richard Fisher, Master Hilles man of Redrife, there is reference to whales.

" In our course to the West of Cape Briton we saw exceeding great store of seales, and abundance of porpoises, whereof we killed eleven. We saw whales also of all sortes as well small as great; and here our men took many berded coddes."

In " a briefe and summary discourse upon the intended voyage to the hithermost parts of America; written by Captaine Carlile in April, 1583," for the information of the merchants of the Muscovy Company and others, there is reference to the prospect of good fishing for whales in northern regions.[1]

One of the earliest voyages by an English ship to the whale fisheries was made by the *Grace* of Bristol,[2] a barque of thirty-five tons, owned by M. Rice Jones, whereof Silvester Wyet, Shipmaster of Bristol, was master. This voyage was up into the Bay of St Lawrence, to the northwest of Newfoundland as far as the Island of Assumption, for the barbs or fins of whales and train oil. The *Grace*, with a crew of twelve men, left Bristol on the 4th April, 1594. In St George's Bay (north side of Nova Scotia) they found the wrecks of two large Biscayan ships which

[1] Hakluyt's, " Voyages," Dent's Everyman Edition, Vol. vi., p. 80.
[2] *Ibid.*, p. 98.

had been cast away three years earlier, from which they extracted seven or eight hundred whale fins; all the train oil was lost though the casks remained. After this Wyet was informed that whales which had been wounded in the Grand Bay and escaped capture eventually stranded on shore on the Isle of Assumption or Natiscotec " which lieth in the very mouth of the great river that runneth up to Canada." So he sailed across without, however, meeting with any stranded whales. They then went back to Newfoundland to fill up with codfish, returning safely " first in Combe and staid there a seven night, and afterward in Hungrod in the river of Bristoll by the grace of God the 24 of September, 1594."

Prior to the voyage of the *Grace* it appears to have been customary for English privateers to lay in wait for Spanish ships on the return voyage from Newfoundland, whither they went for fish and train oil. Thus in April, 1591, the ship of Peter de Hody, merchant of Bayonne, returning from Newfoundland laden with dry and green fish and fourteen hogshead of train oil, was taken by a ship of war appointed by Sir Walter Raleigh and brought to Uphill near Bristol.[1] The same year the ship *Holy Ghost* of St Jean de Luz belonging to Martin, Adam, John and Michael Haurgues, laden with fish and oil from Newfoundland, was captured by the *Elizabeth Bonaventure* and *Dudley*, English men-of-war, and taken to Milford and there sold. She appears to have been improperly

[1] *State Papers, Eliz., Domestic*, Vol. ccxlii., p. 231.

moored since she became a wreck in the haven. This episode was followed by petitions to the Privy Council and a case before Dr Cæsar, Judge of the Admiralty.[1] Some of the oil was eventually sold to a shoemaker at Haverfordwest.

The manufacture of train oil in England cannot at this time have been important, since in May, 1594, a licence was granted to Elizabeth Matthews, widow, for twenty-one years on surrender of the licence granted to her late husband, Richard Matthews, yeoman of the poultry to have the making of train oil of blubbers and fish livers for a rent of twenty shillings. The shoemaker and other inhabitants of Scarborough petitioned to the Council against this grant of monopoly.[2]

Spitsbergen, the scene of the first extensive whaling enterprises and even to-day visited practically every year by whalers, was discovered by Willem Barendts (Barents). Barents'[3] log is still in existence, as are also affidavits by Arent Martenssen of Antwerp and Anthoine Classen Herman, ship's captain, of Leyden, who took part in the expedition.[4]

In previous years, especially in 1594 and 1595, expeditions were sent out from Holland, with financial assistance from the Dutch Government, to

---

[1] *State Papers, Eliz., Domestic*, 1591-94, pp. 248-251.
[2] *Ibid.*, 1581-90, p. 709.
[3] Extract uit het scheeps journal van Willem Barendsz, betreffende de ontdekking van Spitsbergen. Printed by Muller, N.C.
[4] Getuigenissen van twee reisgenooten, van Jan Cornelisz. Rijp over de noordpoolreis van 1596-97. Printed by Muller, N.C.

seek a passage to China by the north-east route. These expeditions failing in their main object, the Government declined to assist the expedition of 1596, which was therefore financed by private enterprise. Barents sailed from Vlieland on the 18th May, 1596, and after touching at Bear Island on the 9th June, they thought they saw land on the 14th but were not certain till the 17th, when they undoubtedly discovered Spitsbergen. Probably the ships (there were two of them) were not fitted out for whaling, and the solitary reference to whales by Barents is on the 15th June, when he records *" Passions une grande Balaine morte, sur lequel y avoit plusiers meauves."* Herman records a landing when they found among other things " *des dens de Baleines.*"

The first mention of train oil in the accounts of the Muscovy Company is in the years 1604-6. This was obtained from Cherie Island (Bear Island) from " Sea-Morses " (Walrus). In 1604 the good ship *God Speed* of sixty tons set sail from London with Thomas Welden as master; who also went in 1605 and 1606.

In 1609 Jonas Poole in the *Lionesse* sailed from Cherie Island, where he " set up a pike, with a white cloth upon it, and a letter signifying our possession for the right worshipfull Company trading to Moscovie." By this time sea-horses were becoming scarce, though Poole observed " the multitude of whales, that shewed themselves on the coast of Greenland." In 1609 the gain was thirty per cent,

EARLY HISTORY OF WHALING 79

although the voyage in 1608 had shown forty per cent profit.

Apparently it was in 1610 that the Muscovy Company first made a serious attempt to exploit the whale fishery in Arctic waters. In that year the Company set forth a voyage to Cherry Island; and for a further discovery to be made towards the North Pole in the ship *Amitie* of seventy tons, of which Jonas Poole was master, having with him fourteen men and a boy. With her was the *Lionesse*, Thomas Edge commander. On the 9th March Poole weighed and put to sea (blessed bee God). They saw the North Cape on the 2nd May and on the 6th encountered much ice, being then in the neighbourhood of Cherry Island. On the 16th May they saw land (Greenland or Spitsbergen as it is now called). They saw great store of whales particularly in Deere Sound and to the northward of Knottie Point. Those in charge of this expedition were censured by the Company for having brought home blubber instead of oil, the dividend paid for 1610 being only twenty per cent. At this time train oil was in great demand for the manufacture of soap so the Company at once decided to fit out a whaling expedition for 1611.

The two vessels sent out were the *Elizabeth* and the *Mary Margaret*, the former a small bark of fifty tons under the command of Jonas Poole, the latter a ship of one hundred and fifty tons commanded by Steven Benet (Edge being on board as agent of the Company). The former was fitted for discovery, the latter for whaling, and fortunately the instructions given by the Company to the masters are still extant.

Poole was told to find whether the said land (Spitsbergen) be an island or a main, and which way the same doth trend, either to the eastward or the westward of the Pole, as also whether the same be inhabited by any people, or whether there be an open sea farther northward than hath been already discovered. His further instructions were to sail in company with the *Mary Margaret* " till God send you to the places where she may make her voyage, which by your report should be at a place named by you the last yeare 1610, Whale Bay." " And God sending you to the said place, we would have you to stay there the killing of a whale, or two or three, for your better experience hereafter to expedite that businesse, if through extremitie of the ice you should be put from your discoveries."

While the whale killing was in progress Poole was told to search the coast with his sloops for whale fins (really the whalebone), morses teeth, ambergris or any other commodities. " And in this your coasting the land, we doubt not but you will endeavour with your Shallops to gather up all the whale fins you can finde, to kill the Morses which you can come on by land, and to reserve the teeth and blubber to the most advantage that may bee, the better to bear out the great charge which you know we are at in these Discoveries. And to that

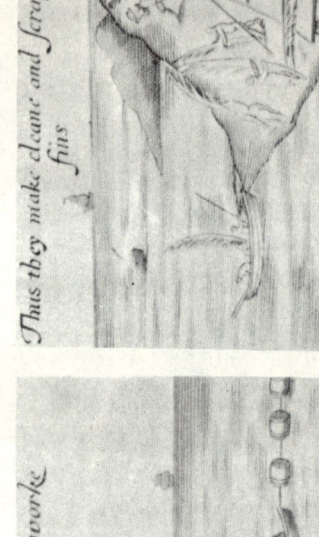

EDGE'S DESCRIPTION OF THE SPITZBERGEN FISHERY, II.

EARLY HISTORY OF WHALING 81

end we have laden in you eleven tunnes of emptie caske."

After a certain time spent in this voyage of discovery the *Elizabeth* was ordered to rendezvous at the place where she left the *Mary Margaret*, and if the time of year permitted to melt their blubber into oil " to avoid the great trouble and inconvenience you know we fell into the last yeere 1610 by bringing the same hither in blubber."

If the *Mary Margaret* was full fished and gone before the *Elizabeth* returned, Edge was instructed to leave a copper at Cherry Island. The detailed instructions specify that the ships should proceed together on the outward voyage to Cherry Island, kill morses there if possible, and then go on together to Whale Bay. On the return journey they were again to rendevous at Cherry Island, waiting the one for the other until the last day of August. They were to fill in the time of waiting by killing morses or searching the island for lead ore, or any other minerals. Since previous voyages had been spoilt owing to the ships returning home through fear of shortage of food the Company on this occasion set down the amount of provender supplied, to wit, " Beefe, 22c. 3 quarters, 18 li. Bisquit. 30c. Beere 14 tunnes. Fish, 200 of Haberdin,[1] and halfe a hundred lings. Cheese 300c weight. Butter three firkins. Oyle three gallons. Pease ten bushels. Oate-meale five bushels. Candels, sixe dozen. Aquavitæ, thirtie gallons. Vinegar, one

[1] Dried, salted cod, originally prepared at Aberdeen.

rundlet of twentie gallons." This was estimated to last them seven or eight months, and of course they could pick up fish, fowl and beasts as they went along.

Jonas Poole was appointed grand pilot; Steven Benet, master of the *Mary Margaret*, having to follow his directions.

The Commission to Thomas Edge[1] to go as Factor in the *Mary Margaret* for the killing of whale and morses upon the coast of Greenland or any other place in the North Ocean dated the 31st March, 1611, is probably the earliest set of instructions for a whaling voyage and is quoted here in some detail.

The adventures and losses in the first voyages are enumerated. Of two prior voyages to Cherry Island the first resulted in a loss of one thousand pounds, by reason of one Duppers, a brewer of London, together with certain men of Hull going thither and " glutting the said place." The second voyage (1609) by reason of ice was also unsuccessful, resulting in a loss of five hundred pounds. For this reason Edge is urged to encourage and stir up his mind to do his utmost endeavour to further the business in this his third employment, that the Company might recover the losses it had sustained. " And for that end we have made choice of you again to goe as our factor." Six men of Saint John de Luz accustomed to the killing of the whale were engaged for the voyage; " whose names are as

[1] Purchas, " His Pilgrims," Vol. xiv., p. 30 (1906 edition).

followeth, *videlicet,* Juan de Bacoyne, Juan de Agerre, Martin de Karre, Marsene de Horisada, Domingo de Sarria and Adam de Bellocke." Edge was warned to use them " very kindely and friendly during this their voyage," but at the same time to omit no opportunity of learning " that businesse of striking the whale, as well as they." " And likewise to know the better sorts of whales from the worser, whereby in their striking they may choose the good, and leave the bad."

The kinds of whales, eight in number, are next enumerated.

" The first sort of whales is called the Bearded Whale, which is black in colour, with a smooth skinne, and white under the chops; which whales is the best of all the rest; and the elder it is, the more it doth yield. This sort of whale doth yeelde usually four hundred, and some five hundred finnes, and between one hundred and one hundred and twenty hogsheads of oyle." Obviously this is the Greenland Right Whale.

" The second sort of whale is called Sarda, of the same colour and fashion as the former, but some what lesse, and the fins not above one fathom long, and yeeldeth in oyle, according to his bignesse, sometimes eightie, sometimes a hundred hogsheads." This whale is the " Nordcaper."

" The third sort of whale is called Trumpa, being as long as the first, but not so thicke, of colour grey, having but one trunke in his head, whereas the former have two. He hath in his mouth teeth of a span long, and as thicke as a man's wrist, but no fins; whose head is bigger than either of the two former, and in proportion far bigger than his body. In the head of this whale is the spermaceti, which you are to keep in caske apart from your other oil; you may put the oyle you find in the head and the spermaceti altogether, and marke it from the other oyle, and at your comming home, we will separate the oyle from the spermaceti. The like is to be done with the oyle of this sort of whale which is to be kept apart from the oyle of the other whales. The reason is, that the oyle of this sort of whale being boyled, will be as white and hard as tallow, which to be mingled with the other oil being liquid, would make the same to show as footie oil, and so consequently spoyle both, and be of little value; you are therefore to be very carefull to keepe the oyle of this sort of whale apart, as well of the head as of the body, for the reasons before mentioned. In this sort of whale is likewise found the Ambergreese, lying in the entrals and guts of the same, being of shape and colour like unto Kowes dung. We would have you therefore your selfe to be present at the opening of this sort of whale, and cause the residue of the said entrals to be put into small caske, and bring them with you into England. We would have the master also to be by at the opening of this whale and to be made privie of the packing of those barils. And although it be said, that the Ambergreese is onely in this whale and in none other, yet we would not have you be absent at the opening of any other; but if you see cause to make a reservation of the entrals of every whale that you shall perceive to be cause of the least suspect to have any of the said Ambergreese, being a matter, as you know, of good worth, and therefore not slightly to be regarded. The teeth likewise of this sort of whale we would have you cause to be reserved for a triall; as also any other matter extraordinarie that you shall observe in the same. This whale is said to yeelde in oyle fortie hogsheads, besides the spermaceti." This is the Sperm Whale which was occasionally encountered even in fairly high latitudes on the way to and from Spitsbergen.

"The fourth sort of whale is called Otta Sotta, and is of the same colour as the Trumpa, having finnes in his mouth all white, but not above halfe a yard long, being thicker than the Trumpa, but not so long; he yeelds the best oyle, but not above thirty hogsheads.

"The fift sort of whale is called Gibarta,[1] of colour blacke like the two first, saving that it hath standing upon the top of his backe, a finne half a yard long. This whale is as big as the first; his fins little or nothing worth, being not above halfe a yard long; and he yeeldeth about twelve hogsheads of oyle, all of which his backe yeelds; as for his bellie it yeelds nothing at all.

"The sixt sort is called Sedeva, being of a whitly

[1] A Finner, see Browne, Goode, *The Fishery Industries of the United States*, Sec. I., pp. 29-30

colour, and bigger than any of the former, the finnes not above one foot long, and he yeelds little or no oyle. The seventh is called Sedeva Negro, of colour blacke, with a bump on his backe; this whale yeelds neither oyle, fins nor teeth, and yet he is of a great bignesse.

"The eight sort is called Sewria, of colour as white as snow, of the bignesse of a Wherrie, he yeelds not above one hogshead or two of Oyle, nor any finnes, and is good meat to be eaten."[1]

Descriptions of the different species of whales by the Dutch will be found in an early pamphlet of Saeghman's[2] and in Zorgdrager.[3] The latter (in 1720) distinguished six or seven species, viz., Vinvisch (*Balena vulgaris*), Walvisch (*Balena vera*), Zwaard-Zaag of Tand-Vische (*Balena Orca vel dantata*), Noortkaper (*Physter*), Potvisch (*Cete*) and Eenhoorn of Hoornvisch (*Narwal*). A short digression is here made to give the various names in vogue from time to time for the whales of Arctic and sub-Arctic waters.

Other accounts of the different species of whales met in northern waters are given by Von Troil[4]

[1] This is the White Whale (*Delphinapterus leucas*). It grows to a length of about twelve feet. White whales were taken by the English, whenever possible. Twenty-four tons of oil were made from white whales in 1670. They were driven ashore by means of nets, and consequently were only taken in the bays.

[2] *Kort verhael van de Gedaente der Walvisschen, En hare Namen, en voorts waer, en hoe, deselve in Zee gevangen worden.* Müller, "Noordsche Compagnie," p. 377, from "Drie Voyagien Gedaen na Groenlandt," Amsterdam, G. J. Saeghman.

[3] *Bloyende Opkomst*, 1st edition, p. 80.

[4] W. von Troil, "Bref rörande en Resa til Island," 1772, Upsal, 1777.

(1772) and Leems[1] (1767), the former dealing with the Icelandic names for whales and the latter with Danish Lapland.

According to Von Troil the natives of Iceland divided whales into two classes, those with, and those without, teeth (tusks).

Those without teeth are divided further into skidis fiskur or smooth bellied and reydar fiskur or wrinkle bellied (roughly, True Whales and Finners). Among the skidis fiskur, who have whalebone instead of teeth, the Slettbakr (*Balæna biscayensis*) whose back is flat, is the largest, and some have been caught one hundred yards (?) in length.

The Hnufubakr (probably *Megaptera boops*) has a hump on his back, and is next in size, from seventy to eighty yards (?) long. Of all the known whales the Steipereidur (*Balænoptera sibbaldi*), which belongs to the class of the reydar fiskur, is thought to be the largest, as there are some one hundred and twenty yards (?) in length. Then follow the Hrafn reydur and the Andarnefia.[2] They are all considered as very dainty food, and the Icelanders say the flesh has the taste of beef.

The whales which have teeth instead of whalebone are also divided into two classes, those which are eatable and those which are not. The names of these are given but not sufficient detail to enable one to identify them with certainty.

[1] Knud Leems, "An Account of the Laplanders of Finmark," originally published in Danish and Latin, Copenhagen, 1767.
[2] Lindeman states that the Andarnefia is the Bottlenose, which is, however, a toothed whale.

Leems distinguished seven species of whale met with in the sea off Finmark. Of these it is possible to distinguish at least four with reasonable certainty, namely, the Ror Hval (a finner), the Nord Kaperen (*B. biscayensis*), the Springere (Dolphin), and Niser (Porpoise).

To return now to the events of 1611, Edge is next admonished to be industrious and diligent and to avoid negligence and idleness, and to see " that every one be imployed in some businesse or other in helping to kill the whale, or in searching the bayes along the coast for whales, ambergreese, morses teeth, or any other strange thing, that may be found upon that coast, or in killing the morses, beares, or anything that may make profit toward our great charges." The *Mary Margaret* is ordered to keep in touch with the *Elizabeth*, and finally Edge is instructed, " You have with you an order set downe by the Lords of his Majesties privie Counsell, for the maintaining of our Charter; which we would have you make knowne to any of our Nation, that you may chance to meet withall either at Cherie Iland, or upon any of those coasts. And if any stranger do offer you violence, or doe disturbe you in your trade, you may both defend yourselves, and maintaine your trade to the uttermost of your powers."

Fortified by these detailed instructions, the *Mary Margaret* and the *Elizabeth* set sail from Blackwall on the 11th April, 1611, accompanied by the *Resolution* on a Russian trading voyage and the

EARLY HISTORY OF WHALING

Amitie, seventy tons, bound for Nova Zembla " to see if they could make a voyage by way of trade, or by killing of Mohorses." Although whaling had undoubtedly been prosecuted in northern waters prior to this, the *Mary Margaret* was probably the first vessel to take part in the " Greenland " whale fishery.

Their voyage was certainly not devoid of incident. Before they reached latitude 65° north, the *Mary Margaret* and *Elizabeth* separated owing to bad weather. Poole reached Cherie Island on the 13th May, and on the 14th spoke the *Amitie*, on the 16th the *Mary Margaret* with whom he kept company until they reached " Greenland." On the 29th May they anchored in Crosse Road (see chart, p. 58) where " we found almost all the sounds full of ice, that the Biscainers could not strike one whale, although they saw divers, which as they said were of the beste kinde of whale."

They cruised about, and on the 12th of June the Biscayners killed a small whale which yielded twelve tons of oil " being the first oyle that ever was made in Greenland." On the 25th June the *Mary Margaret* found a large number of sea-morses in Sir Thomas Smyth's Bay. The crew landed, killed five hundred, leaving a thousand more living on shore. The next day most of the men went ashore to work and make oil of the morses, leaving the master and ten men on board. Some ice drifted into the bay forcing the ship ashore, " where shee, by the master's weake judgment was cast away, and all their bread spoyled not fit to eate." The ship being lost beyond hope of recovery, the crew made ready to leave the place in their boats. Fifty men in all, they left in four small sloops and the ship's boat on the 15th July. After proceeding for some thirty to forty leagues to the southward the boats separated. One sloop and the ship's boat being together, met with a ship of Hull, to whom they imparted the information that their ship was lost and that they had left on land goods to the value of some fifteen hundred pounds. The *Mary Margaret's* men now proceeded with the Hull boat back to Foule Sound to take in the Company's goods and to kill some sea-morses.

This Hull ship, the *Hopewell*, Thomas Marmaduke, master, got back to the wreck of the *Mary Margaret*, where they were ultimately found by Jonas Poole in the *Elizabeth*, as will appear in the sequel.

The main part of the shipwrecked crew of the *Mary Margaret*, including Thomas Edge, the factor, and Steven Benet, the master, held on their course to the southward to Cherry Island, which they reached safely on the 29th July, having been at sea in their sloops for fourteen days, " and comming into the Iland with a great storme at north-west with much difficultie they landed on the south side of the Island." Here they found the *Elizabeth* in the north road, three miles away, " being at that time weighing anchor to set sayle for England."

Poole, who was unquestionably a man of resource, on learning how matters stood with the *Mary*

Margaret, immediately lightened his ship, putting " neere one hundred morse hides on land, and some emptie caske, and haled up a shalop. After hauling up the remaining sloops of the *Mary Margaret* at midnight I set sayle for Greenland, carrying with mee two Biscaine shallops, determining there to try the blubber of those morses we had killed, and bring it to oyle, and to bring all the oyle, teeth and finnes which they had gotten in that country."

Poole left Cherry Island in the *Elizabeth* on the 1st August, and arrived at Foule Sound in " Greenland " on the 14th, where he found the Hull ship, the *Hopewell*, busily engaged in salvage work. As soon as the *Elizabeth* was moored Poole set to work to make the best of things. He determined to get out the blubber and send it ashore to be made into oil, and also to take home the oil and whale-fins as being the more valuable cargo, leaving the morsehides and blubber to the next year. The accounts given by Edge and Poole of this same incident differ in details, though there is an agreement in the main. For instance, Edge gives the date of arrival of the *Elizabeth* at Foule Sound as the 14th August, Poole gives the date as the 3rd.[1] At any rate, Poole lightened his ship too much during these operations, so that " the ship began to held, and with all a great many men went to leeward, there being at that time above forty on board." Poole says he had at this time on board " about nine and twentie tunne weight,

---

[1] But they may have estimated the date, one by the old, the other by the new method.

and to any unpartiall man's judgment, sufficient to shift a bark of sixtie tunnes."

At any rate, the position suddenly got worse, " the hides which lay in the hold slid to leeward, and brought her altogether downe, then every man made shift to save his life, and I being farre from the hatches, could not get up so soone as others did. At which time I saw death before mine eyes two wayes, one if I stayed in hold, I was sure to be drowned; the other if I went up the hatches, I was in election to be slaine; for downe at the hatches fell hogsheads of beere and divers other things, the least of them being sufficient to beate a mans bones." However, Poole escaped, " and, blessed bee God, no man perished at that so dangerous an accident." With their boats they now made for the Hull ship, their sole hope of rescue. There they found small comfort, for Duke told them plainly they were not to come aboard, " and caused pikes and launces to be brought to keepe us out." However, Edge persuaded the Hull man to be reasonable, so that Poole got aboard, " having mine head broke to the skull, and my brow that one might see the bare bones, and by mine eare I had a sore wound, likewise the ribs on my right side were all broken and sore bruised, and the collar-bone of my left shoulder is broken, besides, my backe was so sore, that I could not suffer any man to touch it." An arrangement was eventually come to with the Hull ship whereby the goods which were saved were taken in at the rate of five pounds the tunne. On the 21st August they left Greenland in the *Hopewell*, ninety-nine men in all, arriving at Hull on the 6th September.

This venture, though unsuccessful in itself, held out such great promise for the future that the Muscovy Company determined to embark thoroughly in the whaling trade, a resolution which was speedily copied by various " interlopers " in which term were included not only foreigners but also British subjects, e.g., Hull men, not authorised by the Muscovy Company.

In 1612 the Right Worshipfull the Muscovie Merchants sent out two ships, the *Whale*, one hundred and sixty tons, and the *Sea-horse*, one hundred and eighty tons, under the command of John Russell and Thomas Edge. Leaving Blackwall on the 7th April they arrived at Cherry Island on the 3rd May, where they found a Dutch ship, in which " one Alan Salowes an Englishman was pilot." The Muscovy Company's servant wished to detain Salowes, but eventually he was allowed to depart. On the 22nd May off Black Point and on the 23rd off Cape Cold they saw great store of whales. A few days later they met the Dutch ship again, in company with the *Diana* of London " whereof one Thomas Bustion dwelling at Wapping Wall, was master." The *Hopewell* of Hull, still in charge of Thomas Marmaduke, was also at the whaling this year, and they claimed to have sailed to 82° north. There was also a ship from San Sebastian in charge of Nicholas Woodcock, an Englishman, as pilot, so there were at least six ships at the whaling this year, two of the Muscovy Company's vessels and four interlopers, two English and two foreign. The introduction of the foreign element appears to have been due to English renegades, since the Hollanders " came to Greenland with one ship, being brought thither by an Englishman, and not out of any knowledge of their owne discoveries, but by the direction of one Allan Sallowes, a man imployed by the Muscovia Companie in the Northerne seas for the space of twentie yeeres before; who leaving his country for debt, was entertayned by the Hollanders and imployed by them to bring them to Greenland for their Pylot." Similarly the Spanish ship was piloted by the Englishman Woodcocke, who, however, was subsequently arrested on complaint by the Company, and imprisoned for sixteen months in the Tower.

The Muscovy Company's ships were very successful this year, getting seventeen whales as well as some sea-horses, of which they made one hundred and eighty tons of oil " with much difficultie; as not being experimented in the businesse." The Company for both periods (this and the preceding year) paid two dividends of ninety per cent.[1]

In 1613 great preparations were made, the Muscovy Company alone fitting out five ships and a pinasse for the whaling. These ships were the *Tigre*, Admiral; the *Matthew*, Vice-Admiral; the sea-horse called the *Gamaliel*, Rear-Admiral; the

[1] Scott, " Joint Stock Companies to 1720," Vol. ii., p. 53.

Desire; the *Annula*; the *Richard and Barnard*; with the *John and Francis*, to follow. In all expeditions consisting of more than two vessels, one was appointed to lead, the " Admiral," the other to look out astern, the " Vice-Admiral." By day the Admiral carried a signal and by night a distinguishing light. The officer in command of the fleet was the General, and he sailed in the Admiral. The second in command was the Lieutenant-General, he sailed in the Vice-Admiral. Both of these officers had letters patent from the Sovereign, authorising them to enforce martial law. The journal of this voyage was kept by the famous William Baffin, who afterwards (in 1615) went as pilot of the *Discovery* in search of the north-west passage.

Hearing that a number of foreign ships were fitting out for the fishery, the Company took the precaution of applying for a Royal Charter from King James, to exclude all others, natives and foreigners, from participating in the fishery. It was urged that the industry would be highly beneficial to the country, since every hundred pounds adventured brought trade estimated at five hundred pounds. The claim was based on the right of first discovery and the advantageous character of the occupation.[1] The petition was accepted and a grant embodying the views of the company made on the 13th March, 1613.

This year the Company's ships were under the

[1] " The Humble Petition and Remonstrance of the English Merchants for the Discovery of New Trades," Lands, MSS. No. 142, f. 301.

command of Benjamin Joseph and Thomas Edge. Leaving Queenborough on the 13th May, they reached Greenland in eighteen days. On the 31st they saw a ship which proved to be a ship of Saint John de Luz " which had leave of the Companie to fish," and from whom they learnt that there were eight Spaniards on the coast. They also saw another ship, supposed to be a Frenchman, with Allan Sallas as pilot. On the 2nd June they boarded a small pink and ordered the master and pilot thereof aboard the English General's ship.

The master's name was Clais Martin of Horne, his ship being for Dunkirk, and with him was another ship, whose master was Fopp, also of Dunkirk. According to Edge there were fifteen sail of large ships besides four English interlopers engaged in the whaling this year.

In addition to those mentioned above Baffin records meeting four foreigners on the 6th June at Poopy Bay, of whom two were Hollanders from Amsterdam with a commission granted by the Grave Maurice to fish in that country; one a Rocheller and the fourth a vessel from Bordeaux. When they saw our Kings Majestie's Commission they told our General that they would depart this coast. The English were at this time in great strength. The *Jacques* of Bordeaux agreed with the English that if he were permitted to fish he would hand over half the whales he killed. The Rocheller and the small ship from Biscay agreed (8th June) to leave the coast. On the 9th the English ordered the two

Dutch ships, the Dunkirker, the Rocheller and the Spanish ship from Saint Sebastian out of Green Harbour.

Two Dutch ships were encountered on the 10th at Low Sound, where on the 10th June the English "went on shoare to set up the Kings Majesties Armes upon a low point of land, lying a great way off, called Low-nesse. We set up a Crosse of wood and nayled the Armes upon it." On the 13th the English again molested a number of foreign ships in Horne Sound, compelling them to leave, which they did on the following day, when the English again went on shore and sent up the King's Arms.

In short during the whole of the time of the fishery there were constant altercations ending with the foreigners submitting with bad grace, since they were inferior in strength, and leaving or at least making the pretence of leaving. There was one large ship of Biscay of seven hundred tons " which we expected would have fought with us."

It was in company with two ships of Amsterdam, the masters of which were Cornelius Calias and William Vermogon, Admirals, and John Jacob, Vice-Admiral, " these two would gladly have stood out with us, if the Biscaine would have assisted them." In spite of the enormous waste of time in wrangling with the foreigners, by the 17th July the Company's ships had secured thirty-eight whales (of which eight had been handed over by the Frenchman according to agreement) and one hundred and sixty tons of oil had been prepared. Disputes were, however, continuous, and on the 1st August "for pilfering and some peremptorie two of the Rochellers were ducked at our yard arme, the one on the one side, and the other on the other."

On the 14th August six of the ships left for home, namely, the *Tigre*, the *Gamaliel*, the *John and Francis*, the *Annula*, together with the Bordeaux ship which had fished under permission, and the Biscay ship which had fished in Sir Thomas Smyth's Bay. On the 16th off Cold Cape they fell in with a ship of Alborough belonging to Master Cudner of London, the master being named Fletcher. This was one of the four English interlopers referred to by Edge.

On the whole the voyage produced but poor results for the Muscovy Company, the financial loss being between three and four thousand pounds.

On their return home to Amsterdam the despoiled Dutch ships complained of the ill-treatment to which they had been subject, and representations were made through the ordinary diplomatic channels to King James, who at this time was a convinced believer in the doctrine of *mare clausum*. The Dutch founded their case partly on the right of prior discovery and partly on the general principle of freedom of navigation and fishery.

In all there are six separate accounts of the whaling at Spitsbergen in 1613. These are the accounts by Edge and Baffin published by Purchas; the "Histoire du Pays nommé Spitsberghe" by Hessel Gerritsz, an account by Robert Fotherby, a note in manuscript in the British Museum entitled " A briefe Narration of the Discoverie of the Northern Seas and the Coasts and Countries of those parts as it was first begunn and continewd by the singular Industrie and charge of the Company of Muscovie Merchants of London," and finally the " Corte Deductie ende Remonstrantie van wegen de Bewinthebbers ende Participanten vande respectiue oude Noortse Compagnien ouet Delft, Hoorn, Enckhuijsen, Vlissingen ende Veere, ouergegeuen ænde Hooge ende Mogende Heeren de Staten Generæl Vereenichde Nederlandtse Provintien."[1]

Of these the most valuable account from the whaling standpoint is that by Fotherby. This account is in manuscript in the possession of the American Antiquarian Society, and contains illustrations of the whale fishery together with a description of the fishery. It is really the original description of Fotherby's first voyage (of three).[2] This account has been reprinted twice, and in addition quoted extensively by Conway (" No Man's Land ").

The Dutch version of the occurrences at Spitsbergen in 1612 and 1613 is given by Hessel Gerritsz van Assum.[3]

[1] See Müller. "Noordsche Compagnie," p. 393.
[2] " Transactions and Collections of the American Archæological Society," Vol. iv. (1860), p. 285; reprinted by the Hakluyt Society in a volume entitled " The Voyages of William Baffin," London, 1881.
[3] " Histoire du pays nommé Spitsberghe. Monstrant comment qu'il est trouvée, son naturel et ses animauls, avecques la triste racompte des maux, que nos pecheurs tant Basques que Flamens, ont eu a souffrir des Anglois, en l' esté passée l' An

The Dutch ship this year, 1612, was commanded by Willem van Muijden of Amsterdam, with whom was another ship from Saardam, which, however, only went to Bear or Cherry Island to shoot or catch walrus. In 1613 Van Muijden had two ships, in which were engaged twelve Basque sailors from St Jean de Luz; three master-harpooners, three boatswains, and the remaining six for the preparation of oil and cutting up the whales. There was also a barque from Amsterdam in which was Thomas Bonært, an Englishman, and a few Dutchmen, the majority of the crew being, however, Englishmen. There were also two barques from Saardam. As already related, the English persistently molested the Dutch. Eventually, Muijden showed the English Admiral his Excellency's (Count Maurice) Commission, which stated that he was at liberty to fish, and to defend himself against all who wished to harm him. The Admiral read it, kissed it, and admitted its genuineness, but said he was obliged to execute the charge he had from his king, which was still greater, and which gave him the right to hold for His Majesty, and for their enjoyment, all countries and lands already discovered, and to be discovered, within a line running from the north-west and one from the north-east, drawn with a compass

de grace, 1613." Escrit par H. G. A. " Et en apres une protestation contre les Angloys, et annulation de touts leurs frivols argumens, parquoy ils pensent avoir droict, pour se faire Maistre tout seul, dudict pays," Amsterdam, 1613. (English translation in Hakluyt Society's " Early Dutch and English Voyages to Spitsbergen in the Seventeenth Century," London, 1904.)

placed upon their map midway between Trondhjem and Iceland.

The English Admiral, therefore, not only forbade Muijden to fish anywhere, but took away from him all that he had already caught. The Dutchmen's adventures are related in detail. On the 28th July the English Admiral made Muijden a present of twenty pipes of lard and twenty-one wattles for the eighteen and a half whales which he had captured. And he still retained in his service the vessel from Saardam, which went here and there for him, looking for wood along the banks and bringing the blubber to the Foreland to the other English ships. This vessel was also given a quantity of blubber for its pay, and came home. According to Gerritsz the Muscovy Company accumulated incredible wealth from the despoiling of the Dutch ships.

As will be seen, this success of the English in 1613 was only temporary.

It was evident there would be a keen struggle in 1614, and both sides made great preparations. The Dutch, evidently placing little faith in their diplomatic representations to King James, determined to resort to force to defend their interests. Early in 1614 a new Dutch Company was formed and a charter of monopoly obtained for three years, a period subsequently extended to ten.[1] They obtained the exclusive right " to trade and fish from the United Netherlands on or to the coasts of the

---

[1] This charter is printed in full in " Zorgdrager," 1st edition, pp. 173-175.

lands between Nova Zembla and Fretum Davidis," including Spitsbergen, Beer-en-Eiland and Greenland. A tax of last-money, i.e., a contribution towards the expenses of the common defence based on the tonnage of the vessels participating in the fishery, was levied, and fourteen Dutch whalers set off, convoyed by four men-of-war of thirty guns each.

The Muscovy Company also made a big effort for 1614, and they sent out thirteen great ships and two pinasses for Greenland, under the command of Benjamin Joseph and Thomas Edge, all the ships being well appointed with artillery for defence, as well as the other necessaries for fishing and discovery. The log of one of these ships, the *Thomasine*, was recorded by Robert Fotherby, and from it the following extracts are made. William Baffin was on board the *Thomasine* for this voyage.

On the 14th June the *Thomasine* first encountered the Dutchmen, eleven sail being met off the Foreland, " one of them came roome towards us, and struck her top-sayles twice, whereby we supposed they tooke us for some of their fleete."

Apparently the Dutch were content to leave well alone, so long as they were not molested. At Maudlen Sound Fotherby went ashore and set up a cross with the King's Arms nailed thereon, under which he nailed a piece of sheet lead, with the arms of the Muscovy Company engraved on it. Then cutting up a piece of earth, he said in the hearing of the men there present: " I take this piece of earth, as a signe of lawfull possession (of this countrey of

King James his New-land, and of this particular place, which I name Trinitie Harbour) taken on the behalfe of the Company of Merchants called the Merchants of New Trades and Discoveries, for the use of our Sovereigne Lord James, by the grace of God, King of Great Brittaine France and Ireland, whose Royall Armes are here set up, to the end that all people who shall here arrive may take notice of his Majesties right and title to this countrie, and to every part thereof. God save King James." Later they went ashore on Red Beach, where they found no commodities as they expected to have done, " for here had the Hulmen been in 1612 as we might know by fires that they had made, and gathered the fruites that many yeares before had brought forth. Thus as we could not find that which wee desired to see, so did we behold that which we wished had not been there to be seene, which was great abundance of ice." At a subsequent visit to the same spot they set up a cross and nailed a sixpence thereon with the King's Arms.

The English ships returned half laden, while the Dutch also made a poor fishing. The Muscovy Company, being deprived of the assistance of royalties from foreigners licensed to take part in the fishing, had to reduce their dividend from thirty per cent in 1613 to eleven per cent in 1614.

In 1615 the Muscovy Company sent out two large ships and two pinasses under the command of Benjamin Joseph and Thomas Edge. On one of the pinasses, the *Richard*, twenty tons, of London was Robert Fotherby, who kept a log of the voyage.

This year the Dutch sent out fourteen ships, of which three were States men-of-war of great force; they killed whales in Horn Sound, Belsound, and Fairhaven as they were far too strong to be interfered with by the English. The King of Denmark also sent out three men-of-war to demand toll from the English which, however, was not paid. These were the first Danish ships that went to Greenland being piloted thither by James Vaden, an Englishman.

In a letter written by Fotherby to Edge, dated from Cross Road, 15th July, 1615, there is a reference to a meeting with three ships and a pinasse of the King of Denmark. Fotherby, it must be remembered, was on a very small craft with a crew of ten men. He was " courteously entertayned " by the Danes, who asked him by what right he fished there. Fotherby told them by virtue of the King of England's patent granted to the Muscovy Company of Merchants. The Danes then entreated and finally compelled him to accompany them to meet Edge. Eventually matters simmered down, the Danes being apparently satisfied with their inquiries, " for they seeme to pretend that the right of this land belongs to the King of Denmark, and neither to English nor Hollanders."

This year the English again returned half laden, but the Dutch made a successful voyage.

EARLY HISTORY OF WHALING

In 1616 the Muscovy Company sent to Greenland eight large ships and two pinasses under the command of Thomas Edge. "This yeare it pleased God to blesse them by their labours, and they full laded all their ships with oyle, and left an over-plus in the countrey, which their ships could not take in." By the middle of August they had from twelve to thirteen hundred tons of oil, and all the ships arrived safely in the Thames in September. The Dutch had four ships which made a poor voyage.

Encouraged by this success the Muscovy Company sent out in 1617 fourteen ships and two pinasses to the whale fishing. At this time the Company was showing signs of financial weakness and in January, 1617, it was resolved to send books to the freemen for subscription of a new stock, to be paid up during the ensuing four years, those who failed to take up stock to be excluded during that time.

Moreover, King James himself infringed on the privileges of the Company. On May 24th he granted, by letters patent under the great seal of Scotland, to Sir James Cunningham, his heirs and associates constituting the Scottish East India Company, the right to trade to the East Indies, the Levant, Greenland, Muscovy and all other countries and islands in north, north-west, and north-eastern seas.[1]

The Muscovy Company was chiefly concerned since it was intended in the first instance to take up whaling.

[1] *State Papers*, East Indies, 1., 65.

The actual fishing was again very successful this year in spite of the presence of numerous foreigners and interlopers. Edge himself met with a Dutch ship of two hundred tons, from which he learnt that there were ten Dutch ships on the coast with two men-of-war. Edge warned him not to fish and told him to inform the others, that if he met with him or any Dutch ships hereafter he would take from them what they had got. Hearing later that the Dutchmen had killed a few whales in Horn Sound, Edge ordered his Vice-Admiral to proceed thither, " put the Flemmings from thence and take what they had gotten." This the Vice-Admiral proceeded to do, much to Edge's subsequent dissatisfaction, since the goods taken from the Dutch ships were not worth twenty pounds.

A small English ship of sixty tons with a crew of twenty men under William Heley was more fortunate. Detailed for the purpose of discovery they discovered Witches Island (in 79° north) and also " tooke a ship of Flushing,[1] called the *Noah's Arke* (Master John Versile) in Horn Sound, having out of him two hundred hogsheads of blubber and two whales and a half to cut up, a great copper, and divers other provisions, and sent him away ballasted with stones." Two other Dutchmen and two Danes escaped before Heley appeared on the scene. This year the Company's ships captured one hundred and fifty whales, yielding over one thousand eight

[1] The Noordsche Companie was this year (1617) enlarged by the addition of Zealand partners.

hundred tons of oil, " beside the blubber left for want of caske."

In 1618 the Dutch made another determined attempt to wipe off old scores, and since the Muscovy Company were heartened by the great success of the previous year it looked as if there were to be lively times at the whale fisheries.

The Muscovy Company and Sir James Cunningham's Company joined forces, the East India Company promising the former a loan of one hundred thousand roubles on condition that the whale fisheries should be carried on jointly[1] for eight years. According to Edge this put the Muscovy Company to great trouble and cost " in taking of all the provisions they had bespoken, and paying ready money for the same, having no use thereof, but great part spoyled, and came to little good." There can, however, be little doubt that the Muscovy Company were now hard up, since they were compelled to borrow money from persons not free of the Company. Ultimately, thirteen ships and two pinasses were sent forth again under the command of Captain Edge. The Dutch were represented by twenty-three well-appointed ships, who commenced to fish alongside the English, setting two boats to the English one, " with a full purpose to drive the English from their Harbours, and to revenge the injurie (as they termed it) done them the yeere before."

A letter from Master Robert Salmon dated Sir

[1] *State Papers, Domestic*, James I., xcviii., 2, 9.

Thomas Smyth's Bay, the 24th June, 1618, throws some light on the proceedings. After relating the killing of thirteen whales, which yielded but little oil on account of the difficulty of working in the ice, Salmon goes on: " Here is five sayle of Flemmings which have fourteen and sixteene pieces of Ordnance in a ship; and they doe man out eighteene shallops so that with theirs and ours there is thirtie shallops in the bay, too many for us to make a voyage; there is at least fifteene hundred tunnes of shipping of the Flemmings; we have reasonable good quarter with them, for we are merry aboord of them, and they of us, they have good store of Sacks, and are very kinde to us," yet a little further he says " the Company must take another course the next yeere if they mean to make any benefit of this country, they must send better ships that must beat these knaves out of this country."

The Dutch had, however, evidently intended to continue at the whale fishing, since every ship had Count Maurice's Commission.

Master Sherwin, writing in Bell Sound (29th June, 1618), is also annoyed by the Dutch, " let them all go hang themselves, and although you be not strong enough to meddle with them, yet the worst words are too good for them, the time may come you may be revenged on them againe." Two of the Dutch ships came along, but Sherwin handled them carefully " for fear of after-claps "; had it been later in the year " we would have handled them better." " Now they be gone for Horne Sound, I would that they had all of them as good a pair of hornes growing on their heads, as is in this country." From which it would appear that Master Sherwin was not devoid of humour.

Finally, James Beversham, writing to Master Heley from Fairhaven (12th July, 1618), complains that the Biscainers have stolen one of the sixteen whales they had killed.

Heley was himself by this time in much greater straits, since five of the Dutchmen, namely, the *Fortune* of Camphire, four hundred tons, with eighteen cast pieces beside brass bases and "murtherers," Captain Hubreght Cornelisson; the *Saint Peter* of Flushing, three hundred tons, with eighteen cast pieces, Captain Cornelius Cooke; the *Salamander* of Flushing, two hundred tons, fourteen cast pieces, Captain Adrian Peeterson; the *Cat* of Delph Haven, with sixteen cast pieces, Abraham Leverstick being Captain and General of the Zealanders, and William Johnson of Milliworth in a ship with fourteen cast pieces, after much conference, on the 19th July forcibly set on Heley who was in the *Pleasure*, attended by one English ship and a pinasse. The Dutchmen plied their ordnance, small shot and "murtherers." The English ships, in spite of their resistance, were forced to anchor or run ashore, their ships being rifled, and their casks burnt.

After this, the remaining English ships dispersed, their voyage being "utterly overthrowne." They returned empty, the Muscovy Company putting their loss at over sixty-six thousand pounds besides the spoiling of the ships and the loss of the men.

On their return the English whalers made formal complaint, and the proceedings at the Foreland, Bell Sound and Horn Sound were the subject of separate affidavits.[1]

The statement of events at the Foreland is sworn to by William Heley (London), aged twenty-four years or thereabouts, Robert Salmon of Deptford, Stephen Smith of Gravesend and John Headland of London. At the Foreland it is evident there was considerable wrangling between William Heley, who was the chief representative of the English, and Hubreght Cornelisson, the Admiral of the Flemings.

Heley, though with a numerically inferior force, and with unarmed ships, seems to have attempted to prevent the Dutch from fishing, although the latter were present in overwhelmingly greater force. Heley learnt that this year the Dutch sent nineteen ships to Jan Mayen Island (Hudson's Touches) and that the twenty-three for Greenland (Spitsbergen) were to be distributed as follows: To Horn Sound, five; Bell Sound, seven; Green Harbour, three; the Foreland, five; and Fairhaven, three. There was a man-of-war to ride close to the English Vice-Admiral's side, and if she stirred, then to go with her. It appeared that the Dutch had information of

[1] *State Papers, Domestic*, James I., Sept., 1618, Vol. xcix., No. 40. *Ibid.*, July-Aug., 1618, Vol. xcviii., Docket 44. (Reprinted in "Early Dutch and English Voyages to Spitsbergen," Hakluyt Society, 1904.)

the number of vessels being fitted out in England in the winter of 1617-18 by the Muscovy Company, and were determined to overpower them. Amongst the amenities we read that Cornelius de Cock of the *Saint Peter* said that " our King of England was a Scotchman, and that his picture stood at Flushinge with an emptie purse by his side "; a statement characterised in a marginal note as " a gross and intolerable abuse to his Ma'ty."

The further proceedings at the Foreland, culminating in the attack of the 19th July, are set forth in great detail in the affidavit of Heley and the others.

The events at Bell Sound are sworn to by Thomas Edge of London, Thomas Sherwyn of Wapping, John Thornbush of Wapping, John Martin of Rodrith, John Ellis of Wapping, and John Barker of Radcliffe; and those at Horn Sound by John Johnson of Lymehouse, William Dridle of Redritge, and William Henderson of Lymehouse. At both places the English endeavoured to persuade the Dutch to desist from fishing, but the latter were in great force and took no notice of the English protests, except to produce their commission from the " Grave Morrice," the Prince of Orange. It seems unnecessary to recapitulate all the details of these transactions.[1]

The effect of these events on King James, who was now thoroughly steeped in the doctrine of

[1] " Early Dutch and English Voyages to Spitsbergen," pp. 42-65.

"Dominium Maris," can be imagined. Diplomatic protests were promptly made to the Dutch, who sent ambassadors to England in November to treat on the points at issue.

A detailed account of the discussion of the legal points at issue is beyond the scope of this work. King James appointed two groups of commissioners to treat with the Dutchmen, a Scottish group to deal with the herring fisheries, and the English group to deal with other matters in dispute, including the whale fishery. Pusillanimous James tried to bluff the Dutchmen, but without success. The English case was based on the contention that Spitsbergen belonged to the king, on the prior fishing there, and on the depredations of the Dutch in 1618. The Dutch claimed Spitsbergen by right of discovery, but in order to arrive at a *modus vivendi*, they proposed three alternatives:

(1) That all nations should fish for whales at Spitsbergen, sharing the bays and fishing stations between them.

(2) That fishing should be carried on by the English and Dutch with an equal number of vessels of equal size.

(3) That the island should be divided into two equal parts by an imaginary line, the Dutch to have one part, the English the other.

James would have none of this, and insisted on his right to the sea at Spitsbergen. On the practical point he gave way, consenting that the Dutch should fish at the Island for three years longer.

EARLY HISTORY OF WHALING

In 1619 a joint undertaking of the Muscovy and the East India Companies engaged in the Spitsbergen whale fishery, nine ships and two pinasses being sent out under the command of Captain Edge. The Dutch were also strongly represented. Misfortune dogged the footsteps of the English companies. A letter from John Chambers to W. Heley from Bell Sound, 16th June, 1619, relates a disaster which had occurred to one of the English ships. By this time Salmon had killed ten whales " whereof eight are made into oyle, which hath made one hundred and eleaven tuns and a halfe, the other two were killed the fourth of this present, being very large fish, not doubting but they will make sixe and thirtie or fortie tunnes; we have the hundred tunnes aboard, the rest Master Barker taketh in." The voyage was a great loss to the companies, and as the Dutch brought home large quantities of oil and sold it at low rates, the English companies were compelled to hold theirs over for twelve months and then sell it at a very low price. Moreover, one ship was lost near Yarmouth on the return voyage.

By this time the position of the Muscovy Company was desperate, so that in 1620 a fresh undertaking was formed, new capital being provided by Ralph Freeman, Benjamin Deicrowe, George Strowd and Thomas Edge. The liabilities and assets of the old concern were taken over for a sum of twelve thousand pounds. This included a claim against the Dutch for damage in 1619 amounting to twenty-two thousand pounds.

In 1620 seven ships were sent out under the command of William Goodlad and William Heley. Owing to the great number of Dutch and Danish ships the English were compelled to pass from harbour to harbour, so that they eventually returned half laden with about seven hundred tons of oil.

In 1621 eight ships departed, seven for the whaling and one for discovery, with a partial success, eleven hundred tons of oil being obtained.

In 1622 the Greenland section of the Muscovy Company's trade was put up to auction and sold for an annual sum of five hundred and twenty pounds. The purchasers formed a separate concern known as the " Greenland Adventurers." Eight ships were sent to the whaling and one for discovery.

Bad luck again attended them. One of the largest ships was wrecked on the coast of " King James Newland " and twenty-nine of the crew lost. The remainder returned with one thousand three hundred tons of oil.

Purchas prints three letters concerning the whale fisheries of 1623, from Nathaniel Fanne, Master Catcher and William Goodlad. The last named was Admiral, William Heley being Vice-Admiral.

This year the Dutch were represented by very large ships, up to five hundred tons burden, furnished with material for the building of houses and tabernacles at Spitsbergen, for the living quarters of the shore gang, and preparation of the train oil.

The Dutch Company (Noordsche Compagnie) about this time enlarged its sphere of operations considerably.

It is estimated that in the reign of James I. (1603-25) there were in existence from one thousand two hundred to one thousand four hundred English ships, of which eighteen were engaged in whaling and discoveries in Arctic seas. Marsden's list includes the following names of whalers: *Desire, Dragon, Elizabeth, George, Gods Speed, Hopewell, Jacob, Mary Anne, Mary Margaret, Matthew, Patience, Rainbow, Samaritan, Samuel, Sarah, Tiger* and *Unity*.[1]

Towards the end of the reign of James I. the merchants of Hull complained of the falling off of their trade, and in evidence given by John Ramsden, before the Trades Committee of the Privy Council, it is stated " that the summer trade in fish being ruined by the King of Denmark and the Wardhouse . . . we did seek to revive again by searching and finding out the land called Greenland, where we were the first that found that country, and gave the first hazard of any Englishman to kill the whale, which we hoped would retrieve our fortune; but the Russia Company of London do exceedingly disturb us therein. Another special cause of decay we humbly suppose to be the strict restraint thereof by the Company of Merchant Adventurers and the

[1] For further details see R. G. Marsden, " English Ships in the Reign of James I." *Trans. Roy. Hist. Soc.*, xix., pp. 310-55, 1905, and also Rendel Harris, " The Last of the *Mayflower*." Manchester University Press, 1920.

Eastland Company of London, who abridge and monopolise the whole trade of these countries into their own hands, though many of them are of small ability and hinder often those that are better able."[1]

One of the best early descriptions of the whale fisheries is that of Edge (see illustrations, pp. 64 and 80). First of all the ordinary species of whale is described. " The whale is a fish or sea-beast of a huge bignesse, about sixtie five foot long, and thirtie five foot thicke, his head is a third part of all his bodies quantitie, his spacious mouth contayning a very great tongue, and all his finnes, which we call whale finnes. These finnes are rooted in his upper chap, and spread over his tongue on both sides his mouth, being in number about two hundred and fiftie on one side, and as many on the other side. The longest finnes are placed in the midst of his mouth, and the rest doe shorten by their proportionable degrees, backward and forwards, from ten or eleven foot long to foure inches in length, his eyes are not much bigger than an Oxes eyes, his body is in fashion almost round forwards, growing on still narrower towards his tayle from his bellie; his tayle is about twentie foot broad, and of a tough solid substance, which we use for blockes to chop the blubber on (which yields oyle), and of like nature are his two swimming finnes (and they grow forward on him). This

[1] " Causes of the General Decay of Trade and Scarcity of Money in the Town of Kingston-on-Hull, as laid before the Privy Council by John Ramsden, Merchant," 1622 (from Hadley's, Hull).

creature commeth oftentimes above water, spouting eight or nine times before he goeth downe againe, whereby he may be descried two or three leagues off."

This gives the whalemen their opportunity. When the whale is observed blowing, the shallops are sent out after him. It is unnecessary to quote Edge's description in full, since as Purchas says " You may see this story of the whale killing presented lively in the Map, which Captain Edge hath liberally added to this relation." After the whale has been harpooned by the harping-iron he is lanced, and " in lancing him they strike neere the finnes he swimmeth withall, and as lowe under water neere his bellie as conveniently they can; but when he is lanced he friskes and strikes with his tayle so forcibly, that many times when he hitteth a shallop hee splitteth her in pieces."

" The whale having received his deadly wound, then he spouteth bloud (whereas formerly he cast forth water) and his strength beginneth to fayle him." The whale is next towed to the ship, across the stern of which it is laid. The blubber is next cut off, " then to race it from the flesh, there is a crane or capstan placed purposely upon the poope of the ship, from whence there descendeth a rope with a hooke in it; this hooke is made to take hold on a piece of blubber; and as the men wind the capsten, so the cutter with his long knife looseth the fat from the flesh, even as if the lard of a swine were to be cut off from the leane." The blubber is next towed ashore to the cookeries, where it is boiled (see p. 80). The fins are then severed from one another with axes, cleaned, and packed in bundles of fifties.

This description of Edge's applies to the period of the bay fishery, when the whales were abundant close to the shore. At this time whales were present in enormous numbers in Spitsbergen waters. They arrived on the west coasts and in the west bays of Spitsbergen in the early summer, travelling eastward. They entered the bays in large schools, staying a considerable time, until the excessive hunting drove them out into the open sea, where the chase and capture were far more difficult than in the landlocked and smooth waters of the bays.

Segersz, who wintered on Spitsbergen in 1633-34, says that the whales deserted the bays on the 27th October, 1633, returning on the 27th April, 1634.[1]

---

[1] Segersz, Jacob, van Brugge. Journael of Dagh Register, gehouden by Seven Matroosen, In haer Overwinteren op Spitsbergen in Maurits-Bay Gelegen in Groenlandt. A zedert het vertreck van de Visschery-Schepen de Geoctroyeerde Noordtsche Compagnie, in Nederlandt, zijnde den 30 Augusty, 1633, tot de wederkomste der voosz. Schepen, den 27 May, Anno 1634. Beschreven door den Bevel-hebber Jacob Segersz, van der Brugge. Amsterdam, 1634. *Eng. Trans. Hakl. Soc.*, " Early Dutch and English Voyages to Spitsbergen," 1904.

CHAPTER IV

THE DUTCH WHALERS PREDOMINANT (1623-1750)

The methods of the Dutch whalers at Spitsbergen—Smeerenburg—The French at Spitsbergen—The English Muscovy Company—Anderson and Gray's description of the fishery—The German whalers—The pre-eminence of the Dutch.

ACCORDING to Jansen,[1] the Dutch whalers (1613-1750) did not keep regular written logs. It was not the custom of fishermen to do so, and it was only towards the middle of the nineteenth century that vessels engaged in the Dutch herring fishery kept logs. The whalers went out and home every year, keeping only a slate and no log. The accounts that have been published were written from memory, and were in some cases greatly amplified by those who received them. Fogs prevented accurate observations, and when the fog cleared away boisterous weather drove down the ice from the region of the Pole and compelled the whalers to run before it. Many whalers were lost, and the States General were compelled to make a law to regulate the manner in

[1] Notes on the Ice between Greenland and Nova Zembla; being the results of investigations into the records of early Dutch voyages in the Spitsbergen seas. *Proc. Roy. Geog. Soc.*, Vol. ix., London, 1864-5.

which the whalers were to assist those who had lost their ships.[1]

As a rule whalers did not venture beyond 80° N. Latitude, but entered the west ice at 79° or 79½° N., neither higher nor lower.

The Dutch navigators from 1613 to the end of the eighteenth century were whalers and not explorers. The first period the bay fishery (shore fishery) led to the building of Smeerenburg as an oil boiling establishment. The whalers at this period went straight to Smeerenburg and plied their calling there as described by Zorgdrager (*infra*). A shore fishery was established on Jan Mayen in 1617, and though successful at first, the whales were never so abundant there as at Spitsbergen.

About 1626, when the shore fishery was falling off, the Noordsche Compagnie sent out voyages ostensibly to seek the north-east passage, but really to try and discover new whaling grounds. The results of these voyages were kept secret for this reason.

When the whales were much harried and commenced to leave Spitsbergen they went round the north-west point towards the east, whither the whalers followed them. The new whaling ground was called to the eastward, and the whales caught there were said by the whalers to be different from the species that took flight to the north-west and west

---

[1] Reglement van de Groenlandtsche visscherye, over het bergen der goederen en hetgeene daeren dependeert, nevens haer Ed. Gr. Mog. Resolutie van approbatie, 22 Jan., 1695. *Gr. Placboek*, iv., 1355.

in the ice-bearing southerly current (Greenland current).

The ice between Spitsbergen and Greenland was called West-ice, and the whales in it West-ice Whales. After the slaughter at Smeerenburg these West-ice Whales became very cunning and shy. The other whales, though not differing in appearance, were more abundant in unusual years when the ice east of Spitsbergen and Nova Zembla drifted in greater quantity and with smaller and flatter floes much lower down than in ordinary years. Such an unusual year in which there was great abundance of this peculiar whale was called a south-ice year, and the whale a South-ice Whale. This South-ice Whale was not so shy and cunning as the West-ice Whale, and was even, after a hundred years' slaughter, still more easy to catch than the other.

From this it would appear that south-ice years have been exceptional, otherwise this whale would have changed its habits, like the West-ice Whale.

The whaling ground to the eastward, north of Spitsbergen, was called "Waigat" (blow-hole) because the southerly wind blows strongly through it. The Waygat or Waigat was the north end of Hinlopen Strait.

De Stræt van Hinlopen was first marked on Blæus map (1662); at the same time Colom, Valk and Schenk call it Waygat. The two names were used interchangeably from that time down to Scoresby's day (1820). Martens writes in 1671,

"It is unknown whether the haven of this Weigatt (blow-hole) goeth through the country or no."

In some years this Waygat was blocked with ice, and then the whalers went back round the west ice and anchored at Disco and about the south-east point of Spitsbergen, sending their boats into the ice because there were no whales in the open water. These boats had great difficulty in towing the dead whales, with oars and sails, out of the ice on the east coast towards their ships. If a gale from the east or north-east brought this ice into motion, the ships weighed anchor and retreated into Wybe Jansz Bay.

Whaling was first made a free trade about 1650, by this time the west-ice fishery was being established.

The west-ice fishery was divided into high and low latitude fishery, the former between $79\frac{1}{2}°$ and $73°$ N. Latitude and the latter lower down. At its period of greatest prosperity from one hundred to two hundred ships went along the Greenland ice up to Spitsbergen Voorland (on Prince Charles Island) or straight to $79°$ or $79\frac{1}{2}°$ N., very seldom higher or lower, and thence steered west in the ice-bearing southerly current that is in an ordinary year.

In a south-ice year they did not go so high, but steered east as soon as they found it was a good year for the South-ice Whale. How this was ascertained was doubtful. "Having ascertained from the shape of the ice, its height, size and form, that we were in the south-ice, and that it was a south-ice year, we steered towards the east."

THE DUTCH WHALERS PREDOMINANT 123

The worst year on record was 1668 when the Dutch ships failed to get higher than the Voorland. In an ordinary year the vessels went two hundred and twenty-four miles from Spitsbergen before the real ice fields were found, some thirty-six miles long with smooth water. Sometimes over one hundred ships were attached to the same field. They drifted south with the ice; when free, if full, they went home, if not, they went back again to 79° N. to make the same circuit again, or to the old whaling grounds to the eastward to Disco or Nova Zembla.

If, after a mild winter, there happened to be a hot summer and winds favourable for scattering the ice, then there was a good deal of open water in the ice-bearing current of Greenland, and consequently few whales, for they avoided open water. When the Dutch whalers had been unsuccessful in the west ice and were induced to go to Nova Zembla, it was probably because there was too much open water, and if this assumption be correct, then they only went to Nova Zembla in favourable years.

The most favourable year for going north that way must have been a south-ice year when the ice north and east of Nova Zembla came down towards the North Sea, and in those south-ice years all the Dutch whalers got plenty of whales in the south ice and did not go north. In some years, when the Dutch whalers had been unsuccessful in the west ice the opening in the ice near Nova Zembla was sometimes so great that no ice could be seen.

The general opinion in the seventeenth and

eighteenth centuries was that every winter the water round the Pole was frozen more or less down to 76° N. Latitude, according to the severity of the weather. The whales were supposed to remain in winter near the edge of the ice pack, where the food was scanty, so that the whales captured in the early part of the season were thin. There was an extensive barrier between Spitsbergen and Nova Zembla.

In 1707 a Dutch whaling captain named Cornelis Gillis found, towards the end of the season when looking for whales to the eastward, enough open water to go up north among the seven islands and beyond 81° N. From thence he steered east and south-east round N.E. Land. In the parallel of great island he saw high land at a distance of one hundred miles from N.E. Land.

In some years the Dutch whalers drifted to within a few miles of Greenland in 72° N., but although they often wanted to go ashore, the Whaling Company prevented it. The Dutch whalers have been near the coast of Greenland opposite Iceland.

Usually the Spitsbergen season closed late in August or early September.

Since in 1624 a well-laden Dutch ship, which left the fishing grounds in advance of the remainder of the fleet, was captured on the homeward journey by a Dunkirk privateer,[1] it became the custom for all the fleet to assemble together at a given rendezvous at the end of the season and journey home together for mutual protection.

[1] Wassenaer *Histt. verh.*, fol. 86.

THE DUTCH WHALERS PREDOMINANT

In 1633 the Dutch fleet left Spitsbergen on the 30th August,[1] and Jan Mayen on the 26th August.[2] In 1634 they left Spitsbergen on the 1st September,[3] but generally they left about the middle of August.

At this time the Spitsbergen harbours were shared between the different nations engaged in the whale fisheries.

The English, Dutch, French, and Danes each had their own harbour, where the oil was prepared and the fins cleaned. In the huts the superfluous gear, such as spare boats, were laid up for the winter.

The division of the bays was a source of much trouble. In the first instance the English made an exclusive claim to all the bays and harbours, and, in any case, being the first at the fisheries, they had naturally seized the best fishing places. Reference has already been made (p. 112) to the proposals of the Dutch negotiators in the winter of 1618-19. The different nations frequented selected localities to which they gradually acquired a sort of prescriptive right.

The English claimed from Crosse Roade and Deere Sound right down to Horne Sound. There were English huts (at that time called tents) at the north end of Foreland Sound at both sides, in Greene Harbour, Bell Sound, and on the south shore of Horn Sound. The Dutch occupied

[1] Van der Brugge. *Journal, Hakl. Soc.*, 1904, p. 87.
[2] Van der Brugge. *Twee Journalen*, p. 3.
[3] *Ibid.*, p. 22

harbours north of the English, their principal resort being the bay at north-west angle of Spitsbergen, which they called Mauritius Bay.

The two islands to the west of it, shown on Edge's map, but not named on it, are now known as Amsterdam and Danes Islands; on the former, Hackluits headland is marked. On the east part of the south shore of Amsterdam Island the Dutch built their village of Smeerenburg or Blubbertown. At the commencement of the fishery the Noordsche Compagnie was mainly an Amsterdam venture, but at each renewal of the charter other towns were admitted. Each town had a chamber or committee, and the united chambers formed the company. The older chambers had larger shares and better stations than those admitted later. Each chamber had its own "tent" at Smeerenburg, with a complete equipment for the fishing. The Amsterdam tent had the best position at the east end of Smeerenburg. In order to the west were the following tents: Middleburg, Flushing, the Danes, Delft, and Hoorn.

The Danes afterwards separated from the Dutch. Enkhuisen also had a tent and Van der Brugge mentions a Veere tent.

Each chamber probably had a capstan of its own for hauling in the whales and the ships to their moorings, and for hoisting the blubber and casks. The ships were moored in a row with their sterns to the shore, and room between each for a rowing-boat to pass.

THE DUTCH WHALERS PREDOMINANT 127

Zorgdrager[1] gives a detailed account of the Dutch operations at Spitsbergen at the time when they first took the lead at the Northern whale fisheries. The ships anchored in Dutch Bay, off the flat of Smeerenberg, in a row one behind another, or so near to one another that a sloop could just pass between to tow the oil-casks from ashore on board. An anchor was let go from forward into the bay and the ship made fast astern with a rope to the shore, either to the foundations of the kettles (coppers), or to some large stone, or to the jawbone of a whale, whereof some are still (1720) to be seen in various places as high piles set up for the purpose on the beach. Lying here, as in a desired and safe haven, three or four miles inland from the sea, preserved and protected from all winds, they pursued their fishery with convenience and enjoyment, rowing their sloops round and to the ships in the bay, which in those days was generally full of fish, as their doings and remains sufficiently manifest in various accounts of this fishery, otherwise they would not have settled themselves so solidly by their oil cookeries and laid up their ships so comfortably at anchor. Besides, they brought up double crews of sixty, seventy, and even eighty men, which were apportioned some to the sloops to kill the fish and tow them to the oil cookeries on the shore, others to remain on land and cut up the blubber from the fish, chop it up small, boil down

---

[1] Zorgdrager. *Bloyende Opkomst*, 1st edition, Amsterdam, 1720, p. (in my copy) 174-5; obviously a misprint for 184-5.

the oil, fill it into casks, and roll them down to the water. Others again were on the ships to bring the casks alongside, hoist them aloft with a pulley, and lade them into the ship.

At this time (1623) there came yearly a small fleet of ships from Amsterdam, Rotterdam, Hoorn, and other places, which were arranged in a row along the flat of Smeerenburg, each by its own cookery. Thus there were Amsterdam, Hoorn, Rotterdam, and other oil cookeries with their warehouses and cooperies, wherein a quantity of Greenland implements were stored, casks made, bound and taken away, many things kept ready for future use, and stored away, when the ships sailed home.

According to Müller,[1] the Danes left Smeerenburg in 1623, their place being taken by the Hoorn, Enkhuisen and Flushing men from 1625 onwards. This place lay to the west of the Amsterdam " tents." The Danes protested, but without effect.

In 1626 there were five big Dutch tents at Smeerenburg. In 1633 all the chambers of the Noordsche Compagnie had tents there.[2] Amsterdam alone, had two large tents, the other towns, such as Middleburg, Veere, Flushing, Enkhuisen, Delft, and Hoorn, one each.

All these cookeries and warehouses (Zorgdrager, p. 191) along the flat of Smeerenburg resembled the neighbourhood of a small town, which consequently was named Blubbertown, after the industry.

[1] " Geschiednis der Noordsche Compagnie," p. 143.
[2] *Ibid.*, p. 144.

TYPE OF EARLY DUTCH WHALER, WITH WHALING IMPLEMENTS.

THE DUTCH WHALERS PREDOMINANT 129

It is not clear how many oil cookeries and warehouses there were in all. In 1720 the foundations and ruins of eight or ten oil-coppers were distinguishable, and those of the warehouses. The rest were all decayed by the passage of time so that no trace remained.

Seeing that the ships, as previously stated, brought up double crews, it was very dull, not only on the ships and boats, but also on shore. There came up, therefore, as in a camp, some sutlers, who sold their wares, such as brandy and tobacco and the like, in their own huts or in the warehouses. Bakers also went there to bake bread. In the morning when the hot rolls and white bread were drawn from the oven, a horn was blown, so that some enjoyment was then to be had at Smeerenburg.

In addition to the buildings for the carrying on of the whalers' business, there was a church and a fort with several batteries.[1]

The great days at Smeerenburg were those following 1633, when the place was annually visited by over a thousand whalers, in addition to what may be considered the camp-followers.

There is evidence that the buildings at Smeerenburg were commenced in 1619; twenty years later the place was in a condition of decay.[2]

During the time the fishing was confined to the Dutch chartered companies, the number of ships

---

[1] Müller. "Noordsche Compagnie," p. 147.
[2] Müller, p. 148.

employed was annually about thirty; soon after the fishery was thrown open this number considerably increased. There is no detailed account of the conditions at Smeerenburg at the period of its greatest prosperity. Dirck Albertsz Raven of Hoorn[1] describes a few days spent there in 1639, when, according to Müller, decay had already set in. Raven's ship was wrecked in the ice off Spitsbergen, most of the crew losing their lives. The survivors were taken off by another Dutch whaler, of which Gale Hamkes was master. Gale Hamkes' ship, the *Oranje Boom*, put into Smeerenburg harbour. "On the 4th July we came into West Bay; the sloops of Gale Hamkes then brought us to our tents, where we at once set to work and got ready our three sloops with all their accessories, wherewith we afterwards still caught three whales. On the 26th our one sea-fisher came to us in the Bay, with a good quantity of blubber. On the 22nd August our second sea-fisher also came to us in the Bay, with his ship full of blubber, whereat we were very glad; we then divided our men on the two ships, and got ready to depart again." It is evident at this time that whales were captured partly at sea and partly in the bay.

It is impossible to give a full account of each

---

[1] Journael ofte Beschrijvinge van de reyse ghedaen by den Commandeur Dirck Albertsz. Raven nae Spitsbergen in den Jare 1639, ten dienste van de C. Heeren Bewindt-hebbers van de Groenlandtsche Compagnie tot Hoorn. Waer in verhaelt wordt sijn droevighe Schip-breucke sijn ellende opt wrack, en sijn blijde verlossinge. Met noch eenighe ghedenckweerdige Historien. Hoorn, 1646.

THE DUTCH WHALERS PREDOMINANT

year's proceedings at the Spitsbergen fishery. In 1624 five English ships going to the fishery met two Zeelanders, and would have attacked them, but for the opportune appearance of a Dutch man-of-war.[1] More Dutch ships, to the number of twenty, arrived, so the English were compelled to retire. One of these Dutch ships was a small vessel of eighty tons, in charge of Simon Willemsz, with Jacob Jacobsz of Edam as pilot, with instructions to sail along the north coast to Cape Tabin, and try for a north-east passage. They could not have gone very far, since they were back in time to take part in the season's fishing. The Dutch made a good voyage this year, but sending a laden vessel home imprudently in advance of the others, she was captured by a Dunkirk privateer and held to ransom for ten thousand guilders.

In 1625 the Muscovy Company sent twelve ships to the fishery, under command of Captain William Goodlad, who, arriving at Whale Head, found that nine ships of York and Hull had been there and taken away the Company's shallops left over from the previous season, burned their casks and spoiled their material for the fishery, besides demolishing their houses and fort. On his return, Goodlad applied to the Privy Council for warrants

---

[1] Claes Wassenaer. Historisch verhael alder ghedenckweerdichste Geschiedenisse, die hier en daer in Europa, als in Duitsch-lant, Vranck-rijk ... en Neder-lant, Asia, America en Africa, van den beginne des jaers 1621 tot Octobri des jaers 1632, voorgevallen sijn. (Met platen kaarten en portretten.) Tot Amstelredam, by Jan Evertsz, Kloppenburgh, 1622-4, J. Hondius, 1624, en Jan Jansz, 1625-35, 21 dln., 7 bdn., 4to.

against Richard Prestwood and Richard Perkins "the principal agents in this contempt."

From this time onwards the British whale fisheries at Spitsbergen declined gradually. The whales in the Bays were now scarce and shy, so that it became the custom of the Dutch and Basque whalers to seek them on the edge of the ice to the northward and westward. The English whalers clung to the Bays long after fishing there had ceased to be profitable, and this, combined with squabbles at home between the "Company" and the "Interlopers," led to the disappearance of the British whalers, so there is a distinct gap between the first period of British whaling and the effort by the South Sea Company to resuscitate the trade in 1724.

In 1626 Charles I. licensed Nathaniel Edwards and his partners as a Scottish Company, and their competition had to be bought off by the Greenland Company; for instance, materials for the equipment of the whalers were bought by the latter from Edwards. The competition of the Hull interlopers was a further drawback. In the interests of King Charles's soap monopoly the use of of Greenland oil for soap-making was prohibited, so that the conditions were not very favourable for the growth of an industry already threatened by the severe competition of the Dutch.

The "Society of Soapmakers in the City of Westminster in the County of Middlesex" had the monopoly of soap manufacture and the right of search. Proceedings had soon to be taken against

THE DUTCH WHALERS PREDOMINANT

the old soap boilers, who, in disobedience to the proclamation, used fish oil, and refused to have their soap tried or marked by the assay-master, and who also, though not a body corporate, presumed to assemble in taverns in London and to confer about the sale of their soap and the buying of fish oil from the Greenland Company.

In 1633 a charter incorporated the Governor and Company of the English Colony of Rhodé and Providence Plantations in New England in America. This grant encouraged whale killing.

The French, apart from the Basques, participated but slightly in th- Spitsbergen whaling. Even the Basques went mainly as harpooners in Dutch and English vessels, until the seamen of those nations had learnt the art of killing the whale. Still there were a few attempts, both by the French and by the Basques, to take part in this lucrative fishery.

A " Compagnie du Pole Arctique " was founded secretly in Paris in 1609, not for discovery, but for occupation, and for securing a short passage to the East Indies. It seems to have been fantastically conceived and nothing came of it.

Apparently it was due, to some extent at any rate, to the initiative of this company, that the three Basque ships, *La Grace-de-Dieu* of St Jean de Luz, *Les Quatre-fils-Aymon* of Rochelle, and the *Jacques* of Bordeaux, went to the Spitsbergen fishery of 1613 (see p. 96), where whales were reported to be *comme carpes en un vivier!*

Reference has already been made to the exploits of these vessels, which were commanded by Mignet de Haristiguy, Michel d'Etchepare, and Silhouette. These vessels fished in Bell Sound, which was even then known as the Bay of the French, this pointing to the existence of previous expeditions. All record of these expeditions is now lost, and in fact there is little evidence that the French participated to any extent in the first phase of the Spitsbergen fishery.

The history of the early French adventures in the Spitsbergen whale fishery is obscure, although some research into the history of the subject has recently been undertaken, notably by Hamy.

In 1621 there was founded a society in France entitled " Royale et Generale Compagnie du commerce pour les voyages de long cours es Indes occidentales, la pesche du corail en Barbarie et celle des baleines." The history of this French company is imperfect; the records of the voyages have disappeared, leaving hardly a trace behind. The great French market for whale oil at this time was Havre de Grace, whither the Bayonne ships, for example, took their cargoes. The leader in French whaling enterprise was Jean Vrolicq, whom we first hear of in 1631, entering into partnership with Johann Braem of Copenhagen who had obtained a charter from Christian IV., giving him the right to send six ships to Spitsbergen.

Vrolicq, who had already applied to the French King for a charter, fished in partnership with the Danes in 1631. The following year Vrolicq went to Spitsbergen under the sole patronage of the French King and Cardinal Richelieu, where he attempted to fish in the Bay of Basques, south of Magdalena Bay. He was, however, ordered off by the Dutch, so he went to Iceland whence he made a poor voyage. On his return to France he complained, so the French Government made representations at the Hague, strongly supporting his right to take part in the Spitsbergen whale fishery. The States General eventually recommended the Noordsche Compagnie to allow him to fish outside the limits of their fishery. In 1633 and 1634 Vrolicq was again at Spitsbergen, but he was interfered with by the Dutch and eventually ruined.

Fourteen French ships went to the fishery in 1636, but these were all captured by the Spaniards in the autumn of that year when they sacked St Jean de Luz, Cibourre, and Soccoa. In 1637 a Danish warship drove the French ships out of Spitsbergen waters so that the Havre Company, having sustained a loss of one hundred and sixty thousand livres, was forced into liquidation. The French were unwilling to drop out altogether from such a lucrative trade, so in 1644 Cardinal Mazarin founded the Compagnie du Nord établie pour la pesche des ballaines, which in 1648 amalgamated with the Compagnie de mer de St Jean de Luz. So for a few years longer the French flag was seen in Arctic waters. The charter was renewed in 1669, but shortly afterwards the Company abandoned the business.

In the seventeenth century the Dutch developed

two extensive fisheries, the Grand Fishery, which was the herring fishery in the North Sea, and the Small or Lesser Fishery, which was the whale fishery at " Greenland " (really Spitsbergen). The former was the subject of minute regulation, the latter, though subject to various orders, was comparatively a free fishery, except that at first it was confined to the Noordsche Compagnie. The whalers, unlike the herring fishermen, could fish when and where they pleased. The Dutch Government, at the same time, was interested in the development of the whaling, and made frequent grants of convoy to and from the fishing grounds. There were also prohibitions on the export of whaling ships and implements, and the whalers were forbidden to take service in foreign ships. In time of war the whalers were not allowed to leave port, and they were not exempt from the financial and other burdens placed on the fishing trade in general. For instance, the whalers were ordered to carry home the whole of their blubber, oil, and whalebone, and sell them in the Dutch markets, for the conservation of the custom-house duties and the market tax.[1]

Except for this regulation there does not seem to have been any regulation on the fishing; there was no fishing season prescribed by law, neither were there any rules for branding the produce, i.e., the barrels or casks of train oil.

[1] Placaet, waerby den Groenlandts-Vaerders gelast wert tot conservatie der neeringen, licenten, convoyen ende veylgelt, hier te Lande met haer ghevangen visch, traen, etc., te komen, sonder eerst elders te mogen Zeylen. *Groot Plac.-boek.*, i., 683.

THE DUTCH WHALERS PREDOMINANT 137

The whalers, until the Bounty system was introduced, had to rely solely on their own energy and initiative. There was never any code of regulation for the whaling at all comparable to the code for the herring fishery.

Nevertheless, the herring fishery was the first to decline; the whaling continued to flourish long after there was an unmistakable decline in the former fishery. During the wars which were so frequent at this time the herring fleet, which fished the North Sea, was far more liable to attack by privateers than the whalers in the distant waters at Spitsbergen. In fact, the latter were only liable to attack on the outward or homeward journey, particularly the latter. For their protection during these voyages the convoy system was adopted.[1]

The war with England in 1652-4 was prejudicial to the " Greenland " trade. In April, 1652, before hostilities commenced, the Dutch resolved to continue in the whaling during the coming season, and took steps to secure the supply of able seamen. In July the advisability of calling home the whaling fleet was considered, but for the time the Dutch Government warned the whalers to keep together for safety.

Although it appears that the whaling was kept going in 1652, it was forbidden the following year,[2]

[1] Rapport van de Raadpensionaris van de bedenking der Generaliteit om de geheele visscherije op te ontbieden, van haar neering tot preservatie hunner apparente schaade en ruine door de engelsche vloot; ook de Groenlandsvaarders adverteeren, haar bij form van admiraalschepen te voegen om de gedreygde swaarigheid te ontgaan, 21 July, 1652.

[2] Waerschouwinge ende verboth, waerby omme pregnante

not only to keep the ships safely in port, but because the men were required for the navy.

The "Greenland" warehouses in Amsterdam are described by Filips von Zesen.[1] They belonged to the Greenland (Noordsche) Company, and were situated in the Keisers-gracht. The Greenland Company originally boiled down their oil at Spitsbergen, but other traders, not members of the Company, at this time brought the blubber home to boil it down. The land in the Keisers-gracht was bought by the Company in 1620, and it is probable that the warehouses were erected soon after, when the Company was at the height of its prosperity.

The warehouses were spacious and well suited for the accommodation of the requisites of the fishery and the general merchandise of the Company. There were great stone cisterns[2] in the cellars for the storage of train oil, which was better preserved there, and less subject to leakage than in vats. These warehouses are illustrated in Conway's "No

redenen den Walvisch-vanghst voor het jaer 1653, geschorst wordt, 25 Maart, 1653. *Gr. Plac.-boek.*, ii., 506.

[1] Beschriebung der stadt Amsterdam, darinnen von derselben ersten ursprunge bis auf gegenwärtigen Zustand, ihr unterschiedlicher anwachs, herliche vorrechte, und in mehr als 70 Kupferstükken entworfene führnemhste Gebeue, zusamst ihrem Stahtswesen, Kaufhandel und ansehnlicher macht zur See, wie auch was sich in und mit Derselben märkwürdiges zugetragen vor augen gestellet werden Zu Amsterdam, Gedrukt und verlegt durch Joachim Noschen. Im Jahr, 1664. See also Muller, Noordsche Compagnie," p. 121.

[2] "Gemetzelde Bakken." See *Le Moine de l'Espine and Isaac de Long*. De Koophandel van Amsterdam, Rotterdam, 1780, Vol. ii., p. 198.

Man's Land." They are still in existence and in a good state of preservation. Practically all trace of the blubber-houses or cookeries, which must have been built all over the West European coast from Lübeck to the north of Spain, has now vanished. After the period of the bay fishery at Spitsbergen was over, all the whalers, with the exception of the Basques, brought the blubber home to be boiled down. The first German oil cookeries were erected at Hamburg in 1649; not much is known about them, but they were developed and increased until 1675, when they were burnt down. In 1753 Conrad von Uffenbach described those on the banks of the Elbe near the Altona gate at Hamburg. These blubber factories, which belonged to Mennonites, are fully described and figured by Uffenbach.[1]

The first Dutch cookeries were built at Oostzanen, on the Twisk near the Overtoom, they are illustrated in Conway's " No Man's Land."

The Noordsche Company lost their monopoly in 1642, and immediately the Dutch whaling showed signs of rapid improvement. Meanwhile the English trade languished. The Civil War exercised a detrimental effect on the commerce of the country, and from this even the whaling was not exempt. The disputes between the Monopolists and the Interlopers dragged along interminably.

After the Dutch whaling became free to all (*circa* 1645), a great number took part in it, and for that very reason the increased quantity of whale

[1] " Merkwürdige Reisen durch Niedersachsen," 1753.

products caused a fall in price, which again jeopardised the whale fisheries.

It became customary, in order to avoid the customs duty of two per cent, to land the oil and bone in foreign countries, but this was forbidden by a law of 1652, according to which all Dutch whalers were required to land their cargoes at their home ports. In 1661 all the Dutch whalers were forbidden to go into foreign service, or to sell their sloops, casks, sails, harpoons, or other gear to foreigners. The trade was assisted in 1675 by the passing of two orders, one of which admitted the Dutch whaling products free, and the other taxed foreign imports into Holland with double the original duty (of two per cent). There was an immediate and marked revival, and soon after about two hundred and fifty Dutch ships set out annually to the fishery.

Each ship had to deposit six thousand guilders caution money before starting, as a security that it would return with its cargo to the home port. In war time the whale fishery was either forbidden, the sailors being pressed into the naval service, or the whaling fleet was permitted to start under adequate naval protection.

Commissaries were appointed from South and North Holland, from among the leading men in the trade to see that the regulations were carried out.

The whaling trade generally seems to have been run on a slender margin of profit. True, there were enormous prizes to a favoured few, but, on the whole, the profit was small, and many were able to take part in the trade simply because they supplied the goods which the whalers required. Had they to purchase these goods instead of supplying them at cost price, it is doubtful whether they could have kept on with the trade.

During this period of the Dutch predominance the British whalers were engaged in a series of disputes which may be referred to briefly.

In 1645 the Greenland Company (the successors of the Muscovy Company) petitioned Parliament, which gave notice to all the ports throughout England, by their burgesses, that all should come in and join the Company in guarding the harbours (in Spitsbergen), giving assurance to Parliament to set out yearly a certain proportion of ships. Three months' consideration was given, but, owing to the hazardous nature of the trade, none came in except York, Hull and Yarmouth. It was therefore stipulated that no new adventurers of only two or three years' standing should now be admitted, since London, Hull and Yarmouth have, at great cost, defended Bell Sound, Horne Sound, Green Harbour, Cross Road, Mettle Bay, and Sir Thomas Smyth's Bay. The late intruders, Warner, Whitwell, and others, have for two years only sent into the Company's harbours two or three small vessels, which not only refused to join them to keep out the French and Dutch, but brought in Dutch strangers to manage their stock and adventure, the consequences of which will be most dangerous to English navigation.

The dispute between the Greenland or Muscovy Company and the " Interlopers," as they were called, was really an important trade quarrel between monopolists on the one hand and free traders on the other. Briefly, the Muscovy Company claimed the sole right to the whale fishery at Spitsbergen on the following grounds:[1]

Their discovery of the trade and its protection from the Dutch, their chartered rights confirmed by the Navy Commissioners and the Committee for Trade, and their vested interests. In 1654 a strong effort was made to put an end to these everlasting disputes, which naturally exercised a detrimental influence on the whaling trade. A petition to the Protector was drawn up (17th January, 1654), by Francis Ashe, Governor of the Muscovy Company, in which an appeal is made for regulations for the trade, so that rival interests should not clash in certain harbours, and more harbours might be opened up for whaling. The Company wished to retain possession of Horne and Bell Sounds, urging that private adventurers could not succeed, because the erection of storehouses is needful to store the oil of a successful year, which will occur every three or four years, when the whales come in shoals, and

---

[1] To give full details of this dispute would require a special volume. See *The Calendar of State Papers, Domestic*, from 1611 to 1671.

THE DUTCH WHALERS PREDOMINANT 143

compensate for two or three losing years, and these storehouses involve great expense which could not be faced by private individuals.

The free adventurers (Edward Whitwell and Richard Eccleston of Hull being the leaders) chiefly Hull men, commenced an agitation. They appeared before the Committee of the Council of State appointed to inquire into the question, and in addition printed a broadside addressed to Parliament and every member thereof. They were not above introducing politics into the dispute.

"We conceive the right which such as seek to ingrosse the trade and harbours to themselves, pretend to have, is onely grounded upon a monopolising pattent; which came from prerogative power, and not consistent with the freedome of a Commonwealth and the members thereof. In the late King's time the Company used all unjust, illegal and arbitrary means possible to suppress all but themselves."

The free traders' claim was based on the plea that the trade was discovered by Hull men forty years ago; that there is ample room for all who desire to fish, and that it is inconsistent with the public welfare to restrain the fishing to fifty people, who enhance the price of oil by their inability to bring in a sufficient quantity, that Bell Sound, one of the harbours claimed by the Muscovy Company, is thirty miles long by fifteen broad, and Green Harbour still larger, and that by the admission of all there would no longer be any need to import oil or fins from Holland, and the state would be strengthened by the increase of shipping.

In reply, the Greenland Company stated that where several ships fish in the same bay there are bound to be disputes and quarrels.

According to the Company's agents the whales at this time came into the bays in schools of from two to three hundred " to gender, feed, and rubb themselves," staying many days. The schools consisted of families of two, three or four together; when one was struck with a harpoon the other members of the family dispersed, but whales not of the family paid little attention. " So that when one interest is onely there, they can take or pursue such as are most likely to goe first out, and to follow the rest at leisure; whereas if there be divers interests, each party disturbs the fish wheresoever it appeares, having onely respect to their owne profitt, and so suddanily scares or drives away the whales."

In the light of modern opinion the demands of the Greenland Company seem quite unreasonable, and it must have been evident to the Company that Parliament would not exclude the free traders entirely from the fishery. The free traders wanted all the harbours open to everyone, first comers to have a choice of place, and only a certain number of boats to fish in each harbour. Eventually a compromise was arrived at.

Twelve ships of an aggregate tonnage of three

THE DUTCH WHALERS PREDOMINANT 145

thousand tons were to be sent to the fishery; five to fish in Bell Sound, three in Horn Sound, two in Ice Sound (Green Harbour), two in Cross Road and Sir Thomas Smyth's Bay. There were four hundred and twenty seamen and one hundred and sixty landsmen distributed as follows: two hundred and fifty men at Bell Sound, one hundred and forty men at Horn Sound, one hundred and ten men at Ice Sound, and eighty men at Cross Road and Sir Thomas Smyth's Bay. The shipping was to be supplied in the following proportion: the London Company, one thousand six hundred tons; Hull and York, four hundred tons; Horth for Yarmouth, five hundred tons; Whitwell and partners, three hundred tons, and Batson and partners (with L. Anderson), two hundred tons. The dispute dragged on without much prospect of being settled in time for the approaching season, so the London and Hull adventurers petitioned to be allowed to send up six ships with a pinasse.

This was the year in which the Dutch sent up seventy sail escorted by three men-of-war.

Soon after this the British whaling trade became practically moribund, and the home market for oil depended on captures made by privateers from the foreign whalers, and on the home-grown supply of rape seed. There are numerous references in the State Papers of this period to this privateering, of which a few may be quoted.

In September, 1666, the *Constant*, *Warwick*, and *Victory* put into Plymouth with three French prizes from Greenland, laden with whale oil, one of them being upwards of two hundred and fifty tons, and containing fourteen pieces of ordnance. In May, 1667, the *Mermaid* brought in two French prizes in ballast, bound for Greenland. This was not customary, as it paid better to seize full ships on the return voyage. In August a French ship laden with oil was taken off the coast of Holland and brought into the Humber by the *Hampshire* and the *Oxford*. The same month a Scottish privateer brought into Scarborough a Dutch prize of two hundred tons from Greenland, laden with oil and whalebone. On 3rd October a Frenchman laden with oil is in the roads off Deal, and on the 5th a Frenchman (a prize) with Greenland oil has gone up the Thames, and this presumably refers to the same vessel.

In 1668 the Greenland traders in Holland had such bad luck in their fishing that rape seed " rises apace " and great quantities are shipped from Hull to Holland, four vessels partly laden therewith having sailed by 4th October, and more daily were making ready. In 1671 Hull reports that " in rape seed it fails much of our expectation by reason the Holland Greenland fleet are so well fished that the price has fallen to nothing."

When the Greenland Trade was eventually thrown open by statute in 1672 the trade was quite lost, and wholly engrossed by foreigners.

In 1658-59 the Dutch helped the Danes in their war against Sweden, and in the latter year whaling

THE DUTCH WHALERS PREDOMINANT 147

was first of all forbidden,[1] and then permitted under certain conditions.[2]

Shipowners and captains in the trade were to put fifteen hundred able seamen at the disposal of the Dutch Admiralty, or buy them off at fifteen florin per head. These repeated wars adversely affected the Dutch whalers to such an extent that it became customary to put the ships under a foreign flag. This was forbidden again in 1661.[3]

At this period (*circa* 1660) we have two interesting manuscripts describing the " Greenland " whale fishery, by Anderson[4] and Gray,[5] the latter illustrated by small sketches.[6] The former manuscript is in the British Museum, the latter in the Register Book of the Royal Society. The Royal Society of London, which was incorporated by charter in 1662, interested itself in Spitsbergen and its whaling.

Both accounts are of great interest, as they prove that the English followed the bay fishery (in Bell

---

[1] Placaet, in welcke de Walvischvangst, ende vaert daerop tot nader orde geschort werd. *Gr. Plac.-boek.*, ii., 507.

[2] Nader Placaet, in welcke onder seeckere limitatien de vaert op Groenlandt toegelaten en andere equipagien ter zee bij provisie ende tot nader ordre verboden werden. *Gr. Plac.-boek.*, ii., 507.

[3] Placaet, houdende verbodt, om schepen te laten bevrachten, omme by uytheemsche natien tot den walvischvanghst gheemployert te worden. *Gr. Plac.-boek.*, ii., 2639.

[4] An account of Greenland from Capt. Lancelott Anderson, a Hull merchant who has made thirty-three voyages thither. British Museum, *MS. Sloane*, 3986, ff. 78, 79.

[5] *Register Book of the Royal Society*, Vol. ii. (1662-3), p. 308.

[6] These sketches, as well as the two manuscripts, are reproduced in the *Geographical Journal*, London, June, 1900.

Sound) long after it had been abandoned by the Dutch and French.

Lancelott Anderson was a whaling captain of Hull. He was on the whaling ship which rescued in May, 1631, the eight English whalemen who had been left behind on Spitsbergen the previous year, and were the first to winter there.[1] He is also mentioned in a list of those engaged in the whaling in 1654. His account of the whaling follows:

"First, that they usually went out of Hull in the beginning of May, and that it proved three weeks or four voyage to the place they went to which lay in 78 gr. of Latitude.

"Secondly, that they saild between great masses of ice of seventeen or twenty fathomes thick part of which stood out high above the level of the main mast, off which ran spouts of fair fresh water, when the sun shind upon them. To some of these masses of ice (which were of far lesser bulk) they often times fastened their ships by the Ankor when the winds were higher than ordinary to hinder it for running too swiftly that it might not split itselfe upon those great ices.

"Thirdly, that they caught their whales in some large Bay or other and particularly in the Bay call'd Bell Sound.

"That they always swome to them in their Boates with harping irons of this shape ○→ to strike them,

---

[1] "God's Power and Providence shewed in the Miraculous Preservation and Deliverance of Eight Englishmen," London, 1631. Reprinted, *Hak. Soc.*, 1855.

THE DUTCH WHALERS PREDOMINANT

and always strive to avoid their tayles (because with that part they strike and if they hitt a boate will break it in pieces) but if you bear up to their head and foreparts, then are you more secure.

"The whales are there of quick hearing (though they have but little ears) and if they bee suddenly surprised will quake and shiver, and strive to avoyd you by sinking down in the sea.

"After they are struck they presently dive and run down towards the Bottom.

"Now their harping irons are fastened to a Cord (which lyes coyled up in the Boate, so that it may not run fould) of three hundred fathoms. Which the whale will draw all after it and they follow hir with the Boate which way soever shee draw the cord, and it be not of length enough they are ready (with another Cord in another Boate) to fasten to the end of it before the whale has drawn it quite out to its full Length both of which may extend to one thousand fathom.

"The whale will toyle and weary hirselfe thus till she be weary or not able to stay longer under water (and she will sometimes stay one hower or more under water before shee appear at all) yea and will run under great Ilands of Ice which are floating there, but will come back againe to the open sea and aire.

"Lastly, when shee is dead and floates they lett hir alone for two or three days in which tyme shee swells and so a greater part of hir Back appears on the water.

"Then they goe to hir and cut off Collops of hir back as deepe as the fatt reaches and as far as the water permitts, which done they turn up one side and then the Belly and lastly the other side and so spades hir round and then leaving the rest of the body (except the whalebone which they take out of hir mouth) to the mercy of the sea.

"Then they take these Collops and Boyle them in their Coppers and so the fat runs all into oyle.

"And an ordinary whale will yield twelve tun of oyle, some twenty tun (if large and taken at a seasonable time)."

Mr Gray was one of the crew of the *Salutation*, Captain Mason, which was at the Spitsbergen fishery in 1630. He wrote an account of the whale fishery, which is in the Register Book of the Royal Society (1662-3), entitled, "The Manner of the Whale-fishing in Greenland, given by Mr Gray to Mr Oldenburg for the Society."

"We have according to the bignesse or smalnesse of our ships, the more or fewer Boates; a ship of two hundred tuns, may man six boats; A vessel of eighty or one hundred tuns, four boats; A vessel of sixty tuns, three boats or more, not lesse; three boats being as few as may be with convenience to kill a whale. Each boat hath six men; A Harpeneir, Steersman, and four Oars; to which men the merchant giveth (besides their wages) for every thirteen tuns of Oyle (which we call a whale) when there is so much for each boate, to the Harpenier

THE DUTCH WHALERS PREDOMINANT

6 li. 10s., the Steersman 3 li., and to each Oar 30s., in all for each boat 15 li. 10s., which we call whale money.

" We have several men and boats upon several convenient places, which we call Look-outs, that constantly remain looking out by turnes for the Whale, which when we fish in Harbour, cometh into a smooth Bay, where there is a good Harbour for our ships; and having discovered the Whale, which swimmeth with her back above the water, or is descried by the water which she bloweth into the Air, one Lookout maketh signes to another, by hoysing up a basket upon a Pole, and then all the boats row after her, and having opportunity to row up with her before she goeth down, strike a Harping-iron into her, to which is a staffe joyned being about six foot long, called a harping-staffe, to the Socket of which Iron is a white rope, with an eye seazed very fast; This Rope is about five fathoms long, which Lying upon the forepart of the Boat (which we call a Shallop) always coyled over a little pin, ready to take up, to give scope to the iron, when it is thrown at the Whale; and to this hand-rope is a warpe of three hundred fathoms seazed, to veer after the whale, lest, when she is struck, by her swift motion (which is often down to the ground, where the water is sixty, seventy, or eighty fathom deep) she should sink the boat.

" Thus having gotten our Iron into her, our boats row where they think she will rise (after she hath been beating her selfe at ground) and get two or three more irons into her, and then we account her secure.

"Then when she is neer tired with striving and wearied with the boats and ropes, we lance her with long Lances, the Irons and stands wereof are about twelve or fourteen foot long, with which we prick her to death; and in killing her, many times she staveth some of our boats, beating and flourishing with her tayle above water, that the boats dare scarce come nigh her, but oftentimes in an hours time she is dispatched. Thus having killed her, our boats tow her (all of them rowing one before another, one fast to another like a team of Horses) to the ships stern, where, after she hath layn twenty-four hours we cut off the blubber, and take the finns (which we commonly call the whalebone) and her tongue out of her mouth, and with a great pair of slings and tackle, we turn her round, and take all that is good off her, and then we turn her carcass adrift and tow the blubber (cut in pieces) to the shore where works stand to mannure it.

"Having made fast the blubber to the shore, we have a Waterside-man who stands in a pair of boots, to the middle leg in water, and flaweth such flesh as is not clean from the blubber; Then we have two men with a barrow, that when the Waterside man hath cut it in pieces about two hundredweight, carry it up to a stage standing by our Works, like a Table; then we have a man with a long knife, who we call a Stage-cutter, who sliceth it into thin pieces about halfe an inch thick, and a foot long or longer, and throws it into a Cooler, we call a slicing-cooler, betwixt which and another cooler (called a chopping-cooler) we have men called choppers placed; five or six men, who upon blocks cut about a foot and halfe square (made of the tayle of the whale, which is very tough) do take the sliced blubber and chop it very small and thin, not above a quarter of an inch thick, and an inch or two long; and thrust it off from the blocks into the Chopping-cooler, which holds two or three tuns.

"Then upon a platforme is built a Copper-hole, about four foot high, to which there is a stokehole, and on this Copper-hole is a broad Copper which containeth about a Butt, hanged with mortar and made tight round the edges. And over the stokehole, upon an Arch, stands a Chimney which draws up the smoke and flame. And we have one we call a Tubfiller who with a Ladle of Copper, whose handle is about six foot long, taketh the Chopt blubber out of the chopping-cooler and puts it into a hogshead made with straps for that purpose, and he drawes this hogshead from the chopping-cooler's side to the Copper and putteth it in; under which having once kindled a fire of wood and boiled a Copper or two of Oyle, the scruffe which remains after the oyle is boiled out of the blubber (which we call fritters) we throw under the Copper, which makes a fierce fire and so boyleth the Oyle out of the blubber without any other fewell.

"Then when we find that it is boyled enough, we have two men which we call coppermen who with two longhandled copper ladles take both oil and fritters out of the Copper, about halfe, and put it into a Barrow (we call a Fritter-barrow) made with two handles and barrell-boards set about halfe a-quarter of one inch from the other, through which the oyle runneth and the Fritters remain; from which the oyle being drained whilst another Coper of oyle boils, they are cast into the stokehole and burnt, and the barrow stands ready again on the first Oyle-cooler, to receive what is taken out of the next Copper. Out of this barrow the oyle runs into a great thing we call a Cooler made of Deal-boards, containing about five tuns, which is filled within an inch of a hole (made in the side for the oyle to run into the next spout) with water to cool the oyle, and so the oyle runs upon the water, through this hole into a spout about ten or twelve foot long, into another cooler filled as aforesaid and out of that, through a long spout into a third filled as aforesaid and out of that, in a long spout into a Butt laid under the end of this spout, which being full, the hole of the Cooler, next the Butt is stopt till another Butt is laid under, and then the plugg being taken out, it filleth another, till we have done boyling. Then we fill up our Oyles, when they are thoroughly cold, and marke them and roule them into the water, rafting twenty together, and so tow them aboard, hoyst them into our ships, and stow them to bring them home.

" And for our finns, which grow in two Gumms in the whales mouth (whereof in a whales mouth, great

THE DUTCH WHALERS PREDOMINANT 155

and small are about six hundred, four hundred and sixty whereof being merchandable) we cut them one by one out of the gumms and having rubbd them clean we bind them up sixty in a bundle, and so taking account of them ship them aboard in our Long-boat.

" Upon the shoar we have a Tent for our Landmen, built of stone, and covered with Deals, and Cabbins made therein for our Blubber-men to lodge; And we have a great Working-tent with a Lodging-room over it, where, about six Coopers work to get ready Cask to put the Oyle into."

The Germans first participated in the whale fishery in 1640, by which time the first prosperous period (the bay fishery) was over. The first oil-houses were built in Hamburg in 1648; in 1674 there were nine in existence. Hamburg whalers did well in the period 1669-98, especially in the years 1669, 1671, 1672, 1673, 1682, and 1697. In these years the average was from seven to eleven whales per ship. Whaling at this time does not appear to have been such a hazardous occupation as one would have thought, for of one thousand five hundred and forty-nine ships which voyaged to the Arctic regions, only fifty-six, i.e., three and a half per cent, were lost. The merchants, however, frequently sustained other losses owing to the action of privateers. One of the oldest accounts of the German fishery is given by Martens in 1671.[1] Martens, in the capacity of

[1] Friedrich Martens. " Spitzbergische Reise-beschreibung,"

ship's-barber (doctor) made four journeys to Spitsbergen in whalers, and his book, unlike many whaling treatises, is an account of his own personal experience. His first ship was called *Jonah in the Whale* (*Jonas im Walfisch*). They left the Elbe on the 15th April, 1671; on the 27th they sighted the ice, Jan Mayen being ten miles distant bearing southwest by west. Many ships were engaged at this time in this neighbourhood, and it was customary for the vessels to hail one another, the most frequent question being as to the number of fish (whales) caught. In his reply Martens quaintly says, after giving the number, "*sollte er auch noch einen oder mehr, als er hat, dazu setzen, schadet eben nichts.*"

When the complement of whales was obtained the ship flew a special flag, illustrations of which are given by Martens. On the 7th May the *Jonas im Walfisch* sighted Spitsbergen, on the 14th there were twenty ships whaling in 75° 22' north. On the 15th they sighted their first whale, but failed to secure it, on the 30th they were successful.

After rescuing the crew of a wrecked whaler they obtained their second (13th June) and third (22nd

---

Hamburg, 1675. First translated into English by Sir John Narborough and others, and published in 1694, as an account of several late voyages and discoveries to the south and north, etc. Dedicated to Samuel Pepys.

Also translated and published in the Hakluyt Society's publications for 1855. A collection of documents on Spitsbergen and Greenland, under the title "Voyage into Spitsbergen and Greenland."

THE DUTCH WHALERS PREDOMINANT

June) whales. After securing five more "fish" they sailed for Bear Harbour, where twenty-eight ships were at anchor, twenty Dutch and eight Germans. They returned home on the 21st August. The fishery conditions at this time are not well described. Zorgdrager[1] gives a general account of the extent of the whaling grounds, which comprise the waters from Davis Strait, past Greenland, Iceland, Spitsbergen to Nova Zembla. Martens says the whales are more abundant in the spring towards the west, off Greenland and Jan Mayen, later they move east to Spitsbergen. According to Zorgdrager there was a considerable fishery north of Jan Mayen in 74° north from 1611 to 1633. In the eighties of the seventeenth century there was a prosperous fishery in Gael-Hamkes Bay in Greenland.

The ice fishery has been well described by Martens and Zorgdrager, for the period at the end of the seventeenth and the commencement of the eighteenth century. The treatment of the whale's carcass was apparently evolved by the Dutch, the other nations copying their methods.

[1] The full title of Zorgdrager's book, which was published at Amsterdam in 1720, is, "Bloyende Opkomst der Aloude en Hedendaagsche Groenlandsche Visschery, waar in met eenege geoeffende ervaarenheit de geheele omflag deezer Visscherye beschreeven, en wat daar in dient waargenomen naaukeurig verhandelt wordt." A German translation (with different illustrations) was published at Leipzig in 1723, under the title, "Alte und neue Groenlandische Fischerei und Walfischfang." A second enlarged edition was published at the Hague in 1727, a third edition at Amsterdam in 1728, and a second German edition at Nürnberg in 1750.

The types of vessel in use at this time were of the following dimensions:

Ship 100 feet long	by 26	by 11½	carried	4	boats and	28	men.
100	,, ,,	28 by 12	,,	5	,,	35	,,
112	,, ,,	29 by 12¼	,,	6	,,	42	,,
118	,, ,,	30 by 12½	,,	7	,,	50	,,

The hull of the vessel was strengthened to resist ice pressure, and provided at the bow with an iron " breast-plate " which corresponded in function with the false or ice stem described by Scoresby.

Fitting-out began in March with the preparation of the so-called hard bread, consisting of two-thirds rye and one-third wheat. At the beginning of April the soft bread was made. A ship with thirty-five men and five boats required for the voyage: fifteen casks of hard bread, sixteen sacks soft bread, twenty-eight sacks peas, eight tons meat, thirteen quarters butter, one thousand pounds cheese, five hundred pounds bacon, nine hundred pounds stock fish, twenty-eight barrels of beer, two and a half ankers of brandy, and so on. The empty casks for the reception of the blubber were prepared and placed in the hold, the interstices being filled with firewood for subsequent use in boiling the oil at the factories on shore. The two lowest rows of casks, about two hundred in all, were filled with water. The fore-part of the hull was strengthened inside. At the end of March the master appeared to take the vessel over, and to make ready for sea. The mustering of the crew usually took place at some water-side inn. Zorgdrager specifies in full detail

THE DUTCH WHALERS PREDOMINANT 159

the fishery equipment of the whaler, including four hundred and fifty new casks, sixty new whale-lines, fifty oak harpoon stocks, cloth for sails, forty new and ten old harpoons, fifty new lances, ten blubber knives, and so on.

His list is so meticulously correct that he does not forget the porcelain coffee service and the mirrors and serviettes for the cabin. Evidently the old whaling masters were by no means uncivilised.

Between the 6th and 8th April the crew were mustered in the captain's cabin before the owner and skipper. Advances in pay were made. The captain received one hundred to one hundred and fifty guilders, and twenty-five guilders towards his equipment. His share was also fixed at from twenty to twenty-five guilders per whale and a percentage on the oil. The mate (steersman) received sixty to sixty-five guilders advance and an agreed percentage on the oil, the harpooners fifty to fifty-five guilders advance and a percentage on the oil, but nothing for the whalebone. The monthly pay of the crew was carpenter, thirty-six to forty guilders, boatsmen twenty-eight, cook twenty-eight, butcher twenty-eight, barber (doctor?) twenty-six, quartermaster (Schiemann), who looked after the lines, twenty-five, experienced seamen eighteen to twenty, younger seamen fourteen to fifteen, cooks' assistants twelve, and cabin boys ten to eleven guilders. The steersman of each boat capturing a whale received in addition three guilder. On the 15th to 20th April the ships put to sea, those for Davis Strait, however, starting a month earlier than this. When the vessel reached the latitudes of 61° to 66° north, the whaling apparatus was got ready, the distribution of the various duties at the whaling also being settled. For the flensing the cutters, harpooners, a "blubber king" and "blubber queen" were appointed. Each harpooner had his boat provided with seven lines, each one hundred and twenty fathoms long, of the best hemp. The whaling apparatus was at this time primitive, Martens describes the harpoons and lances, the best harpoons being of steel. Zorgdrager divides the fishery into three main parts: (1) The capture of the whale. (2) The flensing. (3) The treatment of the blubber.

The officers and harpooners keep a sharp look out for whales. The crew are also on the *qui vive* for a dead whale, the first sighting of which was rewarded with a ducat. As soon as a whale is seen the cry "Val Val," is raised, and the men tumble into the boats. When the boat is near enough to the whale, the harpooner throws his weapon. Attached to the harpoon is a line of the best hemp, the "Voorganger," to which five other lines can be attached in succession, after which another boat can be called up, and its lines in turn attached. The line is wound round a bollard (Slupsteven), a wet cloth being kept at hand to prevent the bollard from taking fire from the friction of the lines. Care has to be taken that the line passes out over the bow and not over the side, as in the latter case there is danger of capsizing.

THE NORTHERN WHALE FISHERY (ZORGDRAGER, 1720).

THE DUTCH WHALERS PREDOMINANT 161

A whale can run out ten lines of one hundred and twenty-five fathoms each, after which it is compelled to come to the surface. This gives the opportunity for the discharge of a second harpoon, and for lancing with the six foot lances. Eventually the whale is killed. Sometimes two boats from different ships share in the killing of the whale, in which case the ships take half shares. The tail is now cut off, a hole made in the whale's body, which is then towed alongside the ship by five or six boats. It is now made fast, the tail end forward and the head aft.

A fish of fifty kardels blubber gives two hundred and forty to two hundred and fifty Maas barten (bone of not less than eleven feet long) and about two hundred Untermaas barten. The blubber is put on board into the hold (Flensloch) and must be prepared within forty-eight hours.

The whalers usually returned home in September, October, or November at the latest. The Dutch made several attempts to winter in the North, at Spitsbergen and Jan Mayen (1633-4); Spitsbergen (1630-1) successfully, and 1633 unsuccessfully; in the latter case the men died of scurvy due to the lack of fresh provisions.

During the next three decades, as already described, the Dutch followed the whale fishery with, on the whole, considerable success, while the English took a very minor part. Already the whales were becoming scarce in Spitsbergen waters, and the ships had to go farther out to sea to make their captures. The three Dutch wars with

England 1652-54, 1665-67, and 1672-74, interfered considerably with the Dutch whalers, but the trade was resumed in 1675. The next ten years were very prosperous for the Dutch. There was a slight falling off until 1691, when the fishery was again prohibited on account of the war.

Feeble and unsuccessful attempts were made by the English in 1672 and subsequent years to wrest this valuable monopoly from the Dutch. In 1672 an Act of Parliament allowed British whalers to land their products free; colonials were admitted at a reduced rate, while foreigners had to pay a customs duty of nine pounds per ton for oil and eighteen pounds per ton for whalebone.[1]

In 1693 Sir William Scaven formed the "Company of Merchants of London trading to Greenland"[2] with a capital of forty thousand pounds, afterwards increased in 1703 to eighty-two thousand pounds.

According to Anderson,[2] in 1696 the new Greenland Company, which had been established in 1693 with forty thousand pounds as its original capital stock, had afterwards increased its capital to eighty-two thousand pounds, the completion to be made at any time before the year 1703.

By reason of the war with France, and the scarcity of seamen, the company could not employ all its capital in this trade, so it was enacted that the company, during its term of fourteen years, ending

---

[1] "History of Commerce," Vol. ii., p. 521.
[2] *Ibid.*, p. 626.

in 1707, should be free of all duty, custom or imposition whatsoever, for any oil, blubber or whale-fins caught and imported by them during the said term.

The company, however, was so unfortunate partly through bad management, partly through real losses, as to expend their whole capital some years before the expiration of their term, so that they broke up entirely. This failure was all the more surprising because in 1697 the Dutch whale fishery was universally successful. The superintendent of this fishery reported that when lying in one of the bays with his ship, the *Four Brothers*, having a cargo of seven fish on board, a richly laden fleet assembled at that place, consisting of one hundred and twenty-one Hollanders with one thousand two hundred and fifty-two whales, fifty-four Hamburgers with five hundred and fifteen whales, fifteen Bremeners with one hundred and nineteen whales, and two Embdeners with two whales, and not a clean ship among them.

Elking[1] attributes the ill success of the English to the following:

(1) The ships were commanded by persons unacquainted with the business, who interfered with the fishery, whereas the chief harpooner ought to have commanded at this time.

(2) The captains had fixed pay; they should have been paid by share.

(3) The blubber taken home was slovenly and

---

[1] Elking, "A View of the Greenland Trade and Whale Fishery, with the National and Private advantages thereof," London, 1722.

wastefully managed in boiling, and the fins were ill cleaned; so that the products offered for sale only fetched an inferior price.

(4) The lines and fishing instruments were injured from want of care and frequently embezzled.

(5) The ships were extravagantly fitted; an exorbitant price paid for materials and large sums spent on incidentals, which ought to have been saved.

(6) The last ship sent out was unfortunately wrecked, after securing eleven whales, a misfortune which accelerated the ruin of the company.

In a translation of " divers passages " from De Witt's " True Interest and Political Maxims of Holland and West Friesland," published by the authority of the States General and translated into English in the year 1702, advocating free trade, it is stated that the authorised Dutch Greenland Company made heretofore little profit by their fishing, because of the great charge of setting out their ships, and that the train oil, blubber, and whale-fins were not well made, handled, or cured, and being brought hither and put into warehouse, were not sold soon enough, nor to the Company's best advantage. " Whereas, now that everyone equips their vessels at the cheapest rate, follow their fishing diligently and manage all carefully, the blubber, train oil, and whale-fins are employed for so many uses in several countries, that they can sell them with that conveniency, that, though there are now fifteen ships for one which formerly sailed out of

THE DUTCH WHALERS PREDOMINANT 165

Holland on that account, and consequently each of them could not take so many whales as heretofore; and, nothwithstanding the new prohibition of France and other countries, to import those commodities, and though there is greater plenty of it imported by our fishers, yet those commodities are much raised in value above what they were whilst there was a Company; that the common inhabitants do exercise that fishery with profit, to the much greater benefit of our country than when it was under the management of a Company carried on by a few. For however much these members sell their commodities dearer than if that trade was open or free, all the other inhabitants that gain their subsistence immediately or by consequence by a foreign competition must bear the loss. Indeed, our fishermen, dealers in manufactures, owners of freight ships, are burdened by all manner of imposts; to impress them yet more in their necessity by these monopolies of Guilds and yet to believe that it redounds to the good of the land, because it tends to the benefit of such companies, is to me incomprehensible. These Guilds are said indeed to be a useful sort of people, but next to those we call idle drones, they are the most unprofitable inhabitants of the country, because they bring in no profit from foreign lands for the welfare of the inhabitants of Holland."

Further details of the Dutch whale fishery during this period are given in an Appendix (p. 308).

Towards the end of the seventeenth century

practically all the Dutch seaports were engaged in the Greenland whaling. Van Oelen gives the names and ports of all the Dutch ships which left for the whaling at Greenland in 1683. The leading ports at this time and the number of vessels fitted out from each is given here.

Amsterdam, thirty-four; Rotterdam, thirty-two and a "hooker"; Hoorn and Saardam, twenty-nine each; Ryp, twenty; Jisp, seventeen; Dordrecht, fourteen; Saendyck, twelve; Enckhuysen, Medenblick and Uytgeest, six each; Texel and Edam, five each; Stavoren and De Coog, four each; Delfshaven, Zeelandt and Knollendam, three each; Schiedam, Westsanen and Haarlingen, two each; and finally De Creyl, one ship.

This year Hamburg also sent fifty ships to the whaling, and sometimes the German ships numbered eighty. The Dutch names at this time are very curious, some vessels, e.g., *De Browery* of Hoorn, if they lived up to their names would doubtless be popular amongst the seamen.

Some Dutch whalers went a great many times to the fishing, the record for a Dutch Commandeur being held by Roelof Gerritsz. Meyer, who went forty-four times, capturing two hundred and eighty-seven whales.

At the end of the seventeenth and the commencement of the eighteenth centuries English whaling was practically extinguished, yet the Dutch, in the ten years, 1699-1708, equipped one thousand six hundred and fifty-two ships, which caught eight

THE DUTCH WHALERS PREDOMINANT 167

thousand five hundred and thirty-seven whales, the produce of which sold for over twenty-six million florins, of which four and three-quarter millions was clear gain.

The publication in London in 1721 of a list of ships employed in whaling to " Greenland " and Davis Strait appears to have aroused interest. This list was:

From Holland	251 ships.
From Hamburg	55
From Bremen	24
From Biscayan Ports	20
From Bergen	5

At any rate, shortly afterwards the South Sea Company took the matter up, with what success the next chapter shows.

In the seventeenth and eighteenth centuries the Dutch fleet left the Y and the Zaan every April for Spitsbergen. In war-time the fleet was protected by warships, i.e., in 1697 the whalers were protected by a Dutch and Hamburg convoy. After 1718 the whalers visited Davis Strait. A list of the whale ships from 1719 to 1770 gives the names of forty-four Dutch ports participating in the whale fishery. The Dutch statistics were:

1669-1778—14,167 ships. 561 lost. That is four per cent.

In 1733 the Dutch East Indian Company imported whalebone into Holland from the East Indies. The Dutch Greenland adventurers immediately protested against this, alleging it would ruin their trade if permitted to go on. Their statement, which gives great detail, is of interest, though naturally, it must be discounted a little since it is obviously partisan.

The Dutch Greenland merchants say that at this time, at an expense per ship of ten thousand guilders, the total was one million eight hundred thousand guilders, or, as they put it, eighteen tons of gold, which must be paid out even if not a single whale be caught. Provisions and gear cost five hundred and forty thousand guilders, advances of pay to captains and crew, etc., one million two hundred thousand guilders. A usual catch is about forty-four thousand quartels of blubber and one hundred and twenty thousand pounds of whalebone, besides walrus teeth and seal-skins, the total value being two million one hundred thousand guilders. Of this, one hundred and fifty thousand guilders must be allowed for the cost of working up the products for the market, showing a total income of one million nine hundred thousand guilders. Of this, one million three hundred and fifty thousand guilders represent the goods sold abroad, and three hundred thousand that consumed at home.

An empty ship represents a loss of twelve thousand six hundred florins.

The Davis Strait fishery commenced in 1719. In the first ten years the Dutch sent seven hundred and forty-eight ships. The Hamburgers sent four ships in 1719, the Bremeners two in 1725. The chief fishery was on the south side of Disco Island where, until quite recently, the whalers of Dundee

THE DUTCH WHALERS PREDOMINANT 169

and Peterhead commenced their season's fishing. The Dutchmen usually made first for South Bay in Greenland in 67° 10′ N., where the ships also assembled for the return journey. In Disco and Liefde Bays there were at this time very rich whaling grounds; even in the mid-nineteenth century the British and American whalers fished regularly up to Melville Bay. According to De Jong,[1] L. Feykes Haan in July, 1715, found the strait was closed with ice at 72° N.; the fishery was nevertheless carried on in these regions up to 79° N. There must at this time have been a considerable Dutch trade with Greenland. In 1691, on account of war (the French defeated the allied British and Dutch fleets off Beachy Head this year), the States General forbade the Dutch whalers to set sail to Greenland; and King Christian V. of Denmark issued a decree prohibiting whaling at Greenland to all but Danish subjects. In the following year Hamburg was compelled to conclude a treaty with Denmark to enable her citizens to fish in Davis Strait. In 1709 Great

---

[1] " Nieuwe Beschryving der Walvischvangst en Haringvisschery," by D. de Jong, H. Kobel, and M. Salieth. 1791.

De Reste's book, " Histoire des peches des decouvertes et des establissemens des Hollandais dans les mers du Nord," 3 vols., Paris, 1801, is a translation of De Jong, with some of the illustrations different. The first volume was ready in 1791, and the second almost ready when the revolution broke out. De Reste got into bad odour with the revolutionists (*ces Cannibals* as he calls them), who objected to his association with the old government, and he only escaped narrowly, the executioners surrounding his house in the Rue du Cherche-Midi half an hour after his escape. Eventually his work was completed, and published in the ninth year of the Republic.

Britain, France, and the Netherlands combined to shut the Hanseatic towns out of the whale fishery. The Hanse towns made diplomatic protests which were, however, feeble and unavailing, so they decided on their own convoy system, a decision which was helped by the losses their ships had sustained in the Mediterranean trade owing to the attack of Algerian pirates. Usually twenty, thirty or even forty ships assembled around the convoyer, the captain of which assumed the responsibility of Admiral of the Convoy. This warship carried a crew of from one hundred and thirty to one hundred and fifty, and sixty to eighty soldiers. There was also a chaplain, a surgeon, a " botteler," and a cook. According to contemporary accounts the proceedings aboard these convoyers were of a puritanical description. There was morning and evening prayer, and on Sundays a sermon and communion in addition. Drinking, brawling, " Lastern," and swearing were forbidden, and cards, dice, and " Weiber " were not allowed on board. In 1691 the Bremen convoyer was a ship one hundred and twelve feet by twenty-nine feet by twelve. She carried fourteen twelve, one eight, nine six, ten four, and four three pounders, as well as four metal cannon of three pounds; eight bombs, one hundred and eighty hand grenades, thirty-one casks of powder of each one hundred pounds, and twenty-one pounds musket balls, forty-two muskets, forty-six pistols, and so on.

In 1777 Cornelis Ris attempted to found a poor house at Hoorn, with a school in which useful

THE DUTCH WHALERS PREDOMINANT 171

practical subjects were taught. Laspeyres[1] describes this interesting practical example of combining philanthropy with commercial desires. The cost of keeping the school going depended partly on the alms of the charitable and partly on the profits to be derived from whaling. A whaling company was formed, the membership being fixed at one hundred florins. Anyone unable to risk the loss of this sum is advised to stand out, since the possibility of a total loss cannot be overlooked. The company was formed, and the whale fishing was successful as described in subsequent writings by Ris, who, nevertheless, put the goodwill and assets of the company at nil. In 1777 he petitions for exemption from certain taxes, but in 1779 the company was still successful, since there is a " Lobgedicht " of that date which describes it as flourishing.

In addition to the account of Martens, which is the best, there are other descriptions of whaling voyages to Spitsbergen in the latter part of the eighteenth century. There is an account by Maarten Mooi[2] of a journey to " Groenland " in 1786 in the

---

[1] Laspeyres, E. Geschichte der Volkswirthschaftlichen Anschauungen der Niederländer, Leipzig, 1863. Preisschrift der Fürstlich Jablonowskische Gesellschaft. The papers of Ris referred to are not in the British Museum.

[2] Maarten Mooi, Journael van de reize naer Groenlandt, gedaen door commandeur M. Mooi met het schip Frankendaal, behelzende zijne uitreize van Amsterdam 22 April, 1786, bezetting in het ijs, zedert den 10 Junij, het voorgevallene met de commandeurs H. C. Jaspers, M. Weatherhead, W. Allen en Volkert Klaassen of Jong Volkert Knudsten, welke twee Engelsche comm. beide hunne schepen verloren hebben; de gelukkige verlossing van den Altonaasvaarder Gottenberger en van hem M. Mooi, met veel aanmerkelyke byzonderheden, Amsterdam, 1787

Frankendaal of Amsterdam. It is a description of a more than ordinarily interesting whaling voyage of the period, since they were beset in the ice from the 10th June to the 27th November. Practically contemporaneous with this is the account taken from the *Journal of Jürgen Röper*,[1] published at Altona in 1778. The titles of these works sufficiently indicate their contents.

It was customary when there were exceptional circumstances attending a whaling voyage at this time for an account to be published on the vessel's return home. Among these are the accounts of voyages by Jac. Janssen on the *Frau Elizabeth* of Hamburg in 1769, by Marten Jansen on the *Witte Paard* in 1777, and by Hidde Dirks Kat in 1777 and 1778. To this period may also be referred the earlier voyage of Johann Michael Kühn, published in 1741. It is impossible to quote from all these voyages. The titles are given in the Bibliography at the end of the book (p. 318). Doubtless a diligent search through the various Dutch libraries would yield further references to voyages of this period.

Posselt's book (note p. 181) gives a good account of the conditions under which the German whale fishery was carried on towards the end of the eighteenth century. Posselt was Prediger zu St Johannis auf Föhr, a small island off the Schleswig-

[1] Wahrhafte Nachricht von den im Jahre 1777, auf den Wallfischfang nach Grönland aufgegangenen und daselbst verunglückten fünf Hamburger Schiffen, gezogen aus dem Journal des Küpers Jürgen Röper, auf dem Schiffe genannt Sara Cecilia, Kommandeur Hans Pieters, Altona, 1778.

THE DUTCH WHALERS PREDOMINANT 173

Holstein coast, the home of a colony of Spitsbergen whalers. His information was collected from the whalers direct. For the ten years previous to 1796 it was only the English who were successful at this fishery. The reasons he gives are (1) the greater courage and skill of her seamen, (2) the better build of her boats which can hunt the whale in the open sea even in bad weather, and (3) the ice-free harbours of Britain enable the whalers to start off early so that they get the best fishing; the Dutchmen and Hamburgers only arriving when the whales have been hunted a lot and are scarce and shy. Posselt says the " Greenland Law " permitted the whaler who was fast to a whale to have the sole right of its capture. This he regards as natural, and " it is only the proud English who look upon themselves as Lords of the Ocean and all its inhabitants, who disobey the law and according to general complaint they do so frequently."

When the English first went to Spitsbergen for the whales in 1609 they took with them Biscayan harpooners, and when in 1724 the South Sea Company decided to resuscitate the whaling industry they had to seek foreign assistance, since by then the original industry had died out, and there was no one in the country skilled at the trade of hunting, killing, and cutting-up whales. This time the English sought expert assistance from the Frisian islanders, and it is interesting to see how these men kept in the trade while it had disappeared entirely in the neighbouring island of Great Britain.

Probably these Frisians learnt their trade in the first instance in the early voyages of the Noordsche Compagnie. The islands of Sylt and Föhr were always unable to sustain a large population, and it was long customary for the adult males to seek employment as sailors in foreign or foreign-going vessels. The Frisians probably shipped in the first place as "green-hands," the expert work being done by the Basques. In 1634 there was a serious dispute between the French and Dutch as to the Spitsbergen fishery, and the French Government forbade the Basques to ship in the Dutch whalers.

This, like many arbitrary acts of government, probably produced an entirely different effect from what was intended. The Frisians after about twenty years' experience of the business were probably nearly as expert as the Basques, and this order of the French Government merely facilitated the substitution of Frisians for Basques as harpooners and specksioneers on the Dutch ships. This same year (1634) there was a tremendous inundation of the Frisian coast, causing enormous damage and widespread distress; forcing more men than ever to seek employment abroad. The whaling trade at this time, expanding rapidly in Holland, absorbed large numbers of these men, who were thus enabled to earn a much better living than if they had remained at home and followed agricultural pursuits. Contemporary writers give moving accounts of the annual setting-out and return of practically the whole of the adult male population of the islands of Föhr and Sylt. During the height of the whaling season these islands were deprived of their able-bodied male population every summer. Old men and young boys took part in the Greenland voyages. Jens Jacob Eschels started on his first whaling voyage as a cabin boy at the age of eleven years two months and twenty-five days. In the second voyage a boy was generally promoted to head cabin boy, and subsequently cook's mate, then ordinary and lastly able seaman.

Intelligent men were promoted boatsteerer and ship's officer, the final rank being that of "Commandeur," as the captains of the whalers were described. A ship's master or captain had to possess "Burgerrecht," but with the rapid growth of whaling it was impossible to find sufficient men with this qualification, so it became customary to style a whaling captain "Commandeur" to avoid friction with the captains of the mercantile marine. The Commandeur had general command of the expedition, the navigating officer being the "Steurmann" who never left the ship, not even when all the boats were away after whales. Many seamen of sixty or even seventy years of age were found on these Greenlanders, some of whom had previously been ship's officers or even Commandeur. Some of these men made very many voyages to the whaling. On Köhler's ship there was a "Schiemann" making his forty-seventh consecutive voyage. That these Frisians regarded whaling as a life-long occupation is certain. They were exclusively whalers, and this fact is still recorded on tombstones in Föhr:

> " Ich schiffte auf dem Meer
> nach Grönland hin und her
> die Fahrt ist abgethan,
> ik bin in Kanaan,
> wo Wellen, Eis und Wind
> nicht mehr zu finden sind."

A navigation school was established for young whalers by Pastor Petri on Föhr as early as 1620-78. In 1733 at least twenty-five per cent of the Dutch crews were Frisians from the islands of Sylt, Amrum, Röm, Hooge, and Nordmarsch. At the height of the fishing's prosperity about three thousand Frisians took part annually, of whom one thousand five hundred were from Föhr and seven hundred from Sylt. When signing on the whalers the names of the Frisians were entered in the Dutch form, so that when they subsequently engaged in Hamburg whalers they were erroneously thought to be of Dutch origin.

CHAPTER V

THE BOUNTY SYSTEM

The whalers apply for State assistance—The South Sea Company and the Whale Fisheries—Development of the British whaling industry as a result of the bounty stimulus—Description of Arctic whaling voyages.

At the very commencement of the eighteenth century a petition was presented to Parliament by the merchants who had raised a joint stock for recovering, and effectually carrying on the Greenland whale fishery with vigour, in which application was made for certain special privileges.

Notwithstanding the encouragement given by the previous Acts (4 and 5 William and Mary; 7 and 8 William; 1 Anne, 1702), the Greenland whale fishery had been neglected by the English and carried on to a vast extent by the Dutch, Hamburgers, and others, employing near four hundred sail of ships in such service; by which they were enabled to import to this Kingdom vast quantities of whalebone and oil, and vend the same at exorbitant prices, whereby the subject was aggrieved and large sums drawn out of the Kingdom. The Greenland whale fishery is of a different nature from all other fisheries, and requires the utmost application of a separate distinct company with a considerable joint stock to bring it to perfection.

The joint stock raised by 4 and 5 William and Mary to form a body corporate for the Greenland trade, and the 7 and 8 William, excusing them from duty, failed because of their small stock, want of experience, and opposition of foreign ships in Greenland Seas, of which there were a hundred or more. So the Act of Anne, 1702, made it lawful for any of Her Majesty's subjects to obtain the privileges of this Company.

"The present Undertakers will, by the great number of adventurers and the extensiveness of their stock, be enabled to surmount the difficulties which overwhelmed the earlier company, whose capital was but forty thousand pounds, and they therefore apply for a bill giving them preference over others"; as they claim to know the procedure of the former company having their books in their possession, they are first in the field and "that the design manifestly tending to the increase of navigation, and the benefit of all His Majesty's subjects, it is humbly hoped, will receive countenance and encouragement."

In a broadside (1720) entitled "Reasons Humbly submitted to the Honourable House of Commons for A Clause to prevent His Majesty's being defrauded of the great Customs on Whalebone," it is stated that those who design to defraud the customs

THE BOUNTY SYSTEM

of the duty on whalebone take care to have the fins cut up fit for use before they are imported, and so being made up in small parcels, usually cast the same overboard, in some marked place, where it lies until a convenient opportunity occurs of taking it up unobserved. This is very generally practised by those who cut their fins beyond the sea.

In a further broadside of this time are set forth reasons humbly offered to the Honourable House of Commons against laying any impositions on whalebone caught and imported by the Greenland Company. The Company say that on the encouragement of certain Acts for the development of the Greenland trade (25 Car. II., 4 and 5 William and Mary, 7 and 8 George I.) they have, nothwithstanding all the difficulties, discouragements, and vast losses by them sustained, continued their endeavours for the recovery and settlement of the said trade.

They complain they cannot carry on the same on equal terms with other nations, for they cannot fit out their ships, nor victual their men at such easy rates as other nations, and yet are forced to employ and pay extraordinary wages to foreigners to help and serve them in their fishery.

The Company import but a very small part of the whalebone consumed in this country; they import all the fins, pieces, and chucks, good and bad, which are all extremely moist and green, and which daily do much diminish in weight, so any imposition would rise very high.

So the Company petitions Parliament for exemption from any custom, duty, or imposition whatsoever on oil, blubber, or whale fins taken, caught, and imported into this country in any ships or vessels belonging to the Company.

These agitations and petitions of interested parties ultimately led to Parliament granting certain privileges to British whalers. These privileges were taken advantage of by the South Sea Company with what result the following pages show.

The South Sea Company, which had been established in 1711, with a view of restoring public credit and providing for the extinction of the floating national debt, which at that time amounted to ten million, had obtained a monopoly of trade to the southern seas. The Company after much debate, having before their eyes the former unsuccessful attempts on the part of several companies to engage in the Greenland whale fisheries, decided in 1724 to engage in this fishery.[1] The better to ensure success the Company obtained an Act of Parliament (10 Geo. I. cap. xvi.) whereby the duty of three pence per pound on whale fins was repealed and whale fins, oil and blubber, caught and imported in British ships, whereof the commander and at least one-third of the mariners were British subjects, should be custom free for seven years, from Christmas, 1724. By an Act of Parliament two

---

[1] The "Court Minutes" Book of the South Sea Company is in the British Museum. MSS. Dept. No. 25,501.

THE BOUNTY SYSTEM 181

years later this freedom from custom duty was extended to "Davis's streights and the seas adjacent," and comprised seal oil, seal skins or any other produce of seals, or other creatures, taken or caught in any of the said seas.

It was, however, too late to make a start in 1724, so the Company directed twelve fine ships of three hundred and six tons each, to be built on the Thames, and proper quantities of hemp from Riga and cask staves from Hamburg to be got ready for the ensuing spring. The Company also hired the Duke of Bedford's great wet dock at Deptford, for the use of their ships and stores, and for curing their oil and whale fins.

In 1725 the South Sea Company commenced operations. The twelve ships brought home twenty-five and a half whales, and although this barely sufficed to pay expenses, it was the best year of the eight during which this fishery was carried on preceding the passing of the first Bounty Act. Owing to the fact that for many years prior to this the English had given up the whale fisheries, it was necessary to procure all the skilled men, such as commanders, harpooners, boat-steerers and blubber-cutters from Holstein.[1] One hundred and fifty-two Holsteiners cost the Company over three thousand and fifty-six pounds, whereas three hundred and fifty-three British subjects employed on the same

---

[1] See K. F. Posselt, "Ueber den Grönlandischen Wallfischfang aus mündlichen Nachrichten Föhringer Seeleute," gesamlet von K. F. P., Kiel, 1796.

ships only cost three thousand one hundred and fifty-one pounds.

In 1726 twelve more ships were built for the Company, and the whole twenty-four were sent out to the whale fishery at Greenland and in Davis Strait, capturing sixteen and a half whales.

The following year (1727) the Company built an additional ship and sent out twenty-five to the fishery with disastrous results. Two of the ships were lost, the remaining twenty-three bringing home twenty-two and a half whales.

A half whale results when two whalers of different nationality strike the same whale which is by custom divided.

In 1728 the same twenty-three vessels procured eighteen whales, undoubtedly a losing voyage. The next year one of the twenty-three was lost, the remaining twenty-two bringing home twenty-seven and a half whales, the net loss this year exclusive of wear and tear being over six thousand nine hundred pounds. In 1730 the same twenty-two ships brought home twelve whales, the net loss being eight thousand nine hundred and twenty-one pounds. In 1731 one of the twenty-two was lost and the other twenty-one ships brought home fourteen whales, which was still a losing voyage. At this time there was invented a gun for shooting harpoons with gunpowder, at a greater distance than they could be thrown by hand. This invention was tried with " some success."

THE BOUNTY SYSTEM

At this time the whale fisheries of New England employed about one thousand three hundred tons of shipping.

The year 1732 witnessed the last attempt of the South Sea Company to prosecute the Greenland whale fishery unassisted by bounty. Their twenty-one vessels brought home twenty-four and a half whales, also a very unsuccessful voyage.

The balance sheet after eight years effort, is interesting:

	£	s.	d.
Total issues or disbursements in 8 years	262,172	9	6
Sales of oil, etc., and also of the ships	84,390	6	6
Total loss	£177,782	3	0

At this time it was calculated that if a Greenland ship brought home the produce of three whales only it would be a successful voyage, but the South Sea Company whalers did not average one whale per ship, taking one year with another. Whalers reckoned that one good year would make up the deficits of six bad years, so it is particularly unfortunate that the whole of the eight years of this interesting experiment were alike bad.

The Company now endeavoured to persuade the Government to grant a bounty to assist them, as it appeared evident to the Directors that otherwise the fishery must be abandoned.

The first Act of Parliament granting a bounty for the whale fisheries was passed in 1733, but too late for the Company to take part in the fisheries of that year. Two ships fitted out privately engaged in the fishery. A statistical return showing the number of ships fitted out for the Greenland whale fishery, together with their tonnage and the amount of bounty paid, is given in the Appendix (p. 306) from the commencement in 1733 to the year 1824, when the bounty ceased.

The bounty first offered consisted of an annual sum of twenty shillings per ton on all ships fitted out in Great Britain, of two hundred tons and upwards, for the whale fishery, and navigated according to law. Just previous to this the Dutch were very successful at whaling, for the forty-six years ending 1721 they employed five thousand eight hundred and eighty-six ships, capturing thirty-two thousand nine hundred and seven whales, which at an average valuation of five hundred pounds gives a total of over sixteen million sterling.

According to the Custom House returns four vessels participated in the fishery in 1736, of these one ship brought home seven whales while one hundred and thirty Dutch ships caught six hundred whales. The number of British vessels engaged in the whale fisheries increased but slowly, so in 1740 the tonnage bounty was increased to thirty shillings per ton, the additional bounty of ten shillings to continue " during our then war with Spain only," during which time it was also enacted that no harpooner, line-manager, boat-steerer, or seaman should be impressed.

THE BOUNTY SYSTEM

Even under this increased bounty the fisheries remained stagnant (p. 306), so that in 1749 a further increase in the bounty was decided upon. The tonnage bounty was now fixed at forty shillings per ton, and immediately there was an increase in the number of ships fitted out, the average for the ten years 1740-9 being 3·7 ships, and that for the ten years 1750-9 43·3. This bounty was also extended to ships built in the British colonies in North America, of two hundred tons and upwards, on their arrival from the whale fishery at some port in Great Britain, subject to certain conditions set out in the Act. In 1755 the Bounty Act was amended so as to provide that every ship should have on board an apprentice for each fifty tons burthen, and that no bounty shall be payable for a greater tonnage for any one ship of more than four hundred tons, and ships under two hundred tons were to be entitled to the bounty.

By 1759 it may fairly be claimed that a regular, if small, Greenland whale fishery had been established for British vessels. Thirty-four British vessels took part in the fishery, the aggregate tonnage being ten thousand three hundred and thirty-seven, while this same year one hundred and thirty-three Dutch ships brought home the produce of four hundred and thirty-five whales, a little more than three and a quarter whales per ship. The Hamburgers with sixteen ships only captured eighteen whales.

By this time also there was a small Scottish whale

fishery as is seen from a reference to the Custom House returns for Scotland. Although the table (Appendix II.) distinctly refers to Great Britain, it is obvious that the return deals with England only, since only English ports are specified in the detailed statement, and since there is a separate table for Scotland. It was in 1750 that the first Scottish whale ship, a Leith vessel, applied for the bounty. The number of Scottish vessels participating in the benefits of the bounty system was never large; there was a steady increase from 1750 with one ship to 1762 with fourteen (the maximum being sixteen in 1755 and 1766), and thence a gradual decline to 1784. Leith, Dunbar, and Dundee were the chief ports engaged in the whale fisheries at this period.

The increase in 1749 of the tonnage bounty for whalers to forty shillings a ton induced many seaport towns to fit out one or more vessels for the whaling, but except in the case of London, Hull, and Whitby with only transient success. Bristol, for instance, though it was engaged for several years in the whaling industry, never sent out more than three vessels in any one year. It is recorded that in 1750 two whales were brought to the Sea Mills Dock at Bristol, and the blubber boiled down there. About this time a Joint Stock Company was formed in Bristol, the capital being divided into ninety shares, all of which were taken up. The Company fitted out two ships, the *Bristol* and the *Adventure*, and Felix Farley's Journal of the 18th July, 1752, reports the return of

THE BOUNTY SYSTEM

the ships from Greenland with a catch of five whales valued at two thousand pounds, " which with the bounty money of forty shillings per ton makes their voyage a very successful one." This cargo was also landed at the Sea Mills Dock. A third ship, the *St Andrew*, was sent out in 1755 and 1756, so encouraging were the results. In March, 1757, an advertisement for men to sail in the ships puffed the healthiness of the voyage, stating that of ninety men in the *Bristol* and *Adventure* only one had died a natural death in six voyages, two others being accidentally killed. Perhaps the fact that the *Adventure* had been held in the ice for over ten weeks in 1756 was better known in the port than the Company imagined. At any rate the trade soon began to fall off, and in March, 1761, the Company was wound up.

The first participation of Liverpool in the Greenland and Davis Straits whale fishery is unrecorded. In 1764 three vessels were engaged in the trade, but it was not until 1775 that the first Greenland ship was built in Liverpool in Mr Sutton's yard.[1] This year sixty-five vessels sailed from English ports for the whale fishing. In 1786 thirteen vessels were sent out from Liverpool. In 1788 twenty-one vessels with a total tonnage of six thousand four hundred and eighty-five tons were employed in the trade, the tonnage ranging from two hundred and twenty to

[1] " Liverpool, its Commerce, Statistics, and Institutions, with a history of the Cotton Trade," by Henry Smithers, Liverpool, 1825.

four hundred. In 1789 seventeen vessels were fitted out from Liverpool, four of which were lost. In 1793 eleven vessels sailed of a total tonnage of two thousand nine hundred and seventy-eight. From 1810 to 1816 two vessels were engaged each year, the *James*, Captain Clough, and the *Lion*, Captain Hawkins. In 1818 there were still two vessels, the *James* and the *Fame*; with the latter the name of Captain Scoresby, Junior, is associated.

The trade was, however, never very successful; for the nine years 1814 to 1822 inclusive the average number of vessels was only two, the number of whales captured averaged seventeen, and the tons of oil brought home averaged one hundred and seventy-seven. In 1817 both Liverpool vessels, the *Lion* and the *Lady Forbes*, were lost, the crews in each case being saved. In 1821 Manby made his voyage to Greenland in a Liverpool ship (p. 205). At this time the trade was firmly established at Hull.

In 1772 we have detailed account of a Whitby ship's voyage.[1] The *Volunteer* was a ship of four hundred tons, carrying eight boats with six men to each boat; the total ship's company being sixty-three. At this time the bounty was forty shillings per ton for Greenland whalers, limited to a maximum tonnage of four hundred.

---

[1] An authentic relation of a voyage to Greenland in 1772 of the *Volunteer* of Whitby, by a Gentleman, Surgeon of the said ship. Durham, N.D.

THE BOUNTY SYSTEM

The rates of pay at this period are as follows:

	Bounties.	For every Fish.	For every ton of Oil.	For striking a Fish.	Monthly Pay.
	£ s. d.	£ s. d.	s. d.	s. d.	£ s. d.
Captain	22 1 0	3 3 0	6 0	—	—
First Mate	—	0 10 6	—	—	3 10 0
Second Mate	—	0 10 6	—	—	2 0 0
Spectioneer	9 9 0	0 10 6	6 0	—	—
Harpooner	8 8 0	—	5 3	10 6	—
Carpenter	—	0 10 6	—	—	3 10 0
Carpenter's Mate	—	0 5 0	—	—	2 10 0
Boat Steerer	—	0 5 0	—	—	2 0 0
Line Manager	—	0 2 6	—	—	1 15 0
Seaman	—	0 2 6	—	—	1 10 0
Surgeon	—	1 1 0	—	—	3 10 0
Cook	—	0 2 6	—	—	1 10 0

The rate of pay, as is customary in nearly all branches of fishing, depends to some extent on a share in the profits of the voyage and only partly on a fixed wage. Even the cook's and doctor's earnings depended largely on the success of the voyage. The *Volunteer* left Whitby on the 24th March, 1772. They saw a Sperm Whale in 69° 20′ N. on the 19th April, which is a high latitude for that species. On the 26th they saw two whales, one close to the ship, of very large size but not of the black kind, " these kind of whales have fins on their backs, and are seldom if ever caught, it being dangerous to attempt it for as soon as they are struck they are so strong and swift in nature that no boats can get up to the assistance of the boat that is made fast to them before they are gone, and there is great danger of the boats oversetting." " I never heard of any that attempted striking any of that kind but a Dutchman some years since, but he was never more heard of, so that it was suspected the whale had run him quite off, and he had perished in the attempt."

Evidently the British whalers of this time left the Finner severely alone.

The ice fishery was still flourishing at this time, the *Volunteer* being in sight of fifty vessels at a time.

The *Volunteer* returned to Whitby on the 19th August, having captured five whales which yielded one hundred and eighty-six butts of blubber, estimated to boil to about sixty-five tons of oil which would sell at the lowest estimate at twenty pounds a ton, so that the oil would yield one thousand three hundred pounds. The whalebone of which they had between four and five tons would yield two thousand three hundred pounds at five hundred

THE BOUNTY SYSTEM

pounds a ton. The voyage therefore yielded four thousand pounds, to which bounty money amounting to eight hundred pounds would be added.

Another account of a Whitby ship's voyage about this period is given by John Laing[1] who went to Spitsbergen in 1806 and 1807 on the *Resolution*, in response to an advertisement which was put on the College Gate at Edinburgh, asking for a surgeon for a ship engaged in the North Sea whale fishery. The *Resolution* was captained by Scoresby senior, Scoresby junior being chief mate. Already the whaling trade at Whitby was declining, and it was only the skill and perseverance of the Scoresbys that prolonged what was really an artifically created trade.

Laing's account is very readable, but is remarkable for two things only. In 1806 the *Resolution* reached, on 28th May, the latitude of 81° 50' north, and it was apparently an extremely mild season since " had our object been the making of discoveries, there was not, apparently, anything to have prevented us from going a good way farther to the north." They also met with a party of Russian trappers who used to make periodical visits to Spitsbergen about this time and were the pioneers of the Spitsbergen hunters of the twentieth century.

[1] " A Voyage to Spitsbergen," containing an account of that country, the zoology of the North, of the Shetland Isles, and of the whale fishery. Edinburgh, date? Also an edition published in London in 1815, with slightly different title.

Bacstrom[1] made two voyages to Spitsbergen for the purpose of killing the black whale fish (1779 and 1780). The first voyage was in the whaler *Sea Horse*, the second in the *Rising Sun*, a vessel of four hundred tons, with a crew of ninety men, armed with twenty nine-pounders mounted on the main deck; with nine whale boats. Bacstrom was surgeon. They left London at the latter end of March, 1780, calling at Lerwick, where there were twenty or more English " Greenlanders " at anchor. It was customary to call at Lerwick to take aboard fresh provisions for the voyage. The custom at this time was to sail thence to 79° or 80° north and then make fast to the ice. In June they killed seven large whales, and went with them into Magdalena Bay to cut the blubber up into small bits to fill the blubber-butts, which is called making-off. After this they sailed north to 82° and beyond, the season being exceptionally open. They saw no whales here, so put the ship about for Smeerenburg Harbour, where they saw plenty of Finners, White Whales and Unicorns, " which is a sign that the season is over for killing the Black Whale, which then retires to the northward."

They landed at Smeerenburg and saw the remains of some brickwork, which had been a furnace, obviously the remains of the old Dutch cookeries. According to the Russian trappers who were encamped in the vicinity, " In winter time the Black

---

[1] S. Bacstrom, " Account of a Voyage to Spitsbergen in the year 1780." *The Philosophical Magazine*, July, 1799.

THE BOUNTY SYSTEM

Whales come into the harbour and play close inshore where we kill now and then one with harpoons fired out of a swivel." The *Rising Sun* left for England in July, arriving in the Greenland Dóck, London, in August.

It was in the second half of the eighteenth century that Hull commenced to take a prominent part in the northern whale fishery.[1] The first ship from Hull for the northern fishery set out in 1598, and there are records of Hull whalers in 1610, 1612, and 1613.

In 1618 King James privileged the Hull merchants with a grant of the Jan Mayen Island whale fishery. The earlier efforts were, however, somewhat spasmodic, and it was not until after the passing of the Bounty Act of 1750 that a regular fishery was established from Hull.

In 1753 a whaling company was established there with a subscription of twenty thousand pounds. From 1754 to 1762 the Hull merchants sent vessels every year to the whale fishery, but the circumstances were not favourable. During most of the time England was at war with France, so the whalers had to be well armed and protected by warships. In 1758 the *Humber* and *York* of Hull, returning from Greenland, were captured off the coast by French frigates and taken to Dunkirk. In 1761 the Hull whaler *Leviathan*, which carried a letter of marque, recaptured a ship off the Scottish coast

[1] See *Hull Museum Publications*, No. 31, "Hull Whaling Relics," Hull, 1906.

from a French prize crew. In 1762 the *Samuel* of Hull whilst engaged in the ordinary trade was captured by the French. Subsequently there seems to have been a decline, partly due to the losses above enumerated, and partly to the American war (1774-81) when most of the Hull whalers were taken up by the Government for transport service. In 1779 only four whalers left Hull, and ten Whitby, all well equipped with guns.

In 1784 the *Truelove*, the most famous of all whalers, made her first voyage as a whaler from Hull. This vessel had so remarkable a career that she deserves more than passing reference. She was built and launched at Philadelphia, U.S.A., in 1764, captured by a British cruiser in the American war and sold by the Government about 1780. First employed in the wine trade between Hull and Oporto, she started a whaling career in 1784. She survived the disastrous seasons of 1835 and 1836, making her seventy-second and last whaling trip in 1868.

In 1873 she made the voyage to Philadelphia, where the citizens held a demonstration and presented her with a flag in honour of her birth there, one hundred and nine years before. According to Barron,[1] who was apprenticed in the barque in 1849, the *Truelove* was of two hundred and ninety-six tons register, and in shape much like the barque in which William Penn arrived in America at the time he made the treaty with the Indians.

[1] " Old Whaling Days," Hull, 1895.

THE BOUNTY SYSTEM

The sides batter in to the top of the gunwales, this making the vessel much broader at the water line than the deck. Her bulwark was called pigsty bulwark, i.e., every other plank out to allow the water to run freely off the deck. The following description appeared in her papers: " One deck, three masts, length from main stem to stern post, ninety-six feet; breadth at the broadest part above the mainwales, twenty-seven feet half an inch; depth of hold sixteen feet two inches; square rigged, standing bowsprit, square sterned, carvel built, no galleries, no figure-head."

The *Truelove* saw practically the whole of the Hull fishery from beginning to end.

By 1786 the industry was thoroughly well established at Hull, twenty vessels being fitted out for the fishery. Three of these met with extraordinary success. Whales were abundant in those days, since the *Gibralter* killed eleven whales, the *Manchester* ten, and the *Molly* six in one day. There are detailed statistics of the Hull whale fisheries from 1772 to 1833 (see Appendix VI.). One of the drawbacks to whaling at this time was the importunities of the press gang, which used to wait for the whalers on their return from the Arctic and board them at sea. Instances of this occurred in 1794, 1797, and 1798, so that it became customary to land some of the crew at Dunbar, leaving on board barely sufficient men to navigate the vessel back to the Humber.

In 1798 most of the whalers were captured by

French and Dutch privateers. In the following year the *Molly* made a record voyage, returning to Hull after an absence of only eighty-seven days.

The first three decades of the nineteenth century were the high water mark of Hull whaling. At the commencement of the century the capture or destruction of the Dutch ships led to the growth and prosperity of the trade from Hull and other ports. According to Scoresby " the greatest cargo ever brought into Hull from Greenland was procured by Captain Sadler in the *Aurora* " in 1805; twenty-six whales yielding six hundred butts of blubber and nine tons of bone, the blubber when boiled yielding two hundred and forty-four tons of oil.

The following year the *Truelove* made her first voyage to Davis Strait, her previous twenty-one Arctic voyages being to the Greenland Seas in the direction of Spitsbergen.

The first participation of Hull in the Southern fishery took place towards the end of the eighteenth century. In 1812, twenty years after Colnett's exploratory voyage, the *Comet* (Captain Scurr) left for the fishery. She took three hundred barrels of sperm oil and put into Talcahuano at the time of the war between the Chilians and the " Patriots." She was requisitioned from time to time and detained for over a year. Afterwards she resumed fishing, made a successful voyage, returning to Hull after an absence of three years and three months.

THE BOUNTY SYSTEM

Towards the end of the eighteenth and commencement of the nineteenth centuries, there was still a considerable Arctic whale fishery from the Dutch ports and Hamburg.

In a letter to Lord Auckland[1] from the Hague dated 2nd December, 1791, Mr H. T. Spencer describes the condition of the Dutch fishery. The statistics show the following returns for the years 1787-91:

THE DUTCH WHALE FISHERIES.

		1787	1788	1789	1790	1791
Ships.	Greenland ..	59	58	50	51	48
	Davis Straits ..	8	11	14	15	14
Fish.	Greenland ..	215½	158½	423¼	105	62
	Davis Straits ..	42	21	51½	10	17½
Casks of Blubber.	Greenland ..	5741	2941	7222	2815	2941
	Davis Straits ..	1725	903	960	456	716
Quardels of Blubber.	Greenland ..	5409	2815	6488	2554	2473
	Davis Straits ..	1785	897	1388	446	716

Of these ships thirty-four have come home empty from Greenland, eleven from Davis Strait and three have been lost. Amsterdam alone sent in the

[1] *Auckland Papers*, Vol. xxix., correspondence Oct.-Dec., 1791. British Museum Add. MSS. 34,440, ff. 291-302.

year 1787, twenty-five ships; in 1788, twenty-three ships; in 1789, nineteen ships; in 1790, eighteen ships, and in the year 1791, seventeen ships. At this time the ships engaged in the Dutch whale fisheries were about one hundred and twelve feet long, twenty-eight and a half feet wide, with a depth in the hold of twelve and a half feet, between decks seven and a quarter feet; the burden being one to two hundred lasts or three hundred and sixty to four hundred tons.

The expense of an Arctic voyage was about nine thousand eight hundred florins, made up of ordinary outfit and victualling, two thousand nine hundred florins, wages advances, one thousand three hundred florins, and further wages, five thousand six hundred florins. It will be noted that there is no account of the cost of repairs, insurance, and other expenses. Details of the wages paid to the crew, who work on shares, are given, but as they follow similar lines to those already given by Zorgdrager there is no need to recapitulate them.

At this period the whale fishery was subsidised by the Dutch Government; a ship that returns empty being allowed five thousand florins compensation, or alternatively fifty florins for every cask of blubber short of a hundred, so that a ship that returns with but fifty casks of blubber receives two thousand five hundred florins. Exact notes of the quantity of whalebone were unobtainable. A full-sized fish is estimated to yield one thousand five hundred pounds, but as they have generally run small for several years the fish of these catchings have yielded on the average only from seven hundred and fifty to eight hundred and fifty pounds. The Dutch ships at this period were not provided with instruments for the capture of seals, nor are the men at all trained to that business. Spencer states that the quantity of oil and fins exported from England to Holland this year was "very inconsiderable," though of importance the four preceding years.

"Your Lordship will premise from the above statement that this is, upon the whole, a losing trade, and that the last year has been less productive than any of the former. It is, however, compensated to some sharers by supplying their ships with tackle, provisions, etc., and the hope of great gains induces others to risk their money in this speculation." Then follow detailed statistics of the fishery, as well as some collected from German sources.

An interesting side-light on the condition of the German whale fishing at the commencement of the nineteenth century is given by Köhler,[1] a sailmaker of Pirna, who took part in an Arctic voyage in 1801. Köhler, one of the world's unconscious humorists, writes in a naïve fashion eighteen years after the event. He warns his readers not to take

[1] Reise ins Eismeer und nach den Küsten von Groenland und Spizbergen im Jahre 1801, nebst einer genauen Beschreibung des Walfischfanges von F. G. Köhler, Seilermeister in Pirna, mit zwei Kupfertafeln, Leipzig, 1820.

part in the Greenland fishery on any account, and his book is certainly the most unsophisticated, and in many respects the most intimate account of a whaling voyage. In a company of eighteen ships he sailed on the three-master *Greenland* from Altona on the 16th March, 1801. From the outset Köhler makes no attempt to conceal his apprehensions; in many features he resembles Tartarin de Tarascon, that inimitable character of Daudet.

Of the crew of forty-two, only five were Germans, so it is evident that the German whaling trade at this time was carried on mainly by " Dutch, Danes, and Jutlanders." Köhler's opinion of sea life is worth recording, " es ist ein Gott recht wohlgefälliges Leben, so lange dass Schiff ruhig auf dem Meere schwimmt."

The ship's crew was divided into three watches, each having four hours on duty and eight hours off. Like Martens on an earlier occasion he describes the method of announcing the results of their fishing to passing whalers. " On these occasions I have often remarked the pride of the English. Every English ship waits until the other ship has first given its account of the fishing, so that they (the English) always give a pair of fish in excess. On one occasion, as I stood on the poop to give the signal our captain said, ' Give the number ten and you will see that the English ship will announce eleven or twelve.' And so it happened." But he pays the English a compliment. " As seamen they are skilful navigators, and I have often observed with pleasure how on their ships they set to work with skill and agility."

Köhler describes the process of committing the body of a dead seaman to the deep, explaining that the corpse is not tied to a board, but sunk by means of a stone or other heavy substance. " Der Seeman halt es fur Schande und Schimpf wenn sein Korper auf der See herum schwimmen sollte." The cook-house (galley) next occupies his attention. " There is no fear of my making my readers' mouths water. At four o'clock in the morning we get coarse groats with some butter, and so one morning like another. Dinner shows very little variation. On Sunday grey peas with pickled meat, Monday yellow peas and Stockfish, Tuesday grey peas and meat, Wednesday yellow peas and Stockfish, Thursday the same, Friday grey and meat, Saturday yellow and Stockfish; and so the loathsome grey and yellow change about one week with the other." Only twice did they get white beans and twice *sauerkraut;* they rejoiced for several days when it was anything but peas. On the 28th May, the captain's birthday, they had a feast with twenty-two bottles of wine, with which they drank the King of Denmark's health. The captain also supplied a few potatoes for some of the crew, and Köhler was in luck's way for once, for he got a whole potato and a piece. " Das war ein kostlicher Leckerbissen."

The ship's bread was bad, and often so old as to

be full of worms. It looked exactly like peat, and had to be washed before it could be eaten. The water was as bad as the bread, since the empty water casks were filled with whale oil, and after a perfunctory cleaning used for water again in the following year. " Manches Fass stinkt wie eine Kloake und dennoch darf kein Tropfen davon vergossen werden."

The feeding conditions on merchant vessels generally were at this period extremely bad, and it does not appear that whalers were much worse off than other sailors. The whalers were overcrowded, poorly ventilated, and very wet when there was any sea on. The sleeping quarters were dark, and provisions as a rule of inferior quality. The men were often without a change of clothing and suffered much from scurvy and skin diseases. Probably the whalers were, if anything, rather better off than the average merchant seaman.

There were, at any rate, possibilities of varying their food. Occasionally whale flesh was tried; Martens tried it, but preferred beef. J. J. Janssen, whose crew were compelled to eat whale flesh, took to it well. Sometimes seagulls were eaten; bear's flesh was also eaten. Christian Bullen, who wrote the first account of a German whaler's voyage to Greenland, complained that it tasted to him " *grimmiglich wie ein Bär*." Bullen was, however, a consistent grumbler, the only dish that pleased him being " seal's heart with liver and lights."

In the bays of Spitsbergen the whalers obtained

many fat ducks (Bergenten) and enormous numbers of birds' eggs. Reindeer were sometimes shot, and a plant known as "Greenland salad" gathered as a preventive against scurvy. The chief drink was beer, *branntwein* being reserved for extraordinary occasions. Tea and coffee were also drunk, each man providing his own supply.

Their amusements when laying to among the ice are graphically described by Köhler. They had gymnastics and trials of strength, and the Germans (*wir Teutschen*) played many a joke on the Jutlanders, and it was their delight to master those under whose orders they were at the time. "Ich will euch nur sehen, sagte der Kapitan, als wir Teutsche einst recht Munter waren wenn wir wieder ins Warme kommen."

Finally, when they saw their first whale off Spitsbergen, Köhler says he was so unfortunate as to be in the boat which set out to harpoon it. "Mein Herz klopfte als wir fortrudeten; ich fing an zu beten, und je naher wir dem Ungeheuer kamen, desto deutlicher horten sein blasen und meine Angst stieg." When they got near the whale got restive and caused some commotion, with the result that it escaped. Köhler openly rejoices at this (*Ich war im Herzen froh*) although the captain was greatly disappointed with the loss, since he estimated the whale at eight thousand thalers.

On the whole Köhler's description of the whaling grounds and operations is good. It is only when his personal feelings are concerned that his description becomes biased, as in the case of the whale which, in its struggles, smashed up three of the " shaloups " and kept the others, in which Köhler was engaged, fighting from twelve to sixteen hours until it was killed. During this time, as Köhler laments, they were without bread or water, and thought that every minute would be their last. The *Greenland* caught three whales in all, from which they extracted sixty-four, forty-five, and two barrels of oil. The first whale, which was fifty feet long, was captured in August towards the end of the voyage. This was the beast that smashed the three sloops above. The forty-five kardels whale was an easier capture, the third was a young whale, still a suckling. Dead whales were occasionally met with. Köhler's ship found one. As they proceeded to flense it, Köhler complained of the abominable stink. One of the ship's company replied that this stink was quite bearable, and nothing to the smell of a dead whale they had encountered on a previous voyage, the odour of which was so powerful that " der Mannschaft waren die Kopfe von den scharfen Ausdunstungen angeschwollen." From which it would appear that the crews of whaling ships occasionally indulge in a little exaggeration.

This pleasant reminiscence did not satisfy Köhler, who goes on to lament " *Das Walfischaas stinkt uberhaupt sehr widrig*," but the most abominable of all is the smell of those whales which have expired for some days prior to their flensing. Had

Köhler been contemporaneous with Mark Twain they might have compared notes in this respect on the relative merits of dead whales and Limburger cheese.

On the 23rd August, being then ice-free, they set sail for home. Köhler says it was impossible to describe their feelings of joy at this welcome news, the ship's doctor breaking out into poetry to commemorate their farewell to the world of ice. Ultimately they reached Heligoland where they declined a pilot, owing to the expense (eighty-eight thalers to Cuxhaven). They held on, and running away from an English convoy, went ashore, only getting off with some difficulty.

Köhler's pay for his services on this voyage (performed under circumstances of the greatest danger) amounted to ten shillings.

In 1821 Manby[1] made a voyage to Greenland in Scoresby's ship, the *Baffin*, from Liverpool, for the express purpose of trying a new gun harpoon. Up to this time there was great prejudice among the whalers against the use of gun harpoons, the hand harpoon being invariably preferred.

At this time it is evident the Greenland whale fishery was rapidly declining; due in the first place to the substitution of coal gas for oil gas, and in a lesser degree to the diminution of the whales and the losses of ships crushed amongst the ice. Manby remarks on the superior advantages of oil

[1] G. W. Manby, "Journal of a Voyage to Greenland in the year 1821," London, 1822.

gas: " The advantage of gas produced from oil, compared with that obtained from coal, is so great that it is astonishing that oil gas is not in general use. The gas from oil has no bad nor disagreeable quality, it gives a far more brilliant light than the other, one cubic foot of gas from oil going as far as twice that quantity of coal gas, and it is, moreover, much cheaper. That from coal, on the contrary, is extremely offensive to the smell, dangerous to the health on being inhaled, and injurious to furniture, books, plate, pictures, etc." In spite of all these advantages whale oil gas was soon worsted in the struggle. There is, however, a considerable volume of evidence that at this time the real drawback to whaling was the increased difficulty of taking whales. To remedy this, the gun harpoon was invented, but it does not appear to have been tried on the voyage, though Scoresby expresses a guarded appreciation of it, remarkable in one respect since he foreshadows the use to which the gun harpoon was put many years later, i.e., " for attacking wicked fish, fish at the edge of packs, finners, razorbacks, etc., these destructive implements might be of uncommon service." As will be seen later, the improved gun harpoon of the Norwegians has led to an extensive fishery of Finner Whales.

CHAPTER VI

THE SOUTHERN FISHERY

The capture of the Sperm Whale—Commencement of a southern fishery—The voyages of Colnett, Beale, and Bennett.

THE first Sperm Whale taken by American fishermen was captured in 1712 by a Nantucket whaleman, who had been blown out to sea by a strong northerly wind.[1] This led to an improvement in American whale boats, which had been previously engaged in coastal whaling. In 1730 there were twenty-five vessels of from thirty to fifty tons engaged in deep-sea whaling. The improved oil obtained from the Sperm Whale induced whalers to endeavour to fit out vessels exclusively for this fishing, and ultimately originated the great southern fishery. The American whalers are said to have extended their operations as follow: Coast of Guinea 1763; Western Islands 1765; coast of Brazil 1774. American tradition says that the first whaler to cross " the line " arrived home on the day of the Battle of Lexington and Concord (19th April, 1775).[2] This, however, does not agree with Burke's famous speech on American affairs (1774), when he stated that

[1] Macy, "History of Nantucket," p. 44, 1836.
[2] Tower, "History of the American Whale Fishery," p. 28, Philadelphia, 1907.

American whalers "are at the Antipodes, and engaged under the frozen serpent of the south."

In 1775 the first British attempt was made at the southern fishery.[1] Ships of from one hundred to one hundred and nine tons burthen were sent to South Greenland, the coast of Brazil, the Falkland Islands, and the Gulf of Guinea, but as the principal resorts of the Spermaceti Whale were not then known they met with little success.

In 1776 the Government extended the benefits of the bounty system to the southern whale fishery, and, consequently, the Custom House returns show the number and tonnage of vessels fitted out in Great Britain. The table opposite shows the number and tonnage from the commencement of the bounty system up to 1783.

A statistical table for the southern whale fishery for the years 1800 to 1834 is given by McCulloch (see Appendix III.).[2]

It will be noticed that there is a marked discrepancy between the number of ships at sea and the number of ships returned in any year.

According to McCulloch the southern whale fishery consisted (in 1835) of three distinct branches; the chase of the Spermaceti Whale (*Physeter macrocephalus*), that of the common black whale of the southern seas, and that of the sea elephant or

---

[1] Beale, "Natural History of the Sperm Whale," p. 143, London, 1839.

[2] "Dictionary of Commerce," 1832 edition. Supplement, 1835, p. 57.

THE SOUTHERN FISHERY

southern walrus. According to information collected by Scoresby the fishery for the Spermaceti Whale was conducted off the coasts of Chile, Peru, and California, in various parts of the Pacific about the Gallipagos and Marquesas islands, in the Indian and

SOUTHERN WHALE FISHERY.[1]

Year.	No. of Ships.	Tonnage.	Place from whence fitted out.	Bounty paid.
1763 to 1775	Nil.	Nil.	[2]	—
1776	12	1977	London	—
1777	13	2103	,,	£2400
1778	19	3038	,,	1500
1779	4	467	,,	500
1780	7	771	,,	2000
1781	3	317	,,	—
	1	340	Liverpool	1400
	2	100	Poole	—
1782	4	660	London	—
	1	100	Bristol	1400
	1	150	Cowes	—
1783	4	660	London	—
	4	280	Poole	—
	1	100	Bristol	—

[1] From Third Report on the State of the British Fisheries, 1785, App., pp. 132 and 133.
[2] There would be no returns in the Custom House Books, because no bounties were paid. Nevertheless it is certain vessels took part in this fishery in 1775.

China Seas particularly about the island Timor. The Right Whale, which was hunted by the Sperm whalers, was found on the Brazil Bank from latitude 36° to 48° S., in the former parallel in the months of November, December, and January, in the latter in February, March, and April. In the same months they are to be found in the Derwent River, New Holland, also about the Tristian Islands; and in June, July, August, and September in Walwick (Walfisch) Bay and other inlets on the African coast. They are also found near the island of St Catharine (Brazil), in some of the bays to the westward of Cape Horn, and to the north of Coquimbo on the west coast of South America.

Detailed descriptions of early whaling voyages in the southern fishery are given by Colnett[1] (1792), Beale[2] (1830-3), and Bennett[3] (1833-6).

The term " southern " was applied to the Atlantic fishery, in fact to all voyages which were not to Greenland (Spitsbergen), these latter being distinguished as the northern fishery. As already mentioned the bounty system originally applied only to the northern fishery but was extended to the southern in 1776.

[1] " A Voyage to the South Atlantic and round Cape Horn into the Pacific Ocean for the Purpose of Extending the Spermaceti Whale Fisheries, and other Objects of Commerce," London, 1798.
[2] " The Natural History of the Sperm Whale," to which is added a sketch of a south-sea whaling voyage, by Thomas Beale, London, 1839 (2nd edition).
[3] " Narrative of a Whaling Voyage round the Globe from the year 1833 to 1836," 2 Vols., London, 1840.

THE SOUTHERN FISHERY 211

Although the southern fishery was at first confined to the Atlantic, after a time whalers rounded Cape Horn, and hunted whales in the Pacific. Precisely when this first occurred is not known. One of the earliest, if not the earliest English whaling voyage to the Pacific was that of Colnett, but there is some reason to think that the Spaniards were there before him for the same purpose. A search of the records at Madrid would probably give further information on this point. We know from the voyage of Anson round the world (1740-4) that there was an extensive Spanish trade in the Pacific at this time. Many of the earlier Spanish voyages were precisely through those areas where the Sperm Whale was most abundant.

The same year that Colnett was fitting out in London for his whaling voyage to the Pacific, Sanez Reguart[1] published his monumental work on the Spanish fisheries. This dictionary contains in the third volume under the heading " Harpon " one of the most complete and best illustrated accounts of whaling as practised in the eighteenth century. Special reference is made to the attempts of the Spaniards to resuscitate their whale fisheries by means of a company founded to fish for whales off the Patagonian coast and the Straits of Magellan, Chiloe, and the Pacific Ocean. The Spanish Company was given a charter by Charles IV. in 1789.

[1] " Diccionario historico de los artes de la pesca nacional," Madrid, 1791-5, 5 Vols., 4to. The third volume containing the section on whaling was published in 1792.

There is, therefore, reason to think that the first Spanish whaling in the Pacific preceded the British.

Colnett was a naval officer, who had taken part in one of Cook's voyages. In 1792 the merchants of the city of London, interested in the South Sea Fisheries, prepared a memorandum, and submitted it to the Board of Trade, in which they planned a voyage round Cape Horn to discover whaling grounds for whalers who had rounded the Cape. The Admiralty were induced to look with favour on the scheme, H.M. sloop the *Rattler* was sold to the merchants, and Colnett was nominated to take command of her, being granted leave for the purpose. A crew of twenty-five men were engaged, and the vessel was equipped and made ready for sea by the 11th November, 1792. Colnett purchased a half-share in the vessel, the other half of the undertaking being in the hands of Messrs Enderby & Sons, at that time the largest firm in the whale fishery. Owing to trouble with the French at this time there was a delay in clearing the *Rattler*, and she was sent to Portsmouth to await her commander, who joined her on the 24th December, 1792. In the meanwhile, owing to the bounty offered by the Admiralty to seamen for enlisting in the navy, the crew of the *Rattler* was depleted by the desertion of three seamen, who left to join the navy. Three landsmen were secured in the Isle of Wight, and the *Rattler* set out on her voyage with a crew of seventeen officers and men, three landsmen, and five boys; her normal naval complement being one hundred and thirty men!

The sloop arrived at Rio de Janeiro on the 24th February, 1793, where they repaired and took on board provisions, including " two live bullocks," and on the 5th March set out for the voyage round Cape Horn in company with another whaler, the *Mediator*. The Cape was doubled on the 11th April, 1793, and a course set for the coast of Chile. On 1st May they saw Sperm Whales off Mocha Island, where the sea was covered with them. The crew of the *Rattler* killed six, four of which were secured alongside, but the weather turning bad, only two were saved.

Colnett next decided to cruise off Mocha Island for several days, during which time large numbers of Sperm Whales were seen. The *Rattler*, however, only killed two additional whales here, of which one was secured. Thence a course was set to 26° 30′ N., keeping the coast in sight, but as far as St Felix and St Ambrose Islands no further whales were seen (20th May, 1793).

Subsequently they sailed to the Peruvian coast near Lima and thence to the Gallipagos Islands. Up to this time their search for whales had not been very successful, so they doubled back to Peru, and then sailed in a general northerly direction along the west coast of Mexico. They cruised off the Cocos Islands which was the most northerly point recommended by the Admiralty, but Colnett disregarded his instructions and explored the coast as far north as the Gulf of California, including the islands of Socoro, Santo Berto, and Rocka Partida. " This was an undertaking that few who had suffered, as I had done, from the yellow fever in the prisons of New Spain, as well as from all the horrors of a rainy season on that coast; and it was very evident that if successful in killing them in the rainy season, it must be much more easily done in the dry season." On the 19th August off Point Angles (Mexico) they encountered a large school of Spermaceti Whales, none of which was captured. Here they cruised for sixteen days, killing three whales. The heart of one was cooked in a large " sea-pye," and afforded an excellent meal. On the 4th October they made the coast of California, where they found the " species of whale on this coast is of no value."

Between Cape Corrientes and the Maria Islands they saw large numbers of Spermaceti Whales, but were again unfortunate, only killing two. On the return journey, near Quibo (January, 1794), they fell in with several Spermaceti Whales, killing four. This induced Colnett to prolong his cruise in this neighbourhood until the 8th February, but without further success. By this time Colnett recognised that his whaling business had definitely failed, largely, it would appear from the unskilfulness of his crew, and he decided to return to the Gallipagos for salt for salting seal skins which he proposed to get at the St Felix and St Ambrose Islands. While at the Gallipagos, however, in April, they saw many Spermaceti Whales, especially young ones. They killed five here, and Colnett believed he had dis-

THE SOUTHERN FISHERY 215

covered the general rendezvous of these whales from the coast of Mexico, Peru, and the Gulf of Panama who came there to calve.

He definitely recommends these islands as the best meeting place for British whalers seeking the Pacific grounds. The *Rattler* returned to England after an absence of twenty-two months. It does not appear that the voyage was successful from a whaling standpoint, though much surveying was done, and this doubtless proved useful to subsequent whalers.

Thomas Beale was a Surgeon and Demonstrator of Anatomy to the Eclectic Society of London. On the 16th October, 1830, he left England on board the South Sea whaler, *Kent*. They sailed straight for Cape Horn, passing it on the 5th January, 1831, and thence up along the west coast of South America to Valparaiso and Coquimbo. The latter town was left on the 16th February, 1831, and a course set for the Pacific whaling grounds, along the Peruvian coast.

The whalers appeared to be in no particular hurry, and it was not until the 28th March, 1831, that they left Monta Christa, four days afterwards encountering their first school of Sperm Whales. Four of these were killed, nearly six months after leaving England. The course was now for the Sandwich Islands, sighted on the 4th May, 1831, en route for the Japan grounds which the captain desired to reach in June.

The " off-shore " Japan fishery lies in the Pacific Ocean between 140° to 160° E. and 28° to 32° N. latitude, the best time of the year being from the beginning of June to the end of September, during which time the usual catch is from eight hundred to one thousand four hundred barrels of sperm oil, though up to two thousand barrels have been taken.

From June to September Beale's ship fell in with large numbers of whales on these Japan grounds, seeing them every day for weeks.

At this time the ships employed in the whaling industry were vessels from three to four hundred tons burthen, with a crew of twenty-eight to thirty-three officers and men, including a surgeon. They started from London at all times of the year fully provisioned for three years. Each whaler carried six whale boats, each about twenty-seven feet long by four beam; sharp at both ends for rapid motion in any direction. Near the stern was an upright rounded piece of wood, the " loggerhead," at the bow a groove exactly in the centre, through which the harpoon line ran. Each boat was provided with two harpoon lines of two hundred fathoms length, coiled in tubs ready for use, three or four harpoons, two or three lances, a keg with lantern, tinder-box, and other small articles, two or three small flags, the " whifts " to be inserted in the dead whale for ready detection in case the whale was abandoned for chase of a second, and one or two " drougues," quadrilateral pieces of board with a central handle by which they are attached to the harpoon line to increase its resistance when running out, and so to check the speed of the whale in sounding or running. Each

THE SOUTHERN FISHERY 217

boat had a crew of six men, two of whom in the stern and bow respectively were the " headsman " and " boat-steerer."

Four boats were generally used in the chase under the command of the captain and mates respectively. The headsman has command of the boat, and steers it until the whale is reached. The boat-steerer pulls bow oar, until near the whale, when he quits the oar and strikes the harpoon into the animal. The line attached to the harpoon runs between the men to the stern of the boat, and after passing two or three turns round the loggerhead is continuous with the coils lying in the tubs in the bottom of the boat.

The boat-steerer now comes aft, and steers the boat by means of an oar passed through a ring attached to the stern, he also watches the line. The headsman at the same time passes forward and takes up the lance to plunge into the whale at the first opportunity.

During the time the ship is on the whaling grounds, men are placed at each mast-head, who are relieved every two hours; an officer is also on the fore-top-gallant-yard, so that there are four of the crew constantly on the look-out from the most elevated parts of the ship.

In mid-September the weather changed for the worse and whales became scarce, until at the end of the month they disappeared. A course was then set for the Bonin Islands in 141° 30′ E. Longitude, and 26° 30′ N. Latitude, where several whales were taken. Beale thought that the whales were now migrating south-west (October, 1831). The Bonins were left on the 10th December, 1831, for New Guinea, and, after passing to the windward of the Ladrones, they fell in with the Carolines on the 24th December, " a range of large islands scarcely known, and not even placed correctly on the charts."

On the 1st January, 1832, the *Kent* crossed the Equator for the third time, and made New Ireland on the 6th, having passed St John's Island on the 5th. On the 7th they found themselves in St George's Channel, separating New Ireland (Neu Mecklenburg of the late German colonies) from New Britain (late German Neu Pommern). No whales were met with here, so the course was continued to the southward, towards the north-east of Australia, passing the Louisiade Archipelago en route. Here again no whales were encountered. On account of the lack of success, the course was now set in a northerly direction and Bougainville Island reached on the 20th January, 1832.

Here, on the 22nd January, the first whale, since the *Kent* left the Japan grounds, was taken, yielding sixteen barrels of oil. The Ladrones were now the next objective, New Ireland being sighted on the 29th January, and St John's on the 31st.

The line was again crossed on the 8th February, 1832, and Rota, one of the Ladrones, sighted on the 21st, Guam the chief island being reached on the following day. Here the *Kent* remained some

THE SOUTHERN FISHERY

time to refit; only leaving for the Japan grounds on the 6th April.

The Bonins were again reached on the 21st April, in which neighbourhood the *Kent* continued to cruise for whales. By this time there was considerable friction between Beale and the captain of the *Kent* on account of the latter's brutal treatment of the crew; so when the London south-sea whaler, *Sarah and Elizabeth*, was fallen in with, off the Bonins, on the 1st June, 1832, Beale effected an exchange with the surgeon of that vessel. The *Kent* subsequently went to the Japan fishery, but met with little success. Off the coast of California they were equally unsuccessful, ultimately reaching England after a voyage of three and a half years with only half an average cargo. The *Sarah and Elizabeth* was much more fortunate, for in about six weeks after Beale joined her six hundred barrels of sperm oil were obtained, sufficient to complete the cargo. The ship then went north-east to the Sandwich Islands, sailing into latitude $40°$ north in order to take advantage of the north-east trades.

During this part of the voyage large numbers of Sperm Whales were encountered, apparently migrating in schools to the southward. The meridian of 180 was crossed in latitude $38° 39'$ north on the 6th August, 1832; and one of the Sandwich Isles sighted on the 30th. The course was now homeward bound, but via the Friendly Islands and the neighbourhood of New Zealand. On the

26th October when near the latter islands the course was set direct for Cape Horn, which was sighted on the 18th November, 1832; Beachy Head being sighted on the 3rd February, 1833. Beale had been away two years and four months, the *Sarah and Elizabeth* thirty-two months only, a very successful and, for those days, brief voyage.

The narratives of Colnett and Beale give a personal touch to the history of the southern whale fishery, and their accounts are supplemented by Bennett, who sailed from London on the 17th October, 1833, on the south-seaman *Tuscan*. The *Tuscan* was a whaler of the usual type, being about three hundred tons burthen. Contrary to the experience of the *Rattler* and the *Kent*, the *Tuscan* met with Sperm Whales in the Atlantic in the latter half of November, in latitude 9° N. and 23° W., one of which was killed and secured.

A second encounter with Sperm Whales also occurred in the Atlantic in 38° S. and 51° W. (off the South American coast) on the 24th December, when another was captured. Bennett rounded Cape Horn on the 19th January, 1834. Early in February, when near Juan Fernandez, the first Sperm Whales in the Pacific were seen.

The course of the *Tuscan* was now to Pitcairn Island, Tahiti, Society Islands, Raiatea, thence to the Sandwich Islands from April to 22nd May, 1834. Subsequently the *Tuscan* met with schools of Sperm Whales to the north-east of the Sandwich Isles in · 40° N., two specimens being secured,

THE SOUTHERN FISHERY 221

each of which yielded fifty barrels of oil. The course was now set for the Queen Charlotte Islands off the west coast of North America in 50° N., but no whales were encountered there.

Returning south they saw a solitary Sperm Whale on 23rd July in latitude 31° N. and 153° W. A few days later many Cachalots were observed, and several secured. The ground north of the Sandwich Islands seems at this time to have swarmed with Sperm Whales, and the *Tuscan* was very successful between 23° and 31° N. and 154° and 160° W.

A return was now made to the Sandwich group, where they remained until the 20th October, 1834, on which date they left again, steering north to get advantage of the prevailing westerly winds from the American coast and the Equator. Off Guadaloupe and Cape St Lucas (California) a fleet of American south-seamen were cruising; from here on an indirect course to the Marquesas many Cachalots were seen, and a few captured by the *Tuscan*.

Bennett devoted much space in his journal of the voyage to a description of the various Pacific Islands touched at, together with an account of their history, and the manner and customs of their inhabitants, and the whaling episodes occupy a relatively small portion of the description of the voyage, but there is an Appendix with a detailed account of the whale fishery.

In the nineteenth century the French Government

assisted both cod and whale fisheries, by means of bounties. Nearly twenty-five and a half million francs were given as bounties to industries in one year, to which must be added nearly three and a half million francs for the fisheries.

The law of the 22nd July, 1851, was voted to keep in existence the French whale fishery, consisting at that time of seventeen vessels with six hundred men. Fishing was encouraged in two ways. The markets in France and the colonies were exclusively reserved and bounties (*budget de secours*) were paid. Lajonkiere[1] complains that the French whalers were no good (*malpropres et indisciplinés*). This system of bounties produced poor results, and was unsuccessful in resuscitating the French whale fisheries.

[1] " Des primes à la pêche."

CHAPTER VII

THE AMERICAN WHALE FISHERIES

Importance of whales to the early colonists—Gradual extension of the fishery—Firmly established in 1775—Set-back caused by the Revolution—Gradual recovery—Checked again by the war of 1812—Subsequent rapid expansion—Mid-nineteenth century American whaling fleet the largest ever known—Gradual decline of the industry, and the reasons for it.

THE American whale fisheries, at one time the greatest in the world, originated, like that of the Basques, as a coastal and inshore fishery. Captain John Smith in 1614 found whales so plentiful along the coast of New England that he turned from the original object of his voyage in order to pursue them. Richard Mather, who went to the Massachusetts Bay colony in 1635, saw " mighty whales spewing up water in the air like the smoke of a chimney, of such incredible bigness that I will never wonder that the body of Jonah could be in the belly of a whale."

The earliest references in the history of the Massachusetts Bay colony refer exclusively to drift whales which had been cast ashore, and it is uncertain when the inhabitants first took part in the capture of these cetacea at sea. It is certain, however, from contemporary records, that the fishing had been inaugurated before the end of the seventeenth century. In 1688 Secretary Randolph wrote home to England: " New Plimouth Colony have great profit by whale killing. I believe it will be one of our best returns, now beaver and peltry fayle us." Whaling was early recognised as a regular vocation in the Connecticut and New York colonies. It seems probable that the first organised prosecution of the whale fishery by Americans was made by the settlers at the eastern end of Long Island. Sometime between 1650 and 1670 the practice of taking only drift whales, that had been cast ashore by the sea, was superseded by the taking of whales by harpooners from small open boats. These boats were designed for whaling along the coasts; they were fitted out for voyages lasting two weeks, but did not venture far out to sea, the men usually camping on shore for the night. The only other place to engage in whaling prior to 1700 was Nantucket. Here the whales came right into the harbour, and early efforts were made to capture them by means of harpoons. With the early years of the eighteenth century Nantucket rapidly became the foremost whaling station. At first whales were so plentiful that all the oil required could be obtained without the boats having to go out of sight of land. Naturally at this time all the captured whales were towed ashore where the trying out works were erected. A look-out was kept from a prominent place on the land, and when a whale was seen the boats were sent out in pursuit. Many

THE AMERICAN WHALER. A SHIP ON THE NORTH WEST COAST, CUTTING-IN HER LAST RIGHT WHALE.

Indians were employed, each boat's crew being composed partly of aborigines.

As already related, in 1712 one of the whalemen was blown out to sea where he captured a Sperm Whale, the first of the species taken by American whalers. This led eventually to a great development of the whaling industry. The people of Nantucket immediately began to build whaling sloops of about thirty tons burden to whale in deep water. These vessels were fitted out for cruises of six weeks' duration, the blubber being stripped off, stored aboard in hogsheads and brought back to the trying out works on shore. By 1715 Nantucket had six sloops engaged in this fishery; by 1730 there were twenty vessels of from thirty to fifty tons employed. About this time schooners were introduced, and the size increased up to seventy tons. The shore fishery now reached its maximum development, the whales near the coast becoming gradually scarcer and scarcer owing to over-fishing.

The introduction of sperm oil, so superior to all other oils, was a great stimulus to the development of the industry. With the addition of larger vessels to the fleet longer voyages were made and more distant areas visited. At first it was the custom of the whalers to go to the southward where they fished until July. Then they returned, refitted, and finished the season to the eastward of the Grand Banks. Davis Strait was visited by American whalemen in 1732, and in 1737 the *Boston News Letter* records the voyages of several vessels to that neighbourhood. It will be understood from the preceding chapters that the Atlantic was fished for Sperm Whales, the order of development of the grounds being Carolina coasts, Bahamas, West Indies, Gulf of Mexico, Caribbean Sea, Azores, Cape Verde Islands, and the coast of Africa, whereas in Arctic waters it was the Right Whale which was sought. This development was very gradual; according to Macy the Nantucket whalers extending their operations as follows: coast of Guinea 1763; Western Islands 1765; coast of Brazil 1774.

The chief product of the fishery in the seventeenth and opening decades of the eighteenth centuries was whale oil. When Sperm whaling was commenced whalebone was not considered to be of much value. The oil trade naturally developed at first between the colonial ports (as they then were); in 1720 there is record of an export of a cargo of Nantucket whale oil in London, but whether that was the first venture is not certain.

With the development of whaling which followed the enterprise of the deep-sea whalers, the export trade in whale products grew rapidly since the whalers obtained far more than was required to meet the limited colonial demand. There is evidence about 1730 of a regular export trade in train and whale oil and whalebone to England and British West Indian ports. In 1737 a dozen vessels were fitted out at Provincetown for the Davis Straits fishery, some of them of one hundred tons burthen. " So many men are going on these voyages that not more than twelve or fourteen men will be left at home." After 1741 the whalers were interfered with by French and Spanish privateers, and for some years the voyages to the distant grounds were interrupted; at any rate, there are no records of the Davis Straits fishery. The participation of England in the war of the Austrian succession gave France and Spain an opportunity of preying on English and English colonial commerce, and this was precisely the time at which the New England whaling interests were developing rapidly. This development was naturally hindered by the presence of these privateers off the North American coast. Under this pressure of adverse circumstances the Davis Straits fishery was entirely abandoned, the Western Isles fishery seriously crippled, so that the bulk of the whalers' operations was confined to the vicinity of the Grand Banks and the Bahamas.

In 1748 the colonial fishermen benefited by a Bounty Act passed by the British Parliament. This bounty amounted to twenty shillings per ton; in order to receive it the vessels had to be built and fitted out in the colonies, and to fish in Davis Strait and the vicinity from May to August unless they secured a full cargo or met with an accident.

At first the colonial whaling vessels were manned almost exclusively by colonists and Indians. As the fishery developed the supply of hands became inadequate, so that in 1750 the Nantucket vessels had to secure men from Cape Cod and Long Island.

The whaling industry gradually spread along the

coast including before the revolution, Cape Cod towns of Wellfleet, Barnstable, and Falmouth; Boston and Lynn; the Rhode Island towns of Newport, Providence, Warren, and Tiverton; New London (Connecticut); Williamsburg (Virginia); Martha's Vineyard, and New Bedford (then Dartmouth), all fitting out vessels for the whaling.

At the time of the outbreak of the Revolution whaling had become firmly established in what were then the American colonies. At New Bedford whaling probably commenced about 1755. Ten years later there were four sloops employed, and in 1775 eighty vessels with a tonnage of six thousand five hundred.

In 1755 the colonial whalemen were restricted by an embargo placed on the Banks' fishermen, and this was continued in 1757 when the Nantucket whalers were given permission to resume their whaling voyages. The Gulf of St Lawrence and Straits of Belle Isle were opened to the colonial fishermen in 1761. By 1762 Nantucket alone had seventy-eight vessels engaged in whaling. About this time the British Parliament laid a duty on all whale products exported to England from the colonies with a view to assist the British whalers in their struggles against the supremacy of the Dutch.

British whalers were also granted a bounty in which the colonists did not share. Shortly after the colonists were forbidden to send their exports to any other markets so they were practically compelled to pay the English duties. Both the colonial and

THE AMERICAN WHALE FISHERIES

London merchants protested against this, sending petitions to Parliament, but it was not until 1767 that conditions were much improved.

Just before the Revolution broke out the American whale fishery was very prosperous. The annual production from 1771 to 1775 was estimated at not less than forty-five thousand barrels of sperm oil, eight thousand five hundred barrels of whale oil, and seventy-five thousand pounds of bone. Sperm oil fetched forty pounds per ton, head matter fifty pounds per ton, whale oil seventy dollars per ton, and whalebone fifty cents per pound on the average. Most of the exports went to Great Britain where the increasing consumption of oil in lamps and in various industries led to a large demand for whale products.

The revolution of 1775 put a stop to whaling, and the trade in oil and bone practically ceased, except to the West Indies. The previous year the colonial whale fishery had reached its high-water mark with a fleet of three hundred and sixty vessels of thirty-three thousand aggregate tonnage. Of these at least three hundred sail belonged to Massachusetts ports. In 1775 in order " to starve New England " the British Parliament passed an Act to restrict colonial trade to British ports, placing an embargo on fishing on the banks of Newfoundland or on any other part of the North American coast. When hostilities commenced the only port to carry on whaling was Nantucket, the people of which town were compelled to endeavour to follow this industry, since it was the only one which yielded them any means of subsistence. The history of whaling during the War of Independence is therefore an account of the struggle of the Nantucket men against adverse circumstances. Early in the war the British vessels made several forays along the New England coast, capturing and burning the whale ships, and destroying property on shore at Nantucket, Martha's Vineyard, and Dartmouth.

The privations at Nantucket were so excessive that in 1781 the British Admiral granted the islanders permission to employ twenty-four vessels unmolested by the British cruisers.

In 1783 the Continental Congress granted permits for thirty-five vessels to engage in whaling, but very soon after the treaty of peace was signed.

The end of the war found the whaling industry practically extinct.

Except at Nantucket the whalers were ruined, and even there not much had been saved. When war broke out one hundred and fifty vessels were fishing from Nantucket. In 1784 only two or three odd ships remained; one hundred and thirty-four had been captured or destroyed by the English and fifteen lost by shipwreck.

The recovery of the American whalers for the first two decades after the signing of peace was slow. The whales were less shy and more easily killed, and whale products fetched good prices for a few years after the war. The boom was short-lived, and prices dropped considerably. The British market was to all intents and purposes closed by an alien import duty of eighteen pounds per ton. Oil which fetched thirty pounds per ton before the war now barely made seventeen pounds, and since twenty-five pounds was the minimum required by the whalers in order to clear their expenses it follows that the industry languished. A number of the American ports which had entered the whaling business speedily withdrew from it, and it was due to the courage and enterprise of the Nantucket men that at this stage the industry did not expire.

When the state of the industry appeared hopeless, the Massachusetts legislature came to the rescue, and in 1785 passed a Bounty Act. For every ton of oil imported into the States the whalemen were to receive a bounty of five pounds on white spermaceti oil, sixty shillings on brown or yellow sperm oil, and forty shillings on whale oil. The vessel had to be owned and manned wholly by the inhabitants of Massachusetts, and landed at a port in that state. During the war the lack of oil had induced the people to use tallow candles, so that the increased landings of oil which were the result of this bounty could not be absorbed by the population, with the result that over-production led to a sharp fall in prices.

Scammon states that by 1787-9 there were only one hundred and twenty-two vessels engaged in whaling from Massachusetts ports, and even this list includes small vessels not engaged in regular voyages.

At this time the English were trying hard to build up a whaling trade, paying heavy bounties for the purpose. A commercial treaty with France in 1789 opened up a prosperous trade, but after a few shipments thither the outbreak of the French Revolution upset all calculations, and once more the whaling industry received a check. Under the stimulus of this French trade the American whalers extended their voyages in the Atlantic, and even rounded Cape Horn in their search for whales. The first American whalers to enter the Pacific did so in 1791, about four years after English ships had opened up Pacific whaling. After 1792 the shipments of whale products from America to France did not pay costs, and this branch of the trade ceased. In 1798 the prospects of war between the United States and France induced French privateers to prey upon American commerce, including the whalers.

From this time to the war of 1812, the whaling industry fluctuated considerably. Up to 1806 or 1807, the Fleet was gradually developing from year to year, but after that the decline was steady.

The embargo of 1807 stopped the exportation of whale products and thus kept down the price of oil and candles in the States. In 1810 things appeared more settled, and whaling was extensively resumed, so that when war broke out between the English and the Americans in 1812 a large number of whalers were at sea, some in the Pacific, whither they had gone on voyages of two and two and a half years' duration. Some of the vessels returned on receiving the news of the outbreak of war, to be laid up for its duration. Others were captured at sea. Nantucket and New Bedford, the chief whaling ports, suffered severely. The war again affected whaling in an adverse manner, though the early years of the nineteenth century witnessed the rise of several influences which benefited the whalers. The general increase in prosperity of America led to a demand for whale oil, and sperm candles in preference to tallow candles. There was an increasing demand from all the seaports on the coast, the export trade, especially to the West Indies, developing rapidly.

The war lasted three years (1812-5) and again the whaling trade shrank to zero, except at Nantucket, where perforce a little coastal whaling was indulged in, and an occasional vessel sent out on a longer voyage.

At the close of the war in 1815, the Nantucket whaling fleet numbered twenty-three vessels; in 1819 there were sixty-one, and in 1821 eighty-four. The success of the Nantucket whalers stimulated other ports to follow their example, and there was a general recrudescence of American whaling at this time. The Pacific whalers, which up to this time had frequented only the "onshore grounds," in 1818 first visited the "offshore grounds." In 1820 the first vessels sailed for the Japanese coasts; by 1822 from thirty to forty vessels were whaling there.

234 A HISTORY OF THE WHALE FISHERIES

Nantucket and New Bedford were now the leading whaling ports.

Between 1820 and 1835 the development of the American whaling was steady; towards the latter portion of this period, owing to the generally prosperous condition of the industry, a large number of ports engaged in the enterprise. In 1835 there were nearly thirty ports, with whalers numbering from two or three to over two hundred sail. Growth by this time was exceedingly rapid, the total number of whalers rising from two hundred and three in 1829 to four hundred and twenty-one in 1834.

The two decades following 1835 marked the zenith of the American whale fisheries. This year whaling was commenced by a Nantucket vessel along the north-west coast of America. In 1848 a Sag Harbour whaler passed through Behring Strait into the Arctic, this being the last whaling ground opened up by the American whalers. In 1835 the Nantucket fleet went mainly to the Pacific, after 1840 it went almost exclusively there, and by 1850 the New Bedford fleet had followed its example.

By this time new uses had been found for whalebone, and the oil was steadily and increasingly in request as an illuminant for sperm candles and whale oil lamps. In fact, it was not until the discovery of petroleum in 1859 that there was any serious rival to whale oil in this respect. This discovery, however, sealed the fate of American whaling. The struggle between the two oils was short and sharp. Kerosene came rapidly in

THE AMERICAN WHALE FISHERIES

general use, lubricating oils were manufactured from the residuum, and the introduction of the wax or paraffin for making candles finally sealed the battle.

But before this happened the American whale fisheries were founded on whale products. From 1835 to 1860 the whaling fleet averaged six hundred vessels annually with an aggregate tonnage of 190,500. The annual imports averaged 117,950 barrels of sperm oil, 25,913 barrels of whale oil, and 2,323,512 pounds of bone—a total annual value of over eight million dollars.

In 1846 the fleet numbered six hundred and eighty ships and barques, thirty-four brigs, and twenty-two schooners, with a total tonnage of 233,262. The value of this fleet exceeded twenty-one million dollars, while the whole business interests connected with the trade were estimated at seventy million dollars, giving employment to 70,000 persons. After 1847 the price of sperm oil never fell below a dollar a gallon for thirty consecutive years.

Although 1846 was the year when the largest fleet was employed, the real value of the fishery continued at a high level for many subsequent years. Between 1846 and 1856 sperm oil rose from eighty-eight cents to $1·62 per gallon; whale oil from thirty-four to seventy-nine cents; and whalebone from thirty-four to fifty-eight cents a pound. In 1857 a financial crisis in the country brought a sudden slump in the price of oil, and this was really the beginning of the end of American whaling, as a decline set in, gradual at first, but more rapid later.

The whaling boom of 1846-7 coincided with the opening of new grounds for Bowhead Whales in the Seas of Okhotsk and Kamschatka, the Arctic fishery commencing two years later.

Detailed statistics and records of American whaling voyages are available.[1] Many ships saw the whole of the fishery through practically from beginning to end. Quite a number of the New Bedford whalers were in commission for over fifty years, the four heading the list being the ship *Maria* (ninety years), the ship *Rousseau* (eighty-seven years), the barque *Triton* (seventy-nine years), and the ship *Ocean* (seventy-five years). The *Maria*, which was built by Ichabod Thomas on the North River in Pembroke, Mass., in 1782, sailed the seas of the globe until 1872, when she was broken up at Vancouver Island.

The record of the New Bedford whaler *Lagoda* is of great interest since she participated in the fishery in the boom years, and was only sold by her owners when the decline had unmistakably set in. The *Lagoda* made twelve voyages between October, 1841, and July, 1886, of which ten resulted in a profit, and two (the tenth and twelfth) in a loss; the net gain to the owners being $652,000. The dividends on the individual voyages were in percentages: 29·6; 120·5; 66·9; 177·2; 100; 96·9;

---

[1] Old Dartmouth Historical Sketches, Nos. 2, 14, 43, 44, 45, and 50, New Bedford, Mass., U.S.A.

363·5; 219; 115·2; loss; about 10; loss. Of course it must be remembered that the voyages lasted several years, but even so, in the case of the seventh voyage, which lasted forty-four months, the average monthly profit was eight and a quarter per cent.

Some idea of the relative importance of the various fishing grounds may be obtained from a consideration of the statistics for 1847. About sixty small barques, brigs, and schooners fished in the Atlantic for Sperm Whales, and there was one ship at Davis Strait. Thirty-two barques cruised in the Indian Ocean for Sperm Whales, and there was one schooner similarly employed in the Pacific. A dozen whalers were engaged in the merchant service or as tenders to the fleet.

The remaining six hundred vessels were on the various grounds of the North and South Pacific, a fifth engaged in Sperm whaling, the rest in both Sperm and Right whaling. Within fifty years of the discovery of the Pacific whaling grounds over six-sevenths of the American whaling fleet were engaged there.

At this time a large number of American ports were engaged in whaling. In 1847 there were thirty-four American ports at which whalers were registered. The total number of vessels was seven hundred and twenty-seven with a tonnage of 230,218. The chief ports were New Bedford, two hundred and fifty-four; Nantucket, seventy-five; New London, Conn., seventy; Sag Harbour, N.Y., sixty-two; Fairhaven, forty-eight; Stonington,

Conn., twenty-seven; Warren, R.I., twenty-three; Provincetown, eighteen; and Mystic, Conn., with seventeen ships.

After 1847 there was a gradual decline in the number of whaling vessels, the smaller ports dropping out rapidly.

The following table gives the number of vessels and the aggregate tonnage for each tenth year after 1846, when the number of vessels was a maximum:

	No. of Vessels.	Tonnage.
1846	736	233,262
1856	635	199,141
1866	263	68,535
1876	169	38,883
1886	124	29,118
1896	77	16,358
1906	42	9,878

Although the smaller ports declined after 1847, New Bedford continued to increase its fleet until 1857, when its maximum was attained with three hundred and twenty-nine sail, valued at twelve million dollars, giving employment to ten thousand seamen.

Soon after the introduction of the mineral oils referred to above, and which of itself was beginning to prove a severe handicap to the American whalers, the outbreak of the Civil War proved a formidable blow to industry. At this time most of the fleet was at sea, some of the vessels being in the Pacific on voyages of four years' duration. The Atlantic whalers soon felt the effect of the war, some of them being captured by Southern privateers as early as

1862. The "Shipping List" for 1862, states: "That Southern pirate, Semmes, has already made frightful havoc with whaling vessels, and his piratical ship—the *Alabama*—threatens to become the scourge of the seas." This privateering continued throughout the war, especially by the *Alabama*, and the *Shenandoah*. The latter entered Behring Sea, capturing and burning twenty-five whalers, taking four others for transport.

Fifty whalers were lost in the war; another forty were purchased by the Government to form the Charleston stone fleet, which was sunk in the attempt to blockade Charleston harbour. The decline in the whaling fleet during the Civil War was fifty per cent in vessels and sixty per cent in tonnage (514 vessels to 263; 158,745 tons to 68,535).

After the end of the Civil War there was a revival of whaling, partly due to the prevailing high prices, and San Francisco now began to take part (1869) in the whaling trade, though by this time the Atlantic whaling ports showed a marked and serious decline, Nantucket—to give one example—practically dropping out altogether.

From 1869 to 1880 the rise of San Francisco as a whaling port was very gradual, the number of vessels averaging eight; after 1880 the growth was rapid.

The English first used steam in whalers in 1857, but it was not until 1880 that the Americans adopted it, when it speedily effected a revolution in Arctic whaling. Prior to this, the Arctic fleet had wintered at San Francisco or some other Pacific port, either re-fitting or engaging in short cruises in neighbouring waters, e.g., in the " lagoon whaling " in the arms of Magdalena Bay. In 1848 no less than fifty boats were engaged in lagoon whaling, the vessels being anchored and the whales captured by boats, thus recalling the early days of the Spitsbergen fishery. In spring the vessels went north, and waited for the ice to break up in Behring Strait. In the autumn the cargoes were transhipped to the east from San Francisco, Panama, Honolulu, and other ports.

With the steam whaler it was customary to remain in the Arctic during the winter so as to be the first in the field when the ice broke up in the spring.

By 1893 one-fourth of the vessels whaling in the North Pacific and Arctic wintered off the mouth of the Mackenzie River.

With the opening of the transcontinental railways, the importance of San Francisco as a whaling port increased, and, although New Bedford still possessed the larger fleet, a great many of its vessels carried on the trade with San Francisco as headquarters.

Originally all the refining of the Pacific oil was done at New Bedford, but in 1883 refineries were built at San Francisco together with works for the manufacture of sperm candles. Since 1880, then, there has been a gradual supersession of the eastern by the western ports. The San Francisco fleet grew while all the other fleets declined, so that in

THE AMERICAN WHALE FISHERIES 241

1893 there were thirty-three vessels at that port, of which about twenty-two were steamers. What really happened was a transfer of the whaling interests. Instead of being owned in New Bedford and New London and working out of 'Frisco, the eastern interests were transferred to vessels registered at the latter port.

For the ten years ending 1905 the whaling fleet averaged fifty-one sail with a tonnage of 10,184, yielding whaling products valued at a million dollars.

In 1906 there were three whaling ports employing fleets, namely, New Bedford—twenty-four vessels, tonnage five thousand six hundred and eighteen; San Francisco fourteen vessels, tonnage three thousand six hundred and twenty-six; and Provincetown three vessels, tonnage three hundred and forty. Norwich, Connecticut, had one brig with a tonnage of two hundred and ninety-four, its first reappearance as a whaling port after a lapse of seventy years.

A few American whalers still follow Sperm whaling in the Atlantic, but the bulk of the fleet, practically all the large vessels, work the Arctic grounds from San Francisco.

One cause of the downfall of whaling has been the uncertainty of the business. In no other occupation does the element of chance enter so largely. In 1866 two New Bedford ships each made a profit of one hundred and twenty-five thousand dollars on a capital of twenty-five thousand dollars.

On the other hand, out of sixty-eight vessels due

to arrive at New Bedford and Fairhaven in 1858, forty-four were calculated as making losing voyages, the total loss being one million dollars. In 1871 the entire Arctic fleet was destroyed by pack ice with a loss of over two million dollars, thirty-four vessels becoming a total loss.

Two other adverse circumstances for the whalers were the discovery of gold in California in 1849, and the commencement of the manufacture of cotton goods in New Bedford in 1846.

It was customary for the Pacific whalers to touch at a Pacific port to refit, and during the gold boom whole crews of whalers deserted, so that shipping on a whaler came to be recognised as a cheap means of reaching the goldfields from the eastern states. The whaling capitalists lost large sums of money through their ships being laid up owing to these desertions. The cotton manufacture afforded a steadier yield to capital than the enormously fluctuating whaling industry, so there can be no question but that its establishment in New Bedford led to the withdrawal of capital from the latter, to say nothing of the diversion of new capital that otherwise might have been devoted to the development of whaling.

In the fifties and sixties of the nineteenth century the Pacific whalers made Honolulu their rendezvous. Twice a year the harbour was full of whalers, firstly in March, when they fitted out for the summer season in the Arctic, in Behring Strait, off Japan, and in the Sea of Okhotsk, and secondly in November, when they fitted out for the Sperm whaling in tropical and sub-tropical waters. Some of the vessels fitted out exclusively for the Sperm whaling, and did not take part in the Right Whale fishery of northern waters—these were known as the " Sperm Whalers."

After fitting out in November and December in Honolulu the vessels engaged in Sperm whaling left late in December or early in January, usually taking the following route: southwards to the Marshall, Solomon, and Caroline Islands, and then northwards to Marian and Bonin groups in Japanese waters. Off Japan there were two courses. Some vessels went into the Sea of Okhotsk, others to the Arctic through Behring Strait. Some vessels went direct from Honolulu to the Marianne Islands, anchoring off Tinian Island in February and March, and sending out their boats after the Humpback. After March the Japan grounds were abandoned.

A small fleet consisting mainly of brigs and schooners sailed from Honolulu to the Californian coast to take part in the Grey Whale fishery (p. 29). At this time the Grey Whale was reported to be very fierce and shy, and consequently difficult to capture. The whalers attempted to capture the young ones first, aiming to wound and not to kill. If the young were wounded the mother endeavoured to protect it, and so rendered herself liable to capture, but if the young were killed outright the mother became so desperate in her anger as to render any approach to her on the part of the whale boats an absolute impossibility. This whaling was dangerous, and a lot of lives were lost at it.

In April these whalers returned to Honolulu, leaving a few weeks later for the north.

A good average catch (in the sixties) in northern waters was ten Bowheads or Right Whales, which yielded one thousand barrels of thirty gallons each of oil, and sixteen thousand pounds of whalebone. Landed in Europe this oil fetched three pounds nine shillings a barrel, and the whalebone three shillings and sixpence a pound. At this time the winter fishery for the Sperm Whales was not of much account. A vessel that obtained one hundred barrels of sperm oil was fortunate, though occasionally much larger captures were made since the Sperm Whale is naturally a gregarious animal.

When a Sperm Whale is in distress its companions seek to succour it, the Right Whales on the contrary, leave a stricken comrade. The Sperm whalers took advantage of this, and once a whale had been struck the other boats endeavoured to kill as many of the school as speedily as possible.

The Sperm Whales in the schools are stated at this time to be small on the average, the older larger individuals keeping more to themselves.

The Bowheads were gradually driven farther and farther north, right up into polar waters where the sailing vessels could not follow them. The whales kept more and more to the ice, leaving it later in succeeding years, so that the whalers were compelled to keep near the ice later in successive seasons.

THE AMERICAN WHALE FISHERIES 245

The Finners were not much chased in these waters on account of the difficulty of taking them with the hand harpoon.

The American whaling industry at the end of the nineteenth century was in a bad way.

A small fleet still hunted the Sperm and Right Whales in the North and South Atlantic. In 1892 this consisted of thirty-two ships; in 1898 of fourteen only. Of these four were from eighty to one hundred tons, six of one hundred to two hundred tons, four from two hundred to two hundred and fifty-five tons. The crew consisted of fifteen on two vessels, sixteen on five, twenty-five on six, and thirty on one vessel. A sad decline from the hey-day of the American Atlantic whale fishery. The vessels still fitted out for a three years' cruise, and garnered their harvest on the old whaling grounds. The decrease in the yield of sperm oil from this fishery was from seventy-three thousand seven hundred and eight barrels in 1860 to twelve thousand five hundred and twenty in 1898.

This industry was very rapidly dying out. The West Indian fishery and that of the Southern Indian Ocean was no longer followed by the Americans. In fact, the only fishery remaining to the Americans of any magnitude was that from San Francisco, which still sent out ships to the North Pacific and Arctic-American Oceans.

The American fishery in Davis Strait and Hudson Bay consisted of one vessel in 1890, one in 1892, five in 1895, one in 1896-97, and two in the summer of 1897, both making losing voyages.

The first American whaler passed through Behring Strait in 1848, and this polar fishery has been well described by Scammon.

At the end of the nineteenth century the fishery in polar waters was to a large extent coastal, in this respect resembling the early days of Spitsbergen. The ice off the north coasts of America and Asia comes down much farther south than in Spitsbergen waters, so that the whalers never went beyond 74° N. in the former waters. The fishery off the north coasts of Alaska and Asia was much more dangerous than in Northern European waters, and the return journey through the narrow Behring Strait much more difficult than the homeward journey of the Spitsbergen whalers, and consequently many more ships were lost at this American fishery.

These American whaling steamers usually made nine knots, sailing vessels with auxiliary engines six only. The whaling grounds were much farther from San Francisco than the Spitsbergen grounds from Norway or Great Britain. From San Francisco to the Diomede Islands in Behring Strait is two thousand eight hundred and sixty miles, from thence to the mouth of the Mackenzie a further eight hundred and seventy. The first part of the journey was usually made under sail alone, the coal being reserved for battling through the ice. A few whalers went even farther than the Mackenzie; one hundred and seventy-five miles to Cape Bathurst, and even two hundred and twenty miles farther to Banks Land.

The whalers aimed to reach the Gulf of Anadyr on

THE AMERICAN WHALE FISHERIES

the Asiatic side of the Strait in the middle of May. In the middle of June they were able to enter the Arctic, and this they usually did on the Asiatic side as the ice conditions were generally more favourable there. Whilst waiting for the ice to disappear from Point Barrow, the whalers cruised westward along the Siberian coast, occasionally getting a whale. After this between-season they went for Point Barrow and thence to Point Hope, north of Behring Strait, and then east along the coast to winter quarters off Herschel Island, which lies near the coast somewhat to the west of the mouth of the Mackenzie. Some went still farther to the north-east to Franklin Bay.

Those vessels which wintered off Herschel Island generally got free of the ice by the 10th July, whereas those frozen up in Franklin Bay were fast until August. Usually there is open water from Point Barrow to Cape Bathurst, north-east of Franklin Bay, for three summer months.

Steamers find very little difficulty in making this passage, but for sailing vessels it is troublesome.

In autumn the whalers went west to Herald Island in north-east of Behring Strait in 70° N. and 171° E.

The details of this fishery show that even at the end of the nineteenth century it was possible to make profitable voyages, though on the whole there is an evident decline.

The statistics show clearly that the American whalers at this time hunted the whale chiefly for the whalebone, and on many occasions took no trouble to recover the oil. This is seen when the number of whales killed is compared with the number of barrels of oil obtained in the earlier and later years:

AMERICAN NORTH PACIFIC WHALING FLEET

	Ships.	Whales killed.	Barrels of oil obtained.
1890	49	197	15,220
1891	46	212	12,625
1892	48	240	11,610
1893	46	309	6,440
1894	35	106	6,650
1895	31	46	2,480
1896	29	124	4,435
1897	27	84	3,230
1898	23	157	2,975

It is perhaps hardly necessary to point out that this is an extravagant method of fishing and a great waste of natural resources.

The average yield of a Polar Right Whale in 1897 was estimated in oil at thirty cents a gallon, and four dollars a pound for whalebone, those being the prices at San Francisco. The total value of the whale was about eight thousand dollars (one thousand six hundred pounds). Against this must be set the very high cost of fitting out ships for this fishery. A sailing vessel with four boats had a crew of thirty-eight men, a steamer with five boats forty-four men. They were provisioned usually for a year. Only the engineers were paid by wage, the others by " lays," i.e., a share in the profits. These lays varied at this time from an eleventh in the case of the captain, to a hundred and fiftieth for a greenhand or cabin boy.

The first engineer received one hundred and twenty-five, the second ninety dollars monthly. Insurance was high from ten per cent for steamers,

THE AMERICAN WHALE FISHERIES

to sixteen per cent for sailing vessels. The cost of fitting out a steamer for a season was estimated at fifteen thousand dollars; the first cost of such a steamer from twenty to twenty-five thousand dollars. To fit out a sailing vessel cost eight thousand dollars. This was much cheaper than the expense of a steamer, for the latter the coal alone cost from six to ten dollars a ton. Before starting from 'Frisco each sailor received an advance of forty dollars, each boat-steerer from five hundred to one thousand dollars. If the ship returned clean, i.e., empty, then the crew were paid off on return at the rate of one dollar per man. A whale which yielded from fifteen to seventeen hundred pounds of whalebone usually gave from seventy to ninety barrels of oil. A certain amount of trade was done with the natives, Esquimaux, and Indians, along the coast. On an average, a whaler could reckon on getting from seven to eight hundred pounds of trade bone from the natives in exchange for meal, biscuit, provisions generally, knives, and old whale boats, the latter being much sought after.

There is much information of this fishery in the San Francisco newspapers of the last decade of the nineteenth century. Though of great interest, the details cannot be quoted here. There was also a small Russian whale fishery at this time in the North Pacific. It does not appear to have attained any considerable magnitude.

Although not an American fishery, it is convenient to mention here that one of the few remaining, flourishing whaling industries was that for the Cachalot or Sperm Whale, at the Azores, by the inhabitants, who killed the whale not far from land, towing the carcass ashore for treatment. In 1898 there were no less than twenty-nine whaling companies working at the Azores. The hunting was done by means of small sailing boats—three feet long—each with a crew of six. Of the six, one was officer and steersman, one a harpooner, the other four sailors. The crew of these boats were paid by share, the boats themselves being the property of the various companies. The statistics of the number of whales killed and the amount of spermaceti obtained are not available, but from 1895 to 1897 no less than 480,000 litres of whale oil were exported from the Azores.

An intimate view of life in American whalers may be obtained by a perusal of the works of Olmstead, Ross Browne, and Nordhoff. There are also a number of other writers; in many cases it is difficult to separate fact from fiction.

It was customary to recruit the whalers' crews from landsmen, the captain and officers alone being experienced seamen and whalers. Advertisements of the following type were scattered broadcast over the eastern states in the hey-day of the American whale fisheries :

> "Wanted Landsmen.—One thousand stout young men, Americans, wanted for the fleet of whale ships now fitting out for the North and South Pacific Fisheries. Extra chances given to Coopers, Carpenters, and Blacksmiths.
>
> None but industrious young men, with good recom-

THE AMERICAN WHALE FISHERIES 251

mendations, taken. Such will have superior chances for advancement. Outfits, to the amount of seventy-five dollars, furnished to each individual before proceeding to sea.

Persons desirous to avail themselves of the present splendid opportunity of seeing the world, and at the same time acquiring a profitable business, will do well to make early application to the undersigned."

It is to be feared that the treatment of these greenhorns was in general of a very brutal nature. Their earnings, too, were contemptible. The system of payment was by " lays." Average lays varied from about a twelfth for the captain to a hundred and seventy-five for a greenhand. It was by no means uncommon for an ordinary seamen to receive two or three dollars, or even nothing at all, as his share after a long and hazardous voyage. He had, of course, been kept, and received advances during the voyage; what the food and conditions were like can be estimated by reading the works above named.

Olmstead's book was published at New York in 1841, and describes a voyage made in the barque *North America* of New London.

J. Ross Browne's book, which, in many respects, is the best personal description of a voyage in an American whaler, was published at New York in 1850; Browne joined a New Bedford whaler as a landsman or greenhand (in 1842). The brutalities to which the greenhands were subjected is relieved by the humour of some of the scenes on board, one of the seamen, Bill Man by name, who had previously been a scene shifter in a Bowery theatre in New York, being by no means without humour when drunk.

Nordhoff's book was published at Cincinnati in 1856, and is a description of whaling life by a man who had previously been a sailor.

In 1918 owing to the prevailing shortage of the world's food supply, the American whaling companies were encouraged to save and market whale meat, and the United States Bureau of Fisheries issued a pamphlet on the use of whales and porpoises as food.[1] The west coast whaling companies provided a cold storage and distributing plant, with a capacity of about three thousand tons, a five hundred ton freezing plant, a refrigeration steamer, and a cannery with a capacity of fifty thousand cases. In 1918 a beginning was made with thirty thousand cases of canned meat, and for 1919 an output of fifty thousand cases of canned meat, and one thousand tons of frozen meat is expected.

The equipment and method of canning are similar to those used in Pacific coast salmon canneries, with certain differences in the preliminary handling. The whales for canning are hauled out on a special concrete slip, constantly flooded with fresh running water, and here the meat is removed in the same way as for freezing. After cooling it is placed in mild brine for about thirty-six hours, which removes all blood, at the same time elimin-

[1] Whales and Porpoises as food. *U.S. Dept. of Commerce, Bureau of Fisheries Economic Circular*, No. 38. Issued 6th November, 1918.

ating the gamy taste. The strips of meat are then passed through a salmon cutter of ordinary type, which cuts up pieces of the right size, for one pound flat cans. The cans are then put through the exhaust box for thirty minutes, sealed and cooked in the retort for an hour and twenty minutes, after which they are ready for labelling and shipping.

The fishery for the California Grey Whale by the Makahs or Cape Flattery Indians has been well described by Swan.[1] Since their methods are distinct from those of Europeans, and have been independently evolved, a short description is appended.

The harpoon consists of a barbed head, attached direct to the rope or lanyard. The rope, which is five fathoms long, is made of twisted whale's sinews, and is about an inch and a half in circumference, covered with twine wound around it very tightly. This rope is exceedingly strong and very pliable.

The harpoon head is a flat piece of iron or copper, usually a saw blade or a piece of sheet copper with a couple of barbs of elk's or deer's horn secured to it, and the whole covered with a coating of spruce gum.

The staff is made of yew in two pieces, joined in the middle by a neat scarf, firmly secured by a piece of bark tied tightly round it. The length is eighteen feet, thickest in the centre at the join, and tapering at both ends. To be used the staff is

[1] James G. Swan, " The Indians of Cape Flattery, at the Entrance to the Strait of Fuca, Washington Territory," Washington, 1869, No. 220, *Smithsonian Contributions to Knowledge.*

inserted into the barbed head, and the end of the lanyard fastened to a buoy, which is simply a seal skin taken from the animal whole, the hair being left inwards. The apertures of the head, feet, and tail are tied up airtight, and the skin inflated like a bladder.

When the harpoon is driven into the whale, the barb and buoy remain fast to him, but the staff comes out and is taken into the canoe. The harpoon thrown into the whale's head has but one buoy attached, but those thrown into the body have as many as can conveniently be tied on; when a number of canoes join in the attack it is not unusual for thirty or forty of these buoys to be made fast to the whale, which cannot then sink, and is despatched by lances. The buoys are fastened together by means of a stout line made of spruce roots, first slightly roasted in hot ashes, then split by knives into fine fibres and finally twisted into ropes, which are very strong and durable. These ropes are also used for towing the dead whale to the shore.

The whaling canoe invariably carries eight men, a harpooner, steersman, and six rowers. The canoe is divided by sticks, which serve as thwarts, into six spaces. The fishery is, of course, carried on near the land, and it is customary to have a look-out on a conspicuous position, and this look-out signals to the canoes when one of their number has struck a whale, so that all may join in the kill. When the whale is dead, it is towed ashore, as near a village as possible, and hauled up on the beach. When the tide recedes all hands attack the carcass with knives, and remove the blubber in blocks about two foot square. The blubber, after being cut up into small pieces, is boiled to extract the oil, which is skimmed from the pots with clam shells. The blubber is then hung in the smoke to dry, and when cured looks very much like citron. It is somewhat tougher than pork, but sweet and not of unpleasant taste.

CHAPTER VIII

THE LAST PHASE OF WHALING

The introduction of steam—The harpoon gun and the capture of Rorquals—The disappearance of the old right whalers—The Norwegian whalers—Gradual extension of their operations—The Scottish and Irish whaling stations—Antarctic whaling.

THE first two steam vessels employed in Arctic exploration were the *Pioneer* and the *Intrepid*, which under the command of Sherard Osborn took part in the search for Franklin in 1850.

The experience gained by these vessels led the whalers to attempt the introduction of steam into the Arctic whalers with extraordinary results. The first attempts were made in the fifties of the nineteenth century, when ships fitted with auxiliary steam engines engaged in combined sealing and whaling cruises in northern waters. The seals were looked for at the west ice off Greenland, and subsequently the ships went to the whale fishery at Davis Strait.

The first Hull whaling steamer set out in 1857; in 1858 there were several steamers mainly engaged in sealing, but it was not until 1859 that a really determined effort was made to establish a steam sealing and whaling trade. The results were almost

THE "ARCTIC," WITH BOATS FASTENED TO A FISH, 1875.

THE LAST PHASE OF WHALING 257

uniformly unsuccessful, and steam whaling suffered a serious setback.

One of the Peterhead whalers attracted much attention. The *Empress of India*, built of iron, was specially fitted out for the trade. She was strongly fortified, being twelve feet thick forward and carried eleven boats. The bottom of the captain's gig was bronze. No expense was spared in her outfit, her crew consisting of one hundred and ten men. All the crew expected to make a small fortune, and looked on the old sailers with contempt. Some of the officers were so sure of getting full of seals that they made all their plans for the future; they were going to fall in with the north end of the main body of seals and sweep through the centre, leaving the rest for those who were fortunate enough to be in their company. However, the first piece of heavy ice penetrated their port bow, and they foundered in four hours, all hands being saved by the despised sailers.

Several iron steamers of Hull, the *Emeline, Gertrude, Corkscrew, Labuan,* and *Wildfire,* proceeded to the seal fishery, but most of them came back empty and damaged. According to Barron this year proved that iron steamers, however strongly built, were not suitable vessels to contend with the Greenland pack ice. A few years later (1861) Barron changed his opinion, and now writes that " this year would prove the death-blow to sailing vessels. Men having experienced the great difference between steam and sail, few will go hereafter in a sailing ship if they can possibly get into a steamer."

In the Davis Strait and Baffin Bay fishing it was customary for the whalers to commence operations off Resolution Island off the south-west extremity of Baffin Land, and afterwards make up through Davis Strait and Baffin Bay to the whaling grounds off Melville Bay and down Lancaster Sound on the east side of Baffin Bay. Now the entrance to the north water was often closed in Melville Bay by pack ice of varying density even though there was open water beyond (to the northward). Working through this pack ice was a laborious and lengthy job for a sailing vessel, though the time varied considerably from year to year according to the state of this drift ice. For a steamer the passage of this ice was in any but the most extraordinarily severe seasons a matter which could be accomplished with certainty and safety in a few days, and it was this fact which, more than any other, proved the immense superiority of the steamer over the sailer. This is quite clearly brought out by Barron in his account of his voyage in 1861, when he was master of the famous *Truelove*. " After toiling all day we only succeeded in getting a mile. The s.s. *Narwhal* came to our relief, and towed us into clear water without the least difficulty. This showed the superiority of steam over sailing vessels."

Markham,[1] writing of his experiences at the Arctic

[1] " A Whaling Cruise to Baffin Bay and the Gulf of Boothia," by A. H. Markham, London, 1875.

THE LAST PHASE OF WHALING 259

whale fishery in 1873, proves in a remarkable manner how much the introduction of steam power in whaling ships has reduced the risk of navigation in Baffin Bay and Barrow Strait. Markham took a passage in the *Arctic* of Dundee, a vessel of five hundred tons and seventy horse power. The Dundee fleet this year consisted of ten vessels all equipped with steam power. Seven were ships varying from three hundred and fifty-eight to four hundred and thirty-nine tons and from sixty to seventy horse power. Of the seven, six were built for the trade, the seventh being a converted ship. The three barques varied from two hundred and seventy-eight to three hundred and ninety-four tons, and from thirty-six to sixty horse power. All three had been converted into steamers for the whaling trade. Incidentally it may be noted that while Markham describes the *Arctic* as a ship the illustrations in his book show her to be barque rigged. At any rate she voluntarily entered the ice in Davis Strait until there were some fifty miles of heavy pack ice between her and open water, and then when no more whales were to be found she fought her way by steam power through the ice fields until the open sea was again reached.

The middle ice, which for over half a century had proved a serious obstacle to the whalers, was easily overcome even by the moderately powered vessels of the Dundee fleet of 1873. The old whaler under sail thought himself lucky in traversing it once in three years, with an enormous amount of labour, in from a month to sixty days. The

Arctic and her sister vessels had for nine years successively got through this middle ice in as many hours.

The crew of the *Arctic* consisted of fifty-five men, a fourth part of whom were Shetlanders, most of the remainder being Scotsmen, principally Highlanders. They carried eight harpooners, including the mate, second mate, and specksioneer (the officer under whose direction the whale was cut up). There were eight boat-steerers, including the boatswain and skeeman, the latter being the officer who superintends between decks the stowing away of the blubber in tanks. The word is derived from the Dutch " Schieman," the captain of the forecastle. There are also eight line-managers.

When all the boats were away whaling there only remained on board the captain, doctor, engineer, ship-keeper, cook, and steward. The men were paid by a combination of wage and share in profits.

At this period the vessels left Scotland in the first half of May, earlier or later according to whether they took part in the sealing or not. They all stopped at the Shetlands to complete the crew and to obtain fresh provisions. Then a course was made for Cape Farewell, the south point of Greenland, where the whalers commenced the so-called southwest fishery in the Frobisher Straits area north of the Labrador coast. Then they followed the plan outlined above for the Hull whalers, working their way through the ice in Melville Bay to the north water, thence to Lancaster Sound and Prince Regent

THE LAST PHASE OF WHALING

Inlet. In August and September the whales were followed on their southerly migration to Home Bay and Cumberland Sound on the east side of Baffin Land. The return voyage commenced in the early days of November, though some lucky ships occasionally obtained full cargoes in September or October. Some ships, both British and American, wintered in Cumberland Sound in order to be ready for the early summer fishery.

The voyage of the *Arctic* was a very successful one, thirteen female and fifteen male whales being captured. The weight of whalebone was fourteen tons seventeen hundredweights, and that of the oil two hundred and sixty-five and a half tons, the total value being eighteen thousand nine hundred and twenty-five pounds.

The Scottish whalers at this time brought the blubber back to Dundee in large tanks. There it was filled into casks and taken to the boiling yards to have the oil extracted. This was done by steam in large coppers holding sufficient blubber to yield ten tons of oil. The seal blubber is so fresh when landed that it is necessary to wait six or eight weeks until it is so decomposed that the oil might be extracted easily. But in 1873 the Dundee Seal and Whale Fishing Company fitted up machinery for cutting and crushing the blubber, so that it could be utilised as soon as landed. For some purposes the oil thus reduced is more valuable. After boiling the oil is allowed to settle in coolers, and then run into storing tanks ready for delivery as required.

Prior to the introduction of steam there was a marked decline in the Arctic whale fishery as shown in the statistical returns from 1830 onwards. Towards the end of the sailing days it was only the Norwegians who took part in it to any extent. The English and Scottish fishery gradually declined. In 1831 the greater part of the English fleet (nineteen vessels) was lost in the ice in Melville Bay. The harbours taking part in the whaling trade declined until practically only Dundee and Peterhead were left. In 1830 there were ninety-one Scottish whalers hailing from thirteen ports; in 1857 the number had declined to sixty from seven ports, and in 1868 to thirty vessels from six ports, and of this thirty Peterhead and Dundee claimed twelve each. The Dundee vessels at this time were steamers which visited the Greenland coasts for seals, and subsequently went round into Davis Strait for the whale fishery. Dundee's interest in this fishery persisted beyond that of other Scottish towns since her chief industry, the jute manufacture, required the whale and seal oil, so that the town's two main industries were in a sense interdependent. Dundee's requirements at this time (*circa* 1858) were two thousand two hundred tons of oil annually.

In 1868 the Scottish whaling fleet consisted of four steamers and eight sailing ships from Peterhead, the former of two hundred to two hundred and ninety-five tons, the latter from one hundred and thirty to three hundred and eighty tons; two sailing vessels of two hundred and ninety-two and two hundred

THE LAST PHASE OF WHALING 263

and ninety-seven tons from Fraserburgh; eleven steamers (two hundred and seventy-eight to four hundred and fifty-five tons) and one sailing ship from Dundee, and one steamer of four hundred and fifty-two tons from Kirkcaldy. This was the year in which Hull finally dropped out of the whaling industry.

At this time the Scottish fleet in part went sealing and whaling between Greenland and Spitsbergen, another part, especially the Dundee steamers, went first to the sealing grounds off Jan Mayen, and returned home starting off in the middle of May for their second voyage to the whaling grounds in Davis Strait up to Cumberland Strait, wintering there so as to be ready for the early fishing in the following spring. In 1868 fifteen ships which took part in the sealing and whaling off Greenland caught only three whales and fifty-one thousand eight hundred and sixty-three seals, altogether six hundred and thirty-seven tons of oil. Ten of the ships returned quite empty, a very bad result. In Davis Strait the results were better, ten steamers catching one hundred and four whales with an oil yield of eight hundred and eighty tons; the Cumberland Strait ships got twenty-two whales and eight hundred and eighty White Whales; of these ships two had wintered out and were away eighteen months. The vicissitudes of the whale fishery are enormous; in 1867 the Dundee whalers in Davis Strait only caught two whales; in 1868 they caught seventy-nine.

Modern whaling dates from the year 1880. At that time the Right Whale (*Balæna mysticetus*) valuable on account of its whalebone, was nearly extinct, and whalers sought principally the Sperm Whale, the other species not being much utilised.

Fin and Blue Whales and the common Rorquals were of little or no value for whalebone, and their oil was of small account. Their great activity rendered their capture by the old methods of harpooning extremely hazardous. Whaling appeared to be dying out completely, when a harpoon gun, invented by Svend Foyn, a Norwegian sailor, came into use. This gun was invented by Foyn in 1860, but does not appear to have come into common use until twenty years later. This invention was considerably improved in the course of time, but the earlier guns were muzzle-loaders of steel with steel coils and mounted on swivels. Its length was about four feet, and it was fired at a distance of twenty-five to fifty yards, the gunner trying to hit the whale between the ribs as near the spinal column as possible.

The gun-harpoon consisted of the shell with charge, the barb-holster and pole. The shell was screwed to the barb-holster, which contained a glass filled with sulphuric acid. To the pole a rope was attached, of four hundred fathoms' length and weighing about three thousand pounds.

The whole apparatus when it left the gun was solid; when the harpoon penetrated the whale the barbs turned so as to crush the glass tube, the sulphuric acid escaping, and causing the shell to explode.

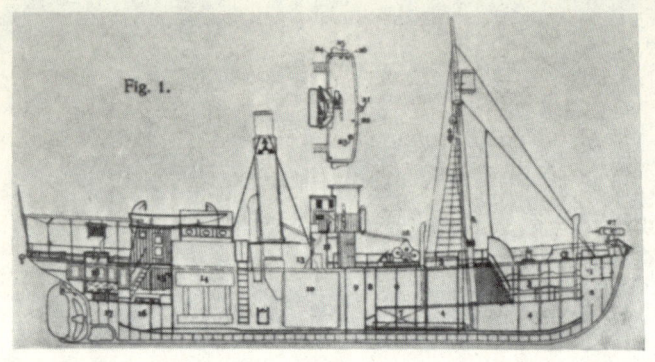
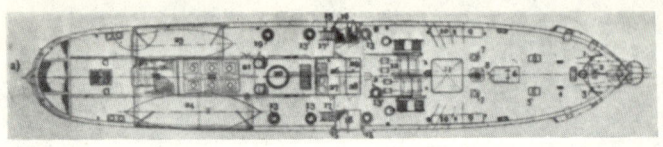
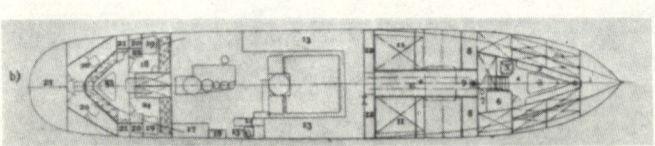

PLANS OF A WHALING STEAMER OF A MODERN TYPE.

THE LAST PHASE OF WHALING

This harpoon gun rendered the capture of the smaller and more active species of whale a commercial possibility, so that what they lacked in weight of oil as individuals, they made up in quantity. Some of these Finners and Rorquals could be captured fairly near to the land, so it became customary to build small, but seaworthy steamers, whose sole function was to shoot the whale, and then tow it ashore to a factory, where all the subsequent operations were carried out.

About the year 1880 the Norwegians built steamers of iron, of about thirty-two registered tons, and twenty-five to thirty-five nominal horse power for this purpose. About thirty feet in length, with a beam of twelve to thirteen feet, and a draught of eight to nine feet, these steamers were rigged as fore and aft schooners. Below deck there was accommodation only for engine, cabins, and stowage for warps, etc., the whales being towed ashore.

The crew consisted of nine men, viz., the captain, three engineers, steward and three sailors; the speed was nine knots.

These vessels were subsequently much improved (p. 264).

Longitudinal section, deck-plan and below-deck plan of a modern type of whaling steamer:

1. LONGITUDINAL SECTION:—
    1. Store-room. 2. Ballast tank. 3. Crew's quarters. 4. Store-room. 5. Hatchway. 6. Space for harpoon lines. 7. Fresh - water tank. 8. Reserve bunker. 9. Coal Bunker. 10. Boiler. 11. Galley. 12. Chart-room. 13. Chain locker. 14. Engine-room. 15. Cabin.

16. Fresh-water tank.   17. Tank.   18. Dining-room. 19. Skylight.   20. Meat safe.   21. Compass.   22. Speaking tube.   23. Engine-room telegraph.   24, 25, and 26. Airpipe for signalling, etc.   27. Harpoon gun. 28. Steam winch for the harpoon lines.

2. DECK PLAN:—

1. Pump.   2. Signal apparatus (to bridge).   3. Speaking tube.   4. Rings.   5. Bits.   6. Gangway to crew's quarters.   7. Chain brake.   8. Mast.   9. Locker. 10. Chain locker.   11. Hatch.   12. Steam winch. 13. Bunker lids.   14. Lavatory.   15. Lid.   16. Salt-water pump.   17. Steps to bridge.   18. Bath-room.   19. Bunker hatch.   20. Funnel.   21. Entrance to engine-room. 22. Engine-room skylight.   23. Boat.   24. Lifeboat. 25. Gangway.   26. Galley.   27. Coal-room.   28. Provision-room.   29. Fresh-water pump.

3. BELOW DECK PLAN:—

1. Ballast tank.   2. Bench.   3. Table.   4. Crew's quarters.   5. Hatch to store-room.   6. Engineers' cabin.   7. Writing-table.   8. Chain locker.   9. Mast. 10. Accumulator for the harpoon line.   11. Fresh-water tank.   12. Reserve bunker.   13. Bunker.   14. Ventilator. 15. Fan for ventilator.   16. Oil tank.   17. Store-room. 18. Captain's cabin.   19. Writing-table.   20. Wardrobe. 21. Store-room.   22. Lavatory.   23. Table.   24. Harpooners' cabin.

Before proceeding to consider the last phase in the history of whaling, the Norwegian fisheries of the twentieth century, it is desirable to summarise the position at the end of the nineteenth century, when whaling appeared to be dying out all over the world.

In the European Arctic waters the capture of the Greenland Right Whale had long been abandoned. Vessels fitting out for the Arctic "fisheries" captured seals, walruses, and any other oil or skin-yielding animals, which would help to make a voyage profitable. Amongst these creatures was

THE LAST PHASE OF WHALING

the White Whale, which appeared in the waters of Spitsbergen and Nova Zembla as soon as the ice began to break up in June. In schools of about two hundred individuals they entered the bays, where the female gave birth to the young in June and the first half of July. The White Whale's visit to Spitsbergen waters is not a food migration, since at this time the stomach is empty. The young when born are from four to five feet long and of a dark brown colour. This colour gradually becomes paler until in the adult it is quite white. The White Whale is valuable, not only on account of the oil it yields, but also for its skin, which can be converted into excellent leather.

When a school is met with in the bays, an effort is made, by surrounding them with boats, to drive them into shallow water, where they are driven on shore or captured by nets. On one occasion fifty whales were driven ashore, killed, and the blubber removed within thirty hours.

The coastal fishery for Finners had by now commenced in Finmark, Tromsö, and Iceland. The whales were killed by means of an explosive harpoon fired from a gun fixed in the bows of a small steamer. These steamers gradually underwent an evolution to the type figured, described, and illustrated above. The whales being killed, were towed ashore to a coastal station for treatment. The Finmark fishery, which commenced about 1889, was concerned with four species of Finner Whale; the Blue Whale, which was estimated at this time to be worth one hundred and fifty pounds, of which the whalebone furnished sixty pounds; the common Finner (*B. musculus*) worth one hundred and twenty-five pounds (whalebone fifteen pounds); the Humpback worth also one hundred and twenty-five pounds; and the Sei Whale worth forty to forty-five pounds, to which the whalebone contributed ten pounds. These estimates are, of course, averages.

In 1896 there were twenty-nine steamers off Finmark, and eighteen off Iceland, engaged in the slaughter of Finner Whales. In 1897 the numbers were respectively twenty-five and twenty-three.

In 1896 the number of Finners slaughtered was two thousand, in 1897, it was one thousand nine hundred.

The average number of Finners killed per annum by the Norwegians was:

For the whole area:—1876-1885	347
1886-1895	1,107
1896	2,081
1897	1,888

In Finmark alone, thirteen thousand four hundred and ninety-one whales were killed in twenty-seven years. A third whale fishery practised in northern waters at this time was that for the Grindhval or Pilot Whale, which was captured by the inhabitants of the Faroes, Orkney, and Shetland Islands. From 1801 to 1879 no less than seventy-eight thousand two hundred and ten Pilot Whales were so killed, an annual average of nine hundred and ninety.

THE LAST PHASE OF WHALING

The hunt for the Bottlenose Whale commenced, according to the Norwegian official fishery statistics, in 1881, when a vessel, which was specially fitted out for this fishery, captured thirty-one Bottlenose Whales. In 1884 nine vessels, one of which was a steamer, captured two hundred and eleven Bottlenose Whales. These vessels were quite small, the average crew being about ten men. The Bottlenose does not swim in schools, usually a small number of individuals, from three to six, swimming together, keeping to water in which the average temperature is 39° F., i.e., where the Gulf Stream and Arctic waters mix. The first hunter of the Bottlenose was the well-known Scottish whaler, David Gray, who, in 1881, in the steamer *Eclipse*, captured twenty of this species. The oil of this whale is of superior quality, and the chase for it consequently developed very rapidly, so that by 1891 there were seventy Norwegian ships in the trade, killing two thousand whales of this species annually. The Bottlenose, in July, was found between 72° and 64° N. Latitude and 2° and 12° W. Longitude, where the temperature of the water varied from 0° to 8° C. In this area the vessels engaged in the chase of the Bottlenose cruised to and fro. It was especially numerous on the boundary of the Gulf Stream and Arctic waters, where the temperature varied greatly in small areas. According to the whalers the Bottlenose goes north in spring and early summer, in midsummer it migrates south, where it is captured off the Faroes in July. The Bottlenose feeds entirely on cephalopods.

The Scottish fishery in Arctic waters and between Greenland and North America has a long and interesting history. By 1898 this industry was obviously moribund. Mainly, and originally exclusively, devoted to the capture of the Greenland Right Whale, the Scottish whalers, towards the end, omitted no opportunity of making a paying voyage, and consequently were not above taking the White Whale, the Narwhal, and the Bottlenose; even seals were captured.

The Greenland Right Whale, the White Whale, and the Narwhal, are exclusively Arctic creatures. In 1870 an average Greenland Whale was worth from one thousand two hundred to one thousand five hundred pounds. Since then the price of oil has materially diminished—the whalebone, on the contrary, increased in price.

According to David Gray the Peterhead whalers killed from 1788 to 1879 no less than four thousand one hundred and ninety-five Greenland Whales; the Dundee fleet for the similar period capturing four thousand two hundred and twenty. These statistics should be contrasted with the slaughter of the Finners by the Norwegian whalers, which at the end of the nineteenth century reached the annual figure of two thousand.

The decline of the Scottish whaling fleet towards the end of the nineteenth century was most marked. In 1868 there were thirty-nine vessels, of which

THE LAST PHASE OF WHALING 271

fifteen were steamers. In 1873 Dundee sent out ten steamers of three hundred to four hundred tons, and thirty-six to seventy horse power. The voyage of the *Arctic* described by Markham, has already been referred to (see p. 256).

The last years of the nineteenth century showed the Scottish Arctic whaling fleet to have practically reached its vanishing point:

	No. of vessels.	No. of whales captured.
1890	17	12
1891	12	17
1892	11	9
1893	7	33
1894	9	20
1895	8	17
1896	9	11
1897	10	13
1898	7	8

In 1901 there were five steamers from Dundee and one from Peterhead. By this time the whalers, finding it did not pay to confine themselves exclusively to whaling, captured any other animal which would help to make a profit. The total catch of these six steamers was fourteen and a half Greenland Whales, seven hundred and thirty-eight White Whales, four hundred and twenty walrus, three thousand four hundred and thirty seals, one hundred and forty-nine polar bears, yielding altogether two hundred and sixty tons of train oil and one hundred and sixty-three and a half hundredweights of whalebone, the price of the latter being one thousand two hundred and fifty pounds per ton.

Coastal whaling has been practised in Japan for centuries, and the industry there is at least as old as the earliest Basque fishery. The whale is extensively used as human food in Japan. There are several Japanese books dealing with this fishery, notably one published by Koyamada at Yedo in 1829. In 1889 the Japanese whale trade was worth seven thousand five hundred pounds. Since then the Japanese have adopted the modern type of whaling steamer, and the industry has developed considerably.

Before the end of the nineteenth century attention was directed to the last virgin field for whalers—the Antarctic.

In the autumn of 1891 the Tay Whale Fishing Company of Dundee sent four of their steamers to the Falkland Islands, and thence to the Antarctic, where they remained from December, 1892, to February, 1893. The Scottish oceanographer and explorer, W. S. Bruce, was on board one of these vessels, the *Balæna*. Many seals but no whales were captured, and the voyages were not successful financially. Right Whales were not observed, but Blue and Bottlenose Whales were numerous. In 1893 a Hamburg company sent a steamer to try whaling and sealing in the Antarctic, and in 1894 two additional steamers. These vessels occupied themselves exclusively with sealing; only a few Bottlenose Whales were seen.

The next attempt was Norwegian, on the steamer *Antarctic*, from 1893 to 1895. This vessel, which

THE LAST PHASE OF WHALING

together with its outfit, cost five thousand pounds, was well equipped with boats, gun harpoons, and all the apparatus necessary for the capture of the Sperm or Right Whale. On their voyage to Kerguelen they encountered large schools of Finners, for the capture of which their equipment was not suitable. After a between-season's Sperm whaling, the *Antarctic* set off in winter (Antarctic summer) of 1894 to a cruise in the Antarctic opposite Australia. Many Finners were again seen.

As a result of an expenditure of over five thousand pounds the Norwegians concluded that the Right Whale was not present in summer-time in the Antarctic pack ice in sufficient numbers to make commercial whaling profitable. In fact, they do not appear to have reported the Right Whale at all in Antarctic waters. The whales they saw off Cape Adare (South Victoria Land) in January, 1895, were Finners.

Only half a century before this Ross (1843), on his return journey to Cape Town from the Antarctic, mentions seeing from five hundred to six hundred whalers fishing off Kerguelen for Right Whales. Most of these ships were American, and the bulk of them made good voyages. Such an enormous destruction had taken place that in 1893 only a few small vessels prosecuted this fishery with doubtful success.

The voyage of the *Antarctic*, however, made it clear that with suitable equipment a profitable fishery for Finners could be carried on in the Antarctic, since hardly a day passed without these whales being observed. The great development of this fishery followed in the twentieth century.

The modern development of whaling through the instrumentality of small specially built steamers for the killing and capture of the whale was extraordinarily successful for a time. From its commencement in 1880 in northern Europe it made enormous strides. From Norway it extended to Iceland (1889), the Faroes (1892), and ultimately to the British Isles. A Norwegian company commenced in the Hebrides in 1895, but it was not until 1903 that the industry became firmly established in the Hebrides and Shetlands. This was a direct result of the prohibition of the pursuit, shooting or killing of whales by the Norwegian Government in the territorial waters of the districts of Nordland, Tromsö, and Finmarken, or the landing of whales in these districts for a period of ten years from the 1st February, 1904. This legislation was due to the protests of the local fishermen of those districts against the whalers, culminating in the "Mehavn Riots." The fishermen believed that the presence of whales was coincident with the appearance of fish off the coast, and they attributed the decline of the fishing to the great destruction of the former by the whalers. Whatever view be taken of the fishermen's complaints, there can be no doubt that this legislation caused the migration of the whalers to the British coasts.

In 1903 two Norwegian companies, the "Norrona" and the "Shetland," commenced operations on Ronas Voe, a narrow winding inlet of the sea on the north-west of Mainland (Shetlands). In 1904 two other companies set up stations in the Shetlands, the "Alexandra" (Norwegian) at Colla Firth, and the "Olna" (Danish) at Olna Firth. The first three had one steamer each in 1904, and the last named four.

In 1904 two stations were also started in the Hebrides, one being Norwegian, the other a Dane. At first these companies worked without any restrictions, but speedily complaints were heard from the local herring fishing interests; so that in 1904 the Secretary of State for Scotland appointed a Committee of Inquiry into whaling and whale curing in the north of Scotland.

The whale first sought by these Norwegians was the large Finner (*Balænoptera musculus*) which is found from thirty to eighty miles from land to the north and north-west of the Shetlands. The next important species was the Sei Whale (*B. borealis*) with occasional Sperm, Blue, Bottlenose, Humpback, and Northcaper Whales. (See return, Appendix V.) The complaints of the local fishermen were of two main kinds: (1) That the harrying of the whales injured the herring fishing. (2) That the treatment of the carcasses caused a nuisance and danger to health.

The latter complaint is clearly one which is capable of being properly controlled and, indeed, the whaling companies practically admitted that any serious nuisance was solely due to the difficulties attending the inauguration of the industry. At the same time it is obvious that any treatment of huge carcasses such as those of the whale is bound to be associated with offensive odours, and the works are only allowable in remote districts as far as possible from human habitation. The real ground of complaint was that of interference with the herring fishing, an important industry in the Shetlands. In 1903 there were one hundred and fifty-seven herring curing stations in the Shetlands, the total herring cured amounting to four hundred and sixty-six thousand and forty-eight barrels; employment being afforded to seventeen thousand four hundred and ninety-one persons.

The herring fishermen object to the killing of the whales because the spouting of the whale is often an indication of the presence of the shoals of herring. There is, however, some conflict of opinion as to whether the whale indicating the presence of the herring is of the same species as that sought by the whalers. The whalers state that their operations are carried on as a rule above thirty-five miles from the land, whereas the herring fishery of the Shetlands is in the main carried on within that distance. The whalers specialise in the capture of the Finner, and they state that it is the smaller " Herring Hog," worthless from their point of view, that points out the herring shoals to the Shetlanders. Other points urged by the herring fishermen were that the whales drive the herrings towards the shore and the nets,

THE LAST PHASE OF WHALING 277

and that the whaling steamers disturb the shoals both with their propellers and their harpoon guns.

The Departmental Committee took evidence at several places in the Shetlands and at Peterhead. They also visited and inspected the Colla Firth and Ronas Voe whaling stations. As a result of their inquiries they decided that while unrestricted whaling might be a possible danger to the herring fishing, there were no valid reasons for the total prohibition of whaling. The latter would probably lead either to the establishment of floating factories or to the working of the Shetland grounds from the Faroes where the whalers would be beyond British control. The Committee believed that the new industry might prove to be beneficial, and afford a source of employment to the inhabitants of the Shetlands. Whaling ought, however, to be restricted. " Unrestricted whaling would be an evil on other grounds than its possible danger to the herring fishery. It could not last long. The Basque and the Greenland whaling industries came to an end by the practical extermination of the species pursued. With the means of destruction now brought to deadly perfection the same fate would overtake the Finners off our coasts in a very short time. That would be an evil in itself, and, while a few companies might go out of the business with a large profit, the local industry would be brought into being only to perish in a few years, and leave the inhabitants worse off than ever." It should be clearly understood that the capital and labour of these companies is entirely Norwegian. The local inhabitants are only employed in insignificant numbers as labourers and unskilled workers. Even the stores are brought from Norway.

The Committee made the following recommendations:

That no person or company shall kill whales off the coast of Scotland or land them in Scotland without a licence from the Secretary of State for Scotland.

That the licensee shall be a British subject or a company registered in Great Britain.

That a licence duty of substantial amount (that in Canada is five hundred pounds) be imposed and paid to the County Council, on which the cost of inspection shall be a first charge.

That no licensee shall have more than one steamer, to be registered in Great Britain, and that tow-boats shall be prohibited.

That the six existing companies may obtain licences for three years, but liable to be withdrawn within that period on payment of compensation, and subject to these other regulations.

That for three years no more licences be granted.

That the licensee shall be bound to make such returns on any matter connected with the whaling business, as the Secretary of State for Scotland shall require.

That the regulations shall not apply to the capture of the small "Ca'ing" Whale, but that

that shall be subject to regulation by the Local Authority under the Public Health Acts.

That regulations for the treatment of carcasses of whales in the stations or factories shall be made by the Local Authority with the approval of the Local Government Board.

That such regulations shall include provisions (*a*) that any whale brought to the station shall be carried into the factory and flenched within forty-eight hours after the arrival of the steamer, and all the meat removed from the bones, and the bones boiled within sixty hours, (*b*) that no part whatever of the carcass, including the blood, is to be returned to the sea or exposed on the beach or ground except as regards the blood, in such quantity as the Local Authority may consider unavoidable and innocuous.

That whaling shall be prohibited within the three mile limit of the territorial waters.

That whaling shall be prohibited from 1st November to the 31st March.

That no person shall pursue or kill a whale within a mile of a boat anchored or engaged in fishing, or half a mile of any other boat.

That it shall be lawful for His Majesty by Order in Council to prohibit the capture and killing of whales during the summer herring fishing, within forty miles from land, and the landing of whales captured and killed within that limit for such period, not longer than five weeks, as he may prescribe.

That it shall be unlawful to kill whales under

forty feet in length, or whales accompanied by a calf.

Many of these recommendations were embodied in the Whale Fisheries (Scotland) Act of 1907, which empowered the Scottish Fishery Board to exercise a general control over the industry.

Whaling is only allowed under licence from the Board; the conditions under which the industry may be carried on are prescribed, as are the penalties to be imposed for infringements of the regulations. The Board are also authorised to collect statistics of the industry.

In 1919 the Scottish Fishery Board appointed another Committee to inquire into the Scottish Whaling Industry. This Committee reported early in 1920, and recommended that, having regard to the practically unanimous belief of the fishing industry, and the inhabitants of Shetland generally, concurred in by the fishing and curing interests of both Scotland and England as to the injurious effects of whaling operations, such operations from stations in Shetland should now be prohibited; and they further recommended that the Whale Fisheries (Scotland) Act of 1907 should be amended, so as to exclude whaling from Shetland.

In 1920 there were three whaling stations at work in Scotland, at Bunaveneadar in the Island of Harris, at Olna Firth and Colla Firth in the Shetlands. There was one whaling station in Ireland, at Elly Harbour in County Mayo. All

MODERN STEAM WHALER. FINNER WHALES BEING TOWED TO THE FACTORY SLIP.

THE LAST PHASE OF WHALING

are under Norwegian management. The whaling stations at Bunaveneadar and Elly Harbour cannot possibly be injurious to the herring fisheries.

RETURN OF WHALING COMPANIES—IRELAND.

WHALES CAPTURED.

	1909	1910	1911	1912	1913	1914[1]	1920
Blue (B. sibbaldi) ..	27	11	10	8	5	13	9
Finner (B. musculus)	54	52	110	38	95	70	101
Sei (B. borealis) ..	9	39	2	4	—	2	3
Humpbacks (Megaptera boops) ..	—	3	—	—	1	—	—
Right (Balaena biscayensis) ..	5	8	—	—	—	—	—
Sperm (Physeter macrocephalus) ..	5	7	9	10	13	4	12
	100	120	131	60	114	89	125

[1] Only one company was engaged in whaling in 1914. There was no whaling in Irish waters in the period 1915-19.

A similar Whale Fisheries Act was passed for Ireland in 1908. It gave the Department of Agriculture and Technical Instruction power to issue licences for the establishment of whaling stations in suitable places, and to impose restrictions for the better control of the industry. The same year a licence was issued to the Arranmore Whaling Company to establish a factory in the Inishkea

Islands. This Company had been at work prior to the passing of the Act, and its operations during 1908 resulted in the capture and treatment of seventy-six whales of five species. This work gave considerable employment to the islanders. A licence was also issued to the Blacksod Whaling Company for a station to be erected at Ardelly Point, County Mayo.

The results of the operations of these two companies are given in the above table.

In 1904 there were six Norwegian whaling stations at the Faroes with ten whaling steamers. The station at Lopra on Sudero was the most successful, its whaling grounds being ten to fifteen miles to the southward towards the Shetlands, where, indeed, whalers from the Shetlands were encountered. The best month for whaling is August.

This year at least two Norwegian companies fished in Spitsbergen waters, one taking eighty-two whales, and the other forty-five whales, in each case mostly Blue Whales (*B. sibbaldi*). The whaling commenced in the middle of June, and lasted till the 25th August. Several companies worked off Bear Island, one steamer capturing seventy whales, of which fifty were Blue Whales.

Newfoundland whaling companies at the time were having small whaling steamers built in Norway, of length ninety-six feet and beam seventeen feet. The crew, consisting of ten men, were Norwegians. These steamers captured

THE LAST PHASE OF WHALING

whales off the Newfoundland coast, towing them ashore, where the preparation of the products took place. It was in 1904 that the Norwegians commenced their operations in South Polar Seas, a company being formed at Buenos Ayres to establish a station on South Georgia. A whaling steamer of considerably larger size than usual (one hundred and five by twenty by thirteen feet deep) was built in Norway for the South Polar whaling. This was necessary on account of the longer distance to be covered. The steamer could carry one hundred tons of bunker coal, and was capable of towing six Blue Whales. There were also two vessels (a barque and schooner) to transport provisions and other material from Buenos Ayres to South Georgia and carry oil back. The personnel was entirely Norwegian, but the capital Argentine.

This year the Scottish whaling fleet from Dundee consisted of seven vessels, which fished in Hudson Bay and Davis Strait. They captured eleven Greenland Whales (Black Whales) with one thousand one hundred and fifty barrels of train oil and twelve thousand five hundred pounds of whalebone, as well as one hundred and sixty-eight White Whales, one thousand one hundred and thirty-five seals, one hundred and nine polar bears, two hundred and eleven foxes, and thirty musk-ox.

In 1904-5 the first Norwegian wintering expeditions to Spitsbergen took place. These expeditions were for general hunting and fishing purposes, and were not confined to whaling.

One expedition captured twenty polar bears, one hundred and five foxes (of which forty-seven were blue fox), nine hundred pounds of bird-down, one hundred and thirty reindeer, and sixty-five ton of blubber. This vessel filled up with whale skeletons, which the whaler had abandoned the previous summer as worthless. A second wintering expedition in Storfiord captured sixty-eight polar bears, twenty-three foxes (of which twelve were blue fox), one hundred reindeer, twenty-five seals (*Phoca barbata*), one walrus, three hundred skins, and four hundred and fifty kilograms of bird-down.

In 1905 the whaling at Iceland was excellent; in Spitsbergen the whalers took from eighty-three to one hundred and twenty-three whales, the latter number including eighty-six Blue Whales, and yielding four thousand seven hundred and eighty-two barrels of blubber.

The total catch of whales by the Norwegians in Spitsbergen in 1905 was five hundred and fifty-three. The number of steamers at work was fifteen, and the barrels of oil produced were seventeen thousand four hundred and sixty, all of first quality.

The total Norwegian catch at Spitsbergen, Iceland, the Faroes, and the Shetlands amounted to two thousand five hundred and ten whales, and seventy-three thousand three hundred and twenty barrels of oil.

The whaling station started in the previous year in South Georgia was extraordinarily successful,

THE LAST PHASE OF WHALING 285

one hundred whales being captured up to June, 1905 (six months' fishing), comprising Finners, Blue, and Humpbacked Whales. This company, the " Sociedad Argentina de Pesca " was managed by a Norwegian whaling captain, Larsen.

Prior to 1906 the Norwegians had gone in extensively for whaling off the Japanese and Korean coast, but in that year the Japanese Government forbade foreigners to whale in Japanese waters. Whaling is only permitted to Japanese companies flying the national flag. At this time, off the Japanese coast near Sendai, the Spermaceti Whale was still captured.

In 1906 the British Government issued an order regulating the whale fisheries of the Falkland Islands and neighbouring waters. A permit or licence to fish had to be obtained at a cost of twenty-five pounds. There was a royalty on each whale caught at the following rates: Right Whale ten pounds; Sperm Whale ten shillings; other whale five shillings. The Ordinance was repealed and the whale industry is now regulated by Ordinance 5 of 1908 and amending Ordinances. A licence fee is payable, but no new licences are granted, other than renewals of annual licences already issued. The killing or shooting of any whale calf, or any female whale, which is accompanied by a calf, is prohibited.

In 1910 whaling was successful at all the customary stations, viz., the Shetlands, the Hebrides, the west coast of Ireland, the Faroes,

Spitsbergen, Iceland, South Georgia, South Shetlands, the Falkland Islands, Kerguelen, the Chile coast, South and West Africa. As this was one of the most successful years for the Norwegian whalers, leading to an enormous development and expansion in the next two years, a short résumé is given.

Seven companies were at work in the British Isles, and these, with sixteen steamers, killed seven hundred and twenty-four whales, yielding twenty thousand eight hundred and sixty casks of whale oil. The average yield per steamer was one thousand three hundred casks of oil, compared with one thousand seven hundred and fifty in 1909, one thousand three hundred and eighty-three in 1908, one thousand five hundred and seven in 1907, one thousand three hundred and eighty-eight in 1906, one thousand four hundred and thirty in 1905, and one thousand four hundred and seventy-seven casks in 1904. In addition to this there was manure and cattle food. Of the rarer whales, eight Sperm Whales and seventeen Nordcapers were killed.

At the Faroes there were six companies engaged with fourteen steamers, yielding ten thousand one hundred and fifty casks of oil, the number of whales is not given. The average per steamer was seven hundred and twenty-five casks against eight hundred and fifteen in 1909, seven hundred and three in 1908, one thousand in 1907, eight hundred in 1906, one thousand two hundred and forty-seven in 1905, and one thousand and eighty-eight in 1904. In 1909 the Sei Whale formed eighty per cent of the total, whereas in 1910 these whales were relatively fewer. In 1909 the Common Finner (*Balænoptera musculus*) was relatively scarce, whereas in 1910 it formed over sixty per cent of the total whales captured. Four Sperm Whales and two Nordcapers were killed in 1910 at the Faroes. In Iceland six companies worked with thirty-two steamers, killing six hundred and forty-nine whales, which yielded twenty-two thousand six hundred casks of oil. Four of the companies had factories for the manufacture of guano. Four of the companies had their stations on the east side of the island, and only two on the west side. The average yield of oil per steamer was seven hundred and fifty casks, compared with one thousand and sixty in 1909, nine hundred and seventy in 1908, one thousand three hundred and seventy in 1907, eight hundred and sixty-four in 1906, and one thousand five hundred and forty-five in 1905. The whales were chiefly Finners, but several Blue Whales and Humpbacks were captured.

At Spitsbergen there were two Norwegian whaling companies at work in 1910 with six steamers, killing one hundred and sixty-five whales, yielding five thousand four hundred casks of oil. One of the companies had a shore station in Green Harbour in Icefiord, the other company working a floating factory. The average yield of oil per steamer was nine hundred casks, compared with seven hundred and sixteen in 1909, four hundred in 1908, six hundred and nineteen in 1907, seven hundred and five in 1906, and one thousand and sixty-six in 1905. The floating factory had only twenty-seven casks of oil per whale, whereas the shore station produced thirty-six casks per whale. The ice conditions in 1910 were fairly good. Most of the whales captured were Blue Whales, but four Bottlenose were among the slain.

The total yield in northern waters in 1910 was about fifty-eight thousand five hundred casks of oil, and about sixty thousand sacks of guano and cattle food.

In southern waters there was a marked increase of whaling. In South Georgia six companies worked with fourteen steamers, yielding one hundred and three thousand casks of oil; two of the companies also producing guano.

One of the shore stations erected here was the largest hitherto known. Over four thousand whales were killed, mostly Humpbacks, the average yield per whale being twenty-six casks of oil.

At the South Shetlands there were three Norwegian companies at work in 1910, with eight steamers, killing one thousand five hundred and sixty-one whales yielding thirty-two thousand five hundred casks of oil. In addition, there was another company worked by Norwegians with Chilian capital, employing three steamers, killing four hundred whales and yielding eight thousand casks of oil. The majority of whales killed here were also Humpbacks, but one hundred and fifty Blue and three hundred Finners were among the slain. The

MODERN WHALING. THE CHASE.

THE LAST PHASE OF WHALING 289

greatest catch was made on the coast of Graham's Land, from whence the whales were towed to Deception Island.

On the Chilian coast there was one Norwegian company working with a shore station at Corral i Valdivia. With two steamers they got seven thousand casks of oil and about three thousand sacks of guano. The whales killed were principally Blues and Humpbacks; Sei Whales were also seen, but not hunted. A second company had a station south of San Pedro, and a third (Chilian) company worked from Puntas Arenas. This last company obtained four thousand casks of oil, killing amongst others twenty Right Whales.

At Kerguelen one Norwegian company was at work with a fixed station, hunting sea-elephants as well as whales. Only eight-two whales were killed, which yielded two thousand eight hundred casks of oil, two steamers being engaged in the slaughter. A floating factory, employing one whaling steamer, utilised the carcasses of forty-one whales yielding one thousand casks of oil. In South Africa a company established stations at Durban and Saldana, at which twenty thousand five hundred casks of oil and large quantities of guano were prepared. Other stations were established in Portuguese West Africa; a summary of the Norwegian stations and the dates of founding is given in Appendix VII.

A company at work in Newfoundland in 1909 employed seven steamers, killing five hundred and eighteen whales (including eighty Blue Whales).

The Dundee Right Whaling Fleet is now reduced to three vessels, which killed respectively five, three, and seven Right Whales, returning with six thousand five hundred, two thousand five hundred, and fourteen thousand pounds of whalebone.

In 1910 the Norwegian Bottlenose Fleet consisted of forty-two vessels, of which six ships from Tonsberg killed one hundred and fifty-six whales, i.e., twenty-six each; twenty from Sandefjord killed six hundred and fifty-seven whales or thirty-three each; thirteen from Aalesund killed three hundred and forty-nine whales or twenty-seven each, and three vessels from Stadten which accounted for forty-two whales. Most of these whales were killed at Spitsbergen. In 1909 there were thirty-eight ships, which killed one thousand three hundred and seventy-eight Bottlenose Whales.

The price realised for whaling products in 1910 was excellent. Most of the whale oil made in Japan and Newfoundland was sold to the United States. The world's production of whale oil can be estimated at three hundred thousand casks in 1910. Of this quantity about seventy thousand casks (barrels) was disposed of in Christiania, one hundred thousand casks or barrels were sold in Germany, Holland, and Belgium, and a similar quantity in Glasgow. The average price for quick delivery was forty-four ore (about sixpence) per kilogram. Most of the oil of the following season was sold in advance at Glasgow at twenty-two pounds ten shillings per ton.

By 1911 it was estimated that over twenty

THE LAST PHASE OF WHALING 291

thousand whales were being slaughtered annually. It is unnecessary to give detailed statistics each year, those just given for 1910 give a fair idea of the position at the end of the first decade of the twentieth century.[1]

At the end of the first decade of the twentieth century the whaling industry had practically passed entirely into Norwegian hands.[2] Prior to the outbreak of the great war (1914-8) this fishery had attained extraordinary dimensions.

The prohibition of whaling off the Norwegian districts of Nordland, Tromsö, and Finmark by the law of the 7th January, 1904, led to a great dispersal of Norwegian whaling interests. This is seen to be particularly noticeable in the southern hemisphere from the following statistical table:

NORWEGIAN WHALING COMPANIES.

CATCH OF OIL.

	Northern hemisphere.	Southern hemisphere.
1906	47,200 barrels	4,200 barrels
1907	57,750	7,500
1908	69,000	21,000
1909	57,000	71,700
1910	45,500	137,600
1911	38,000	306,000

At the commencement of 1912 there were sixty Norwegian companies at work, mostly with their headquarters on the south coast of Norway at

[1] For detailed statistics for 1911, see C. Rabot, " La Nature," 1912. Translated into English in the *Smithsonian Institution Report* for 1913 (1914).
[2] Hval-fangsten i. 1912. Sigurd Risting, Bergen, 1913.

Sandefjord, Larvik, and Tonsberg, though some hailed from Christiania. Two firms were established in the United States of North America and one in Chile. The companies possessed in the aggregate one hundred and fifty-seven whaling steamers of the general type described (see p. 264) with eleven transport vessels and thirty-seven floating factories, thirty land stations, nine guano works with thirteen factories for the preparation of canned whale meat and cattle food products.

The capital of these concerns differs considerably. That of the smallest was nominally one hundred and twenty thousand kronen (about six thousand seven hundred and fifty pounds), the largest two million kronen (one hundred and twelve thousand five hundred pounds). The dividends varied greatly, but that of one company established on the South Georgian coast was one hundred per cent.[1]

The chief whaling areas are in the northern hemisphere, Alaska, the Shetlands, Ireland, Iceland, the Faroes, the Hebrides, Spitsbergen; in the southern hemisphere,[2] the Australian coasts, Chile, South-east Africa, West Africa (Elephant Bay), East Africa (Mozambique), the South Shetlands, South Orkneys, South Georgia, the Sandwich Isles and Kerguelen.

Concessions are obtained for lengthy periods,

[1] See Emil Diesen, " Tabellarisk Oversigt over de vigtigste norske hvalfangerselskaper," Feb., 1912. (I kommission hos Grondahl u Son, Christiania.)

[2] T. E. Salvesen, " The Whale Fisheries of the Falkland Islands and Dependencies," *Scottish National Antarctic Expedition*, Edinburgh, 1914, pp. 479-86, with 4 plates.

THE LAST PHASE OF WHALING

mostly for fifty years. Prior to the outbreak of war the general opinion in whaling circles was that future prospects were good, although, since the industry is highly speculative, there is no certainty about it. In many districts, especially in the extreme south, success is dependent to some extent on the weather, which in the Antarctic is extraordinarily inclement.

A considerable fall in the price of whale oil owing to increased production was at the time not improbable. This price also depends to some extent on what other oils are on the market, such as cotton seed oil, linseed oil and others. In 1911-2 whale oil had declined in a comparatively short time from twenty-four pounds to eighteen pounds per ton.

The table (Appendix VII.) shows the position of the Norwegian whaling companies in 1912, following the boom year in 1911.

Generally speaking, one ton of whale oil fills six barrels. The species of whale yield oil at the following rate: Blue Whale (*Balænoptera sibbaldi*) fifty to sixty barrels; the Greenland Whale sixty to seventy barrels; the Finner (*Balænoptera musculus*) thirty-five to forty; the Humpback (*Megaptera*) twenty-five to thirty-five; and the Sei Whale (*Balænoptera borealis*) five to ten barrels. All these, it will be noted, are whalebone whales. One ton of whalebone would be worth from thirty-nine to forty-five pounds.

Recently the Norwegian whaling interests have

formed a combine "Den norske Hvalfanger-forening" under the direction of members from Christiania, Tonsberg, Sandefjord, Larvik and Haugesund. Just before the war broke out, this combine was seeking to get in touch with other whaling companies and associations. Their main object was to control the selling price of the articles produced by the whaling companies.

Quite recently State control of whaling has been inaugurated in those countries, the coastal waters of which have been the resort of whalers. In Natal the operations of whalers have of late been particularly numerous. Commencing with the South African Whaling Company of Sandefjord in 1908, which paid a dividend of twenty-five per cent after its first year's operations, a second Norwegian Company—the Union Fishing and Whaling Company—was founded in 1910. This company was even more prosperous, paying a dividend of fifty per cent after its first year's work.

The exports of whaling products from Natal were:

In 1909, 27,414 pounds whalebone, value £325, to England.
171,693 pounds whale oil, value £11,184.
In 1910, 10,000 barrels and 1,600 tons oil.
700 tons fertiliser, and 1,600 tons whale meat for preparation of the same.
37 tons whalebone.

For the whole of British South Africa, 1910:

879,852 pounds oil worth	£61,403
Whalebone	1,840
Fatty Acids	18,708
Miscellaneous	1,446

THE LAST PHASE OF WHALING

In 1911 a local company—African Whales, Ltd.—was founded, in Park Rynie between Durban and Port Shepstone, and proposals were afoot for the formation of another company—the Durban Whaling Company, Ltd.—at Durban. Early in 1912 there were four whaling companies in Durban, with fifteen whaling steamers. The chief species of whales off the Natal coast are the Humpback (*Megaptera boops*), the Western Right Whale (*Balæna australis*), the Blue Whale, the Rorqual or Sei Whale and the Sperm Whale. Of these the Humpback is the commonest, the other four being much scarcer.

The yield of the Natal whalers was:

```
1908    106 whales (including 104 Humpbacks).
1909    155    ,,           ,,    149    ,,
1910    308 whales.
```

Up to this time whaling had been carried on near the coast where the whales are found in the winter months, from the middle of June to the middle of November, and in the first two years with two, and in 1910 with four steamers. In summer the whales forsake the coast and seek colder waters. It is reported that they are now getting more and more shy and difficult to approach. There is a distinct tendency on the part of the whales to abandon the coast altogether, so that floating factories are coming more into favour.

Whaling in Natal was in 1912 subject to a licence fee of fifty pounds per annum, this superseding the older tax of five pounds per whale caught. There is no close time for whaling. Up to 1912 there was no evidence of any falling off in the numbers of the most numerous species, the Humpback. There is some reason to believe that the local Government is not prepared to grant further concessions for whaling off the Natal coast.

The Portuguese colonies regulated whaling in the Mozambique waters by a decree dated 27th May, 1911, amended on 31st August, the same year. Up to that time the Government had granted seven whaling licences for the Mozambique coast-line of nine hundred miles.

Of these only one was at work, a Norwegian company at Linga-linga in the district of Inhambane; this company in its first year killed two hundred and sixty-four whales, which were prepared at a floating station.

A station at Angoche, after obtaining eight thousand pounds worth of oil, removed to Mokambo Bay on account of the lack of harbour facilities at the former place. The New Transvaal Chemical Company were about to start on an island off Lorenzo Marques. The other four licences had not been utilised up to the commencement of 1912.

Since the whaling industry in the Dependencies of the Falkland Islands (i.e., South Georgia, the South Shetlands, and the South Orkneys, being the principal centres) is now one of the most important of those yet remaining, a brief résumé of the conditions obtaining there is appended.

This whaling field has of recent years been more

productive than all the others in the world put together, and its regulation is therefore a matter of considerable importance.

Reference has already been made to the first attempts at whaling in the Antarctic and to the first company which worked at South Georgia in 1904. The first whaling, in a modern sense, at the South Shetlands, was in the season 1905-6. From 1909 to 1911 seven other leases were granted at South Georgia. In both these localities whaling was extraordinarily successful. By 1912-3 the number of whale catchers in South Georgia had increased to twenty-one, and in the South Shetlands to thirty-two, to which totals the whalers were restricted by the Government.

The following table gives the return of whales captured at the Falkland Island Dependencies for the nine last seasons for which the statistics are available:

FALKLAND ISLAND DEPENDENCIES.
Capture of Whales.

	Right.	Sperm.	Blue.	Fin.	Humpback.	Sei.	Bottlenose.
1909-10	37	4	26	58	3,391	—	—
1910-11	79	—	85	168	6,197	—	—
1911-12	99	4	1,261	2,321	7,936	—	3
1912-13	0	9	2,277	4,899	3,474	—	5
1913-14[1]	72	21	2,441	4,288	1,598	94	—
1914-15	22	1	4,203	3,894	1,489	—	2
1915-16	18	4	4,871	5,102	1,797	—	—
1916-17	12	35	3,820	2,208	399	—	—
1917-18	48	37	2,268	1,771	131	49	1

[1] Statistics incomplete. 715 whales not accounted for in detailed statistics.

During the war whale oil became of importance as a source of glycerine, so Government restrictions were relaxed and the number of whale catchers allowed at South Georgia was temporarily increased to thirty-two. Floating factories were, however, diverted to war services elsewhere, and the number of whale catchers at the South Shetlands fell off. The whaling fleet suffered severe losses from German submarines.

As will be seen from the above table, the great majority of whales killed are Blue, Fin, and Humpback Whales. There has been a great decline in the number of Humpbacks, and it would not be detrimental to the industry if the slaughter of this species were prevented for a number of years. Experienced whalers can readily distinguish the different species of whales, the Humpback, for instance, being recognised by its spouting a very short and broad jet of vapour.

It is doubtful how soon the ceaseless hunting of the other Rorquals will lead to a serious diminution in their numbers, but judging from the results in other localities the time cannot be far distant when other restrictions will have to be enforced if the industry is to survive in this region, one of the last haunts of the whale.

The practice of granting annual licences is unquestionably correct, since it would be unwise for the Government to tie itself down to granting privileges for a term of years, by which time the industry might become moribund. At South

THE LAST PHASE OF WHALING 299

Georgia the Humpbacks were not to be hunted during the whaling season of 1918-9, and though the Finner and the Blue Whale do not yet require such protection, the statistics need careful study so that Government action may be taken before it is too late.

A close season would also appear to be desirable. From the detailed statistics it is seen that the whaling seasons slackens off considerably during the Antarctic winter, and no hardship would be involved if the period from the 15th May to the 30th September were declared a close season. That the dangers to the continued existence of the whale and *ipso facto* of the whaling industry are not imaginary a reference to the first chapter of this book will prove.

The policy of the Government of the Falkland Island Dependencies is also directed to the prevention of unnecessary waste, since the uneconomical use of material may involve the slaughter of three whales where two would have sufficed to obtain the same results. An extreme instance of the reckless exploitation of a valuable natural asset is given above in the description of the practice of the American whalers off the Arctic coasts of America.

Evidence is forthcoming that the economy effected is in inverse proportion to the number of whales captured.

In seasons when whales are plentiful, the average number of barrels of oil per whale of a given species is conspicuously lower than in seasons when the whales are less abundant. Floating factories are less efficient in working up the products of the whale than the shore stations, and consequently it is desirable to restrict the use of floating factories as far as possible. The fee for a whaling licence is one hundred pounds; for a floating factory not less than one hundred pounds, or more than two hundred pounds.

In 1921, owing to the great fall in the price of whale oil, none of the Norwegian whaling companies associated to the whaling combine (Den Norske Hvalfangerforening) commenced operations at Iceland, the Faroes or the British Isles. One company, Messrs H. M. Wrangell & Company, of Haugesund, worked at the Faroes; this firm was not a member of the combine. I am indebted to the courtesy of Messrs Wrangell and their manager, Captain J. Ellingsen, for a visit to this station at Thorsvig in 1921. This year about ninety-seven per cent of the catch were common finners, the remainder being Blue Whales. Only one Nordcaper had been taken up to the end of July. The Sei Whale was not hunted owing to the abundance of the larger and more valuable species.

A Spanish company, the Compania Ballerena Espanola, opened a station early in 1921 near Algeciras, early reports from this station recorded abundance of whales.

LIST OF APPENDICES

I

GRANT TO THE FELLOWSHIP OF ENGLISH MERCHANTS FOR DISCOVERY OF NEW TRADES, 1576-7.

II

STATISTICS OF THE BOUNTY SYSTEM AND THE GREENLAND WHALE FISHERY, FROM THE COMMENCEMENT OF THE BOUNTY IN 1734 TO ITS TERMINATION IN 1824.

III

STATISTICS OF THE BRITISH SOUTHERN WHALE FISHERY, 1800-34.

IV

STATISTICS OF THE DUTCH WHALE FISHERY (IN DECENNIAL PERIODS), 1670-1794.

V

STATISTICS OF WHALING IN SCOTTISH WATERS, 1904-20

VI

STATISTICS OF THE HULL WHALING, 1772-1852.

VII

RETURN OF NORWEGIAN WHALING COMPANIES, 1912.

APPENDIX I

GRANT TO THE FELLOWSHIP OF ENGLISH MERCHANTS FOR DISCOVERY OF NEW TRADES (1576-7).

(*Patent Rolls*, 19 *Eliz.*, pt. xii.)

ELIZABETH by the Grace of God, etc., To all manner our officers true liege men ministers and subjects, and to all other our people as well within this realm as elsewhere under our obeisance jurisdiction and rule or otherwise, to whom these our Letters Patents shall be seen read or shewn. Greeting.

We being given to understand by our faithful and loving subjects Sir Rowland Heyward and Sir Lionel Duckett, Knights, Governors of the Fellowship of English Merchants for Discovery of New Trades, that the said Fellowship do mind shortly to attempt the killing of whales in the ocean and other seas, for to make train oil to the great commodity and benefit of this our Realm of England, And for that purpose have already to their great costs and charges procured certain Biscayans men expert and skilful to instruct our subjects therein. We well liking and allowing of this their attempt and enterprise as a thing likely to be very beneficial both for the increase of our Navy and mariners and also for furnishing of this our said Realm and Dominions with so necessary a commodity, of our certain knowledge free will mere motion special grace and of our regal authority for Us our heirs and successors by these presents do grant to the Governor or Governors Consuls Assistants and Fellowship aforesaid and their successors for ever That they the said Governors and their successors, by their factors servants ministers deputies and assigns and none other shall and may from henceforth for the space of twenty years next ensuing the date hereof use and exercise the killing of whales within any seas whatsoever, and thereof to make train oil to their most commodity and profit; And further for Us our heirs and successors, We do expressly enjoin prohibit forbid and command all and singular person and persons whatsoever as well denizens as strangers and all other persons being in any wise subjects to the Crown of England, being not of the said Society or Fellowship, that they nor any of them shall kill any whale to make train oil thereof, or shall hire or set on work or cause or procure to be hired or set on work directly or indirectly any person or persons to kill any whale or make any oil thereof Upon pain that all and every person or persons whatsoever doing the contrary shall suffer imprisonment during the will and pleasure of Us our heirs or successors and not to be discharged thereof without special warrant from Us our heirs or successors And also to forfeit and pay to Us our heirs or successors the sum of Five pounds of lawful money of England for every ton of oil so made, one half to be to the use of Us our heirs or successors the other half to the use of the said Fellowship and their successors. And to the intent this present grant may the better effect to the encouragement of the said Fellowship in this their enterprise and attempt our further will and pleasure is and We straitly charge and command all our Customs officers Comptrollers and other our ministers of our ports that they nor any of them in any wise during the said term of twenty years do take any entry or make any composition of or for any oil commonly called train oil which shall be made of any whale that shall be killed or caused to be killed by any Englishman or other person inhabiting within this our Realm and brought into this our Realm of others than the said Fellowship of English Merchants for the Discovery of New Trades or their successors factors or assigns upon pain of our high displeasure. Provided always that if the said Fellowship (etc.) by the space of four years in time of peace shall discontinue or surcease the killing of whales and making of train oil as is aforesaid that then it shall be lawful to and for every other of our subjects whatsoever to enterprise and attempt the killing of whales and making of train oil where they might lawfully have done it afore this our special grant or license Anything in this our special grant to the said Fellowship made to the contrary notwithstanding.

In witness whereof, etc., witness ourself at Westminster the XII day of February, per breue de privato sigillo.

APPENDIX II

THE BOUNTY SYSTEM OF THE WHALE FISHERIES

(England only. The "British" or "Greenland" Fishery.)

ANNUAL AVERAGE

Years.	Rate of Bounty.	No. of Ships.	Tonnage	Bounty Paid.	Remarks.
1734-9	20/- per ton	4·5	1,329	£ 1,085	30/- per ton during war with Spain.
1740-9	30/- ,, ,,	3·7	1,203	1,260	
1750-9	40/- ,, ,,	43·3	13,812	27,175	
1760-9	40/- ,, ,,	35·3	10,909	20,327	
1770-6	40/- ,, ,,	65·2	19,652	36,046	
1777-81	30/- ,, ,,	58·3	16,775	25,096	
1782-86	40/- ,, ,,	94·2	28,756	57,490	
1787-91	30/- ,, ,,	167·0	48,283	—	No information. Documents destroyed in Custom House Fire.
1792-94	25/- ,, ,,	78·3	22,255	—	
1795-1806	20/- ,, ,,	71·8	20,901	—	
1807-13	—	—	—	—	No documents available.
1814-24	20/- ,, ,,	130·0	41,482	40,156	

NOTE.—The number of ships and tonnage (1733-84) are from a return issued by the Custom House, London, of ships fitted out from Great Britain for the Greenland Whale Fishery. The places from which the ships were fitted out are in all cases given and the table clearly refers to ENGLAND ONLY. Moreover, there is a separate return for Scotland. The amount of bounty is from a separate table and refers to the British Whale Fishery (1734-82). There is an additional table showing the amount of bounty (all monies) paid in England for the British Whale Fishery for 1783 and also for the Southern Whale Fishery from 1777 to 1784. For 1789 and subsequent years the statistics are taken from McCulloch "Dictionary of Commerce and Commercial Navigation," London, 1832.

APPENDIX III

THE SOUTHERN WHALE FISHERY (BRITISH), 1800-1834

(AVERAGES)

Years.	Ships at Sea.	Ships returned.	Sperm Oil Imported. Tons.		Common Oil Imported. Tons.		Price per ton. Sperm Oil.	Price per ton. Common Oil.	Total Value Imports.	Average Tonnage of Ships.	Average Crew.
			British	Colonial	British	Colonial	£	£	£		
1800-1809	72·6	28·1	1634·1		3228·4		80·8	32·0	233,393·9	242	28
1810-1819	64·4	25·3	2573·7		2345·8		78·7	37·4	285,389·3	300	30
1820-1822	126·0	46·0	4111·0		3867·0		61·2	22·0	326,518·2	340	32
1823-1832	94·4	32·0	5069·4	582·8	593·9	742·8	60·9	30·0	384,699·1	340-390	32-36
1833-1834 [1]	104·5	23·0	3736·0	2659·0	184·5	2319·5	63·5	24·0	461,643·5	390	36

[1] 1823.—The number of ships for this and succeeding, as well as previous years, are those for Britain only.
1826.—From this year commenced the Imperial measure.

APPENDIX IV
STATISTICS OF DUTCH WHALING

IN DECENNIAL PERIODS

Years.	Vessels sailed to Greenland.	Whales caught Greenland.	Vessels sailed to Davis Strait.	Whales caught Davis Strait.	Remarks.
1670-79	981	5748	—	—	War stopped whaling in 1672-74.
1680-89	1966	9487¼	—	—	
1690-99	900	5331¼	—	—	War stopped whaling in 1691.
1700-09	1628	7935	—	—	
1709-19	1407	4749¼	—	—	
1719-28	1504	3439	748	1251	
1729-38	858	2198	975	1929	
1739-1748	302	1041½	1047	5566	
1749-1758	1337	4531	340	639½	
1759-1768	1323	3016	294	820	
1769-1778	893	3197	426	1339½	
1779-1788	391	1698¼	113	204	War stopped whaling in 1781-2.
1789-1794	287	1011	53	66	Six years only.

NOTE.—The years 1709 and 1719 are included twice over in the above table.

The statistics from 1670 to 1719 are from Zorgdrager "Bloyende Opkomst der aloude en hedendaagsche Groenlandsche Visschery"; 1719 to 1738 from Brandligt "Geschiedkundige Beschouwing van de Walvisch-visscherij" from 1737 to 1750 from the "Europische Mercuur," the remainder from the "Nederlandsche Jaarboeken."

APPENDIX V

RETURN OF WHALES CAPTURED IN SCOTTISH WATERS

	1903	1904	1905	1906	1907	1908	1909	1910	1911	1912	1913	1914	1920[2]
Finner, Balaenoptera musculus..	—	263	450	317	396	379	432	381	344	292	259	325	331
Sei, Balaenoptera borealis	—	7	34	326	151	232	223	190	130	108	159	248	261
Sperm, Physeter macrocephalus	—	5	5	1	10	1	7	1	18	9	8	—	—
Bottlenose, Hyperoodon	—	—	1	1	2	—	2	1	2	8	7	—	5
Blue, Balaenoptera sibbaldi	—	42	37	54	12	17	33	21	5	12	2	19	58
Nordcaper, Balaena biscayensis	—	—	—	6	24	20	21	9	—	11	1	5	1
Humpback, Megaptera	—	10	6	5	5	2	12	12	4	—	1	2	1
Totals	127[1]	327	533	710	600	651	730	615	503	440	437	599	658

[1] Total only available. [2] Includes one Killer (*Orcinus Orca*).

APPENDIX V (a)

DETAILS OF WHALE FISHERIES (SCOTLAND)

	No. of Steamers.	Total Tonnage.	Total Value.	Men engaged on Steamers.	Men employed on shore.		No. of Voyages made.
					British.	Foreign.	
1908	11	307	46,800	108	142	184	490
1909	11	393	48,850	109	145	170	535
1910	11	417	47,000	109	139	163	441
1911	11	497	55,550	110	148	147	406
1912	11	469	51,800	110	143	138	391
1913	13	491	54,000	129	141	129	411
1914	13	550	54,200	130	164	114	412
1915-19			Suspended owing to War.				
1920	9	468	71,600	93	213	66	381

APPENDIX V (b)

PRODUCTS OF THE SCOTTISH WHALE FISHERIES

	1908		1909		1910		1911		1912		1913		1914		1920	
	Tons.	£	Tons.	£	Tons.	£	Tons.	£	Tons.	£	Tons.	£	Tons.	£	Tons.	£
Oil	2601	43349	3170	48037	3007	50796	2111	40191	2060	33396	1723	32348	2334	48748	2525	88358
Cattle food	536	3905	1070	7383	629	4643	317	2392	335	2555	221	1657	263	1939	320	6400
Bone meal	197	761	416	1592	311	1154	180	704	218	863	121	449	176	608	300	3900
Manure	1610	8288	908	4463	1234	6164	1183	9072	956	5810	963	6381	1354	7668	1543	24581
Whalebone	65	6947	71	7260	59	4577	44	2321	44	3562	44	1831	78	2587	67	8445
Salted meat	45	289	10	87	9	105	—	—	—	—	—	—	—	—	—	—
Spermaceti	11	300	100	2400	36	1020	175	4250	102	2462	85	2022	—	—	—	—
		63641		71223		68459		58931		48649		44688		61550		131684

(Fractions omitted).

APPENDIX VI

THE WHALING TRADE OF HULL [1]

ANNUAL AVERAGES

Years.	Bounty.	No. of Ships.	Value of Oil and Bone.	Remarks.
1772-6	40/- per ton	10·	11,328	
1777-81	30/- ,, ,,	5·6	10,552	
1782-86	40/- ,, ,,	10·4	20,209	
1787-91	30/- ,, ,,	27·6	33,418	
1792-94	25/- ,, ,,	18·3	32,522	
1795-1806	20/- ,, ,,	29·3	102,826	
1807-13	20/- ,, ,,	39·7	188,766	
1814-24	20/- ,, ,,	54·5	215,203	
1825-34	No Bounty	29·1	126,937	
1835-44	,,	1·2	2,129	
1845-52	,,	11·7	20,163	

[1] *Munroe. Journal of the Statistical Society, London, March* 1854, *p.* 34.

The years have been grouped to afford comparison with the preceding table of the whaling statistics for England under the bounty system (App. No. 2). It will be seen that the Hull Whaling Trade fluctuated considerably and apparently independently of the bounty system. It was in 1834 that the great decline set in. The number of vessels decreased from 27 in 1833 to 8 in 1834. The annual averages of values of oil and bone are based on estimates made by Munroe and are of doubtful reliability.

APPENDICES

APPENDIX VII — NORWEGIAN WHALING COMPANIES, 1912

Region.	Name of Company.	Headquarters.	Fo'nded	Capital.	Dividends F'mer	Dividends Last
Hebrides	Harpunen	Christiania	1895	200,000	20	20
Shetlands	Alexandra	do.	1904	182,000	10	10
do.	Norrona	Sandefjord	1903	350,000	30	60
do.	Shetland	Larvik	in 90's	170,000	—	—
Faroes	Emma	Tonsberg	1900	190,000	—	—
do.	Norddeble	Christiania	1897	250,000	5	10
do.	Sudero	Sandefjord	1901	400,000	30	60
do.	Verdandi	do.	1901	120,000	25	—
Iceland	Hekla	Haugesund	1902	400,000	15	19
do.	Talkna	do.	—	220,000	—	—
do.	Victor	Tonsberg	1890	400,000	6	25
do.	Victoria	do.	1912	150,000	—	—
Ireland	Blacksod	do.	1910	164,000	—	5
Spitzbergen	Nimrod	Larvik	1906	145,000	—	5
Arctic	Oceana	Sandefjord	1910	200,000	—	10
WEST AFRICA	Bas	do.	1910	350,000	—	—
do.	Haugesund	Haugesund	1911	528,000	—	—
do.	Kastor	Tonsberg	1911	800,000	—	—
do.	South Atlantic	do.	1911	800,000	—	—
do.	Viking	Sandefjord	1909	600,000	50	50
SOUTH AFRICA	South Africa	do.	1907	960,000	50	20
South-east do.	Mossel Bay	Tonsberg	1911	450,000	—	—
East Africa	Capella	Sandefjord	1911	1,200,000	—	—
do.	Mozambique	do.	1911	800,000	—	—
do.	Normanna	do.	1910	500,000	—	—
do.	Quilimane	Larvik	1911	700,000	0	0
Kerguelen	Kerguelen	Christiania	1908	968,000	—	—
AUSTRALIA, S. & W.	Australia	Tonsberg	1911	1,000,000	—	—
do.	Dominion	Sandefjord	1911	850,000	—	—
do.	New Zealand	Larvik	1911	1,000,000	—	—
do.	West Australia	do.	1911	1,800,000	—	—
Tasmania	Spermaceti	do.	1911	700,000	—	—
do.	Antarctic	do.	1911	100,000	—	—
do.	South Pacific	Christiania	1912	800,000	—	—
N. America (east)	Norweg-Canadn.	do.	1911	400,000	—	—
do. (west)	Alaska	Sandefjord	1911	1,125,000	—	—
do.	Standard	do.	1911		—	—
do.	United States	do.	1911	1,500,000	—	—
S. America (east)	Brasilian	do.	1912	500,000	—	—
do. (west)	Corral	Bergen	1911	1,000,000	—	—
do.	Pacific	Sandefjord	1910	750,000	—	12
do.	Soc. Ballenera	do.	1910	500,000	—	0
South Georgia	Bryde and Dahls	do.	1908	—	—	—
do.	Condor	do.	1909	150,000	30	75
do.	Ocean	Larvik	1909	650,000	30	100
do.	Sandefjord	Sandefjord	1906	400,000	—	—
do.	Tonsberg	Tonsberg	1907	960,000	18	60
South Shetlands	Hektor	do.	1910	700,000	—	32
do.	Hvalen	Sandefjord	1910		—	—
do.	Nor	do.	1906	550,000	20	30
do.	Norge	Larvik	1910	650,000	—	50
do.	Odd	Sandefjord	1911	700,000	—	45
do.	Sydhavet	do.	1908	550,000	15	25
South Orkneys	Ornen	do.	1903	500,000	30	60
do.	Rethval	Stabaek	1911	700,000	—	—
Brazil, S. Georgia	Vik	Sandefjord	1911	—	—	—
Tasmania, S. Shetlands	Laboremus	do.	1910	1,000,000	—	$6\frac{1}{2}$
E. Africa, S. Seas.	Ostkysten	do.	1911	700,000	—	—
Okhotsk, S. America	Kosmos	do.	1910	700,000	—	—

BIBLIOGRAPHY

Most of the important works published dealing with the whale fisheries are included in the following list, which is, however, by no means complete, since references to periodical literature are for the most part omitted. For the benefit of serious students of the subject the following notes are given.

In the first place, the earliest organised whale fishery—that of the Basques—has not yet been properly investigated. Research at the Bibliothèque Nationale at Paris or in the Archives of the Ministry of Marine at Madrid would probably yield further material for a proper appreciation of this trade in relation to the maritime affairs of Northern Spain and the Biscayan provinces of France during the time when the Basque whale fishery flourished.

The connection of the oil trade of French towns such as Bayonne with such English ports as Bristol, which were early engaged in the soap trade and for which whale oil was almost certainly used, has also not yet been suitably investigated. Possibly some of the older Bristol Archives or the books of the older trading companies—such as the Society of Merchant Adventurers of Bristol—would repay perusal. So far as is known at present there is one solitary record of a Bristol voyage to the whale fishery of Newfoundland (1594) except for a spasmodic effort on the part of Bristol in response to the Bounty Act of 1749.

Yet it is almost certain that Bristol, with its ancient connection with the soap trade and its former maritime supremacy, must have been closely connected either with the whale fishery or its products. The author has seen in the church of St Mary Redcliffe at Bristol the "Rib of a whale from Newfoundland"[1] which, according to the legend current in the city, was the rib of a cow which supplied the whole of the city with milk.

No connected account of the first British whale fishery, that at "Greenland" (Spitsbergen), has yet been written which can be compared with the corresponding works of Müller (Dutch) or Brinner (German), and the second British venture in these waters, that of the South Sea Company in 1724, is still only accessible in manuscript form (in the British Museum).

There is slight evidence that prior to the supposed first British whale fishery at Spitsbergen, English ships took part in whaling voyages to Norway or Newfoundland. Diligent search may yet reveal evidence of these voyages. Apart from the records of actual whaling voyages, evidence of the train oil and whalebone trade is to be sought in the Port Books, a manuscript catalogue of which is to be

[1] Figured in Traill and Mann, "Social England," Vol. ii., p. 673.

BIBLIOGRAPHY

found in the Literary Search Room at the Record Office, London. The earlier Port Books (from 1275) will be found in the class of Exchequer, K-R, Customs Accounts. The later Port Books, from 1565, are contained in one thousand four hundred and sixty-four bundles which are indexed under the port names.

A careful search of these MSS. would doubtless give evidence of an early trade in whalebone and trayne oil, e.g., there was a discharge of a cargo including trayne oil by a ship of Holland at Kingston-on-Hull in December, 1608, to one James Scotus; on 22nd March, 1631, Richard Parkins & Company, import two hundredweights of whale fins (this man was afterwards prosecuted by the Muscovy Company); on 5th September, 1633, in the *Mayeflower* of Hull, Richard Parkins, junior, from Greenland for the Company, one hundred and twenty-two tons and a halfe of whaile oil, value three thousand six hundred and fifteen pounds.

Another source of information is the Calendar of State Papers. The student will find numerous references indexed under such headings as: " Fish," " Fisheries," " Iceland," " Newfoundland," " Greenland," and so on.

Another aspect of the case which merits careful consideration is the history of the relations between the authorised Trading Companies (e.g., the Muscovy Company) and the Interlopers, the chief of whom hailed from Hull and London.

Later features of the whaling trade are naturally

better known, but since a large amount of the information is scattered in periodical literature, such widely different sources as the San Francisco *Call* and the *Bamburger Wochenblatt* giving valuable material, it follows that here again further research will prove profitable.

ADELUNG, JOH. CHR. Geschichte der Schiffahrten und Versuche welche zur Entdeckung des Nordöstlichen Weges nach Japan und China von verschiedenen Nationen unternommen worden. Zum Behufe der Erdbeschreibung und Naturgeschichte dieser Gegenden entworfen. Halle. J. J. Gebauer. 1768. 4to. Met 19 gegrav. platen en kaarten.

AITZEMA, L. VAN. Saken van Staet en Oorlogh, in, ende omtrent de Vereenigde Nederlanden (1621-1669). s'Gravenhage, 1669. 6 vols. Folio.

ALDRICH, H. L. Arctic Alaska and Siberia or Eight Months with the Arctic Whalemen. 1889.

ALLEN. The Whalebone Whales of New England. 1916.

ANDERSON, AD. An Historical and Chronological Deduction of the Origin of Commerce from the earliest accounts. London, 1789. 4 vols.

ANDERSON, JOHANN. Nachrichten von Island, Grönland und der Strasse Davis, zum wahren nützen der Wissenschaften und der Handlung. Hamburg, 1746. Another edition, Frankfort, 1747. French translation by Rousselot de Surgy. Paris, 1764. Dutch edition, Amsterdam, 1750; later edition, Amsterdam, 1756.

ANDREE, KARL. Geographie der Welthandels. Mit geschichtlichen Erläuterungen. Stuttgart, 1867, 1872. 2 vols.

ANDREWS, ROY CHAPMAN. Whale Hunting with Gun and Camera. New York, 1916.

BAASCH, ERNST. Hamburgs Convoyschiffahrt und Con-

BIBLIOGRAPHY 319

voywesen. Ein Beitrag zur Geschichte der Schiffahrt und Schiffahrteinrichtung im 17 und 18 Jahrhundert. Hamburg, 1896.

BACSTROM, S. Account of a Voyage to Spitsbergen in the year 1780. In Pinkerton's Collection of Voyages. London, 1808-14.

BAFFIN, W. The Voyages of William Baffin. 1612-22. Ed. by C. R. Markham. Hakluyt Society. London, 1881.

BARRON, WILLIAM. Old Whaling Days. Hull, 1895.

BAUDARTIUS, W. Memoryen ofte Cort Verhael der Gedenck-weerdichste Gheschiednissen van Nederland, Vranckrijck, Hoogh-Duytschland, Groot-Brittannyen enz. Van den jeere 1603-24. Arnhem, 1624. 2 vols.

BAYONNE. Archives Municipales. 2 vols. 1911.

BEALE, THOMAS. The Natural History of the Sperm Whale, to which is added a sketch of a south-sea whaling voyage. London, 1839.

BENNETT, F. D. Narrative of a whaling voyage Round the Globe from the year 1833 to 1836. Two vols. London, 1840.

BOSGOED, D. M. Bibliotheca Ichthyologica et Piscatoria. Haarlem, 1874.

BRANDLIGT, C. Geschiedkundige Beschowing van de Walvisch-Visscherij. Amsterdam, 1843.

BRINNER, LUDWIG. Die Deutsche Grönlandfahrt. Einleitung. Die Erschliessung des Nordens für den Walfischfang. Inaugural—Dissertation zur Erlangung der Doktorwürde. Phil. Fac. Berlin, 1912. First part only published, also in the *Hansische Geschichtsblatter*. Jahrgang, 1912. Remainder is in the 7th vol. Abhandlungen zür Verkehrs und Seegeschichte. Karl Curtius. Berlin.

BROWNE, J. R. Etchings of a Whaling Cruise, with

notes of a Sojourn on the Island of Zanzibar. London, 1846. New York, 1850.

BULLEN, CHRISTIAN. Eines Seefahrenden Journal oder Tag-register, Was auff der Schiffahrt nach der Nordt-See und denen Insuln Groenlandt und Spitsbergen täglich vorgefallen im Jahr Christi 1667. Worin ausfuhrlich der Wallfischfang, deren Arth und Natur, auch andere in der See vorgefallene wunderbare Sachen eygentlich und natürlich beschrieben werden. Bremen, 1668.

BURFIELD, S. T. The Belmullet Whaling Station. Rept. British. Ass. Section D. Dundee, 1912.

Calendar of State Papers. (Further references in the text.)

CHAVANNE, KARPF und LE MONNIER. Die Literatur über die Polar-regionen der Erde. K. K. Geog. Gesell. Wien, 1878. (Contains on pp. 50 *et seq.* Bibliography of Polarfischerei und Jagd.)

CLEIRAC, ETIENNE. Us, et coustumes de la mer. Bordeaux, 1647. (Not in British Museum, in Bibliothèque Nationale, Paris.)

COLLECTION OF BOOKS, Pamphlets, Log Books, Pictures, etc., illustrating Whales and the Whale Fishery contained in the Free Public Library, New Bedford, Mass., U.S.A. Second edition, April, 1920.

COLNETT, J. A Voyage to the South Atlantic and round Cape Horn into the Pacific Ocean for the purpose of extending the Spermaceti Whale Fisheries and other objects of commerce, by Captain James Colnett of the Royal Navy, in the ship *Rattler*. London, 1798.

CONWAY, SIR W. M. Early Dutch and English Voyages to Spitsbergen. Hakluyt Society. London, 1904.

No Man's Land. A history of Spitsbergen from its discovery in 1596 to the beginning of the scientific

BIBLIOGRAPHY

exploration of the country. Cambridge Univ. Press, 1906.

CREVECOUR, ST JOHN. Letters from an American Farmer. London, 1782.

DEGENHARDT, W. Wandelingen in de bezielde schepping. Amsterdam, 1872.

DELANO, R. Wanderings and Adventures, being a narrative of twelve years life in a whaleship. 1846.

DELAVOIPIÉRE, ANTOINE. Faits relatifs à la pêche de la baleine. Havre, 1821.

DENMARK. Diplomatic and Consular Reports. Trade and Laws of the Faroe Isles. Foreign Office, London, May, 1903.

DUCÉRÉ, Ed. Dictionaire Historique de Bayonne. Commission des Archives Municipales. Ville de Bayonne. 2 vols. Bayonne, 1911.

Recherches historiques sur la Pêche de la Morue et la Decouverte de Terre-Neuve par les Basques et les Bayonnais. Pau, 1893. (Not in British Museum, in B.N.).

Histoire Maritime de Bayonne Les Corsaires sous l'ancien Regime. Bayonne, 1895. (Not in British Museum, in Bibl. Nat.).

DURO, CESAREO FERNANDEZ. La Marina de Castilla. Madrid, n.d.

ELKING, HENRY. A view of the Greenland Trade, and the whale fishery with the national and private advantages thereof. London, 1722.

ESCHELS, JENS JACOB. Lebensbeschreibung eines alten Seemannes. Altona, 1835.

L'ESPINE and DE LONG. De Koophandel van Amsterdam en andere Nederlandsche steden. Rotterdam, 1780. Amsterdam, 1801-2. 10th edn.

ESQUIROS, A. Nederland en het leven in Nederland. (From the French) Amsterdam, 1858. An English translation in 1863.

FAUCONNIER, P. Description historique de Dunkerque.

Ville maritime et port de mer très fameux dans la Flandre occidentale. Bruges, 1730.

FERNANDEZ DURO (CESAREO). La Marina de Castilla. Madrid, 1882.

FISCHER, F. C. J. Geschichte des Teutschen Handels, der Schiffahrt, Fischerei u.s.w. Hannover, 1793. 4 vols.

FISCHER, M. Cétacées du Sud-ouest de la France. Actes Soc. Linn. Bordeaux, 1881.

FORBES, ALLAN. Special Exhibition of Whaling Pictures from the collection of Allan Forbes, Esq. Peabody Museum, Salem, Mass., U.S.A.

FOTHERBY, ROBERT. Narrative of a Voyage to Spitsbergen . . . 1613 at the charge of the Fellowship of English Merchants for the Discovery of New Trades; commonly called the Muscovy Company. With a description of the country, and the operations of the whale fishery. American Antiq. Soc. Boston, 1860. (For other voyages of Robert Fotherby see Purchas, His Pilgrimes. Vol. III.)

GERRITSZ, VAN ASSUM (HESSEL). Histoire du pays nommé Spitsberghe Monstrant comment qu il est trouvée, son naturel et ses animauls, avecques la triste racompte des maux, que nos pecheurs tant Basques que Flamens, ont en a souffrir des Anglois, en l'esté passée, l'An de grace, 1613. Escrit par H. G. A. Et en apres une protestation contre les Angloys, et annulation de touts leurs frivols argumens, parquoy ils pensent avoir droict, pour se faire Maistre tout seul, dudict pays. Amsterdam, 1613. English translation. Hakluyt Soc. Early Dutch and English voyages to Spitsbergen. London, 1904.

GLOGER, C. W. L. Der Walfischfang und seine Beförderung in Deutschland als vaterlandische Zeitfrage in volkswirthschaftlicher, seemännischer und staatlicher Beziehung. Berlin, 1847.

GOODE, G. BROWNE. U.S. Commission of Fish and

BIBLIOGRAPHY 323

Fisheries. The Fishery Industries of the United States. Sec. I., Whale and Porpoises, pp. 7-32. Washington, 1884. Sec. V., Vol. II., The Whale Fishery, pp. 3-293. Washington, 1887.

GRAND D'AUSSY, LE. Histoire de la vie privée des Francais, depuis l'origine de la nation jusqu'a nos jours. Paris, 1782. 3 vols.

GRAY. The Manner of Whale Fishing in Greenland. Geog. Journal. London, 1900. P. 632.

GREENLAND. An Authentic Relation of a Voyage in 1772, of the *Volunteer* of Whitby. 1773.

HAKLUYT, RICHARD. The principal navigations voyages traffiques and discoveries of the English nation, made by sea or overland to the remote and farthest distant quarters of the earth at an time within the compasse the these 1,600 yeares. London, 1599.

Hakluyt Society. Vol. for 1855, see White *infra*. Vol. for 1904, see Conway *supra*.

Hakluytus Posthumus, or Purchas his Pilgrimes. Contayning a History of the world in sea voyages and lande-travels by Englishmen and others. London, 1625, 1626. 5 vols. Reprinted 1906.

HALDANE, R. C. Whaling in Scotland. Ann. Scot. Nat. Hist. April, 1905. July, 1906. January, 1907. April, 1908.

HAMILTON, J. ERIK. Report on the Belmullet Whaling Station. British Ass. Report for 1914.

HAMY, E. T. Les Francais au Spitsberg au 17e siecle (in Etudes historiques et geographiques. Paris, 1896).

HANSEN, LARENS. Accounts of the Whalers in the year 1777. Ribe, 1780.

HARRIS, RENDEL. The last of the *Mayflower*. Manchester Univ. Press, 1920.

HEUGLIN, TH. VON. Reisen nach dem Nordpolarmeer in den Jahren 1870 und 1871. Braunschweig. 1872. 2 vols.

HIJLKES, R. Merkwaardig verhaal van Reinier Hijlkes

als matroos met het schip; de hopende Visser, commandeur Volkert Janz. ten jare 1777 na Groenland . . . op de walvisvangst. Amsterdam, 1779.

HJORT, JOHANN. Fiskeri og hvalfangst i det nordlige Norge. Aarsberetning vedkommende Norges fiskerier for 1902. Bergen, 1902.

HONIJ JZN. JR., J. Historische, oudheid en letterkundige studien. Zaandijk, 1866.

HUNT, W. The Trade and Commerce of Hull and its Ships and Shipowners. Hull, 1878.

JANICON, F. H. Etat present de la Republique des Provinces-Unies, 1755. Dutch translation published at s'Gravenhage, 1732. 4 vols.

JANSEN. Notes on the ice between Greenland and Nova Zembla, being the results of investigations into the records of early Dutch voyages in the Spitsbergen seas. Proc. Roy. Geog. Soc. Vol. IX. London, 1864-5.

JANSEN, MARTEN. Kort, doch echt verhael wegens het verongelukken van zyn schip, genaemt; het Witte paard, en nog negen andere schepen, dewelke alle verongelukt zijn in Groenlandt ten jaere 1777. Waarby nog copia van een brief van commandeur Hidde Dirks Kat, aan zijn huisvrouw, geschreven uit straat Davis. Amsterdam, 1778. Another edition, Leeuwarden, 1778.

JANSSEN, JAC. Merkwürdige Reise, welcher mit dem schiffe die Frau Elisabeth den 7ten April nach Grönland auf den Wallfischfang gegangen u.s.w. Hamburg, 1770. Also in Dutch, Haarlem, 1770.

JONG, D. DE, KOBEL, H. and SALIETH, M. Nieuwe Beschryving der Walvischvangst en Haringsvisscherij. Amsteldam, 1791.

Journael of Dagh-Register gehouden by Seven Matroosen in haer Overwinteren op Spitsbergen, 1633-34, by Jacob Segersz. van Brugge. Amsterdam, 1634. 2nd edn. Amsterdam, 1635. Translated into English. Hakluyt Soc. Vol. XI., Ser. II. 1904.

BIBLIOGRAPHY 325

Journael ofte Beschrijvinge van de reyse ghedaen bij den Commandeur Dirk Albertsz. Raven, in den jare, 1639 (see under Raven).

KAT, H. D. Dagboek eener reize ter walvisch en robbenvangst gedaan in 1777 en 1778. Haarlem, 1818.

KÖHLER, FR. GOTTL. Reise ins Eismeer und nach den Küsten von Grönland und Spitsbergen im Jahre 1801, und Beschreibung der Wallfischfang. Leipzig, 1820.

KRÖGER. Historisch wahre Nachricht von dem Elend . . . des im J. 1777 . . . nach Grönland abgefahrenen . . . verungluckten Schiffe . . . Wilhelmina. Bremen, 1779.

KÜHN, JOHANN MICHAEL. Merkwürdige Lebens und Reisebeschreibung, dessen Schiffahrten nach Grönland und Spitsbergen. Gotha, 1741.

KÜKENTHAL. Articles in Deutsche Geographische Blätter. 1886. XV., p. 38. White Whale Fishery. 1888. P. 6. Bottlenose Whaling. 1890. XIII., p.14 Finmark Whaling.

LAING, JOHN. An account of a Voyage to Spitsbergen, containing a full description of that country, of the zoology of the North, and of the Shetland Isles, with an account of the whale fishery. London, 1815.

LAJONKIERE, P. DE. Des primes a la pêche. Journal des Economistes. 1852. XXXII., p. 330-7.

LAMBERT, J. M. Two thousand years of Guild Life. Hull, 1891.

LASPEYRES, E. Geschichte der Volkswirthschaftlichen Anschauungen der Niederlander. Preisschrift der Fürstlich Jablonowski'schen Gesellschaft. No. 11.

LECOMTE, J. Pratique de la pêche de la baleine dans les mers du Sud. Paris, 1833.

LESCARBOT, MARC. History of New France. The Champlain Society. Toronto. 3 vols. 1907-14. Whale Fishing in Vol. III., p. 241.

LINDEMAN, M. Die arktische Fischerei der Deutschen Seestädte. 1620-1868. Mitt. a. J. Perthes. Geog. Anst. Erganzungsband VI., 1869-71. Gotha, 1871.
 Die gegenwartige Eismeerfischerei und der Walfang. Bd. IV Abhandlungen des Deutschen Seefischerei Vereins. Berlin, 1899.

LINDSAY, DAVID MOORE. A Voyage to the Arctic in the whaler *Aurora*. London, 1911.

LÜDER, A. F. Geschichte des Hollandischen Handels. Leipzig, 1788. (An abbreviated translation of Lusac's Hollands Rykdom).

LUZAC, E. Hollandsch rykdom of tafereel van Neerlandsch Koophandel en zeevaart, behelzende deszelfs oorsprong, magt en toe neemende vermeerdering. 4 deels. Leiden, 1780-3.

McCULLOCH, J. R. A Dictionary of Commerce and Commercial Navigation. There are numerous editions. (My copy is dated, London, 1832.)

MANBY, G. W. A Journal of a Voyage to Greenland in 1821. London, 1822.

MANDT, M. W. Observations . . . in intinere Groenlandico factæ. 1822.

MARKHAM, A. H. A Whaling Cruise to Baffin Bay and the Gulf of Boothia. London, 1875.

MARSDEN, R. G. English ships in the Reign of James I. Roy. Hist. Soc. Trans. 1905. XIX., pp. 310-55.

MARTENS, F. Spitzbergische Reise-beschreibung. Hamburg, 1675. (English translations, 1694 and 1855. See under White).

MAURY, M. F. The Physical Geography of the Sea. London, 1863.

MICHEL, FRANCISQUE. Histoire du Commerce de Bordeaux. 2 vols. Bordeaux, 1867-70.

MOBIUS, K. Ueber den Fang und die Verwertung der Walfische in Japan. Mitt. der Sektion für Küsten und Hochseefischerei. 1894. No. 7.

MONCK, JOHN. Voyage to Greenland in 1619 and 1620.

Described in J. and A. Churchill's Collection of Voyages. Vol. I., p. 509. 1732. Also in Drie voyagien gedaen na Gröenlandt, printed by G. J. Saegham, Amsterdam, ? n.d.

Mooij, Marten. Journael van de reize naer Groenlandt, gedaen door commandeur M. Mooij met het schip *Frankendaal*. Amsterdam, 1787.

Morinière, Noel de la, S. B. J. Memoire sur l'antiquité de la pêche de la Baleine par les nations Européenes. Rouen (1833?).

    Memoire sur l'Antiquité de la pêche de la baleine. Paris, 1795.

    Histoire générale des pêches anciennes et modernes. 1815.

Muller, F. R. De Nederlandsche Geschiednis in platen. 5 vols. 1863.

Muller, Fz. S. Mare Clausum. Academisch proefschrift ter verkrijging van den Graad van Doctor in het Romeinsch en Hedendaagsch Recht. Amsterdam, 1872.

    Geschiednis der Noordsche Compagnie. Uitgegeven door het provinciaal Utrechtsch Genootschap van Kunsten en Wetenschappen. 1874.

Munroe, Henry. Statistics Relative to the Northern Whale Fisheries from 1772 to 1852. Rept. British Ass. Hull, 1853. Abbreviated from Journ. Statistical Soc., London. Vol. XVII., Pt. I. March, 1854. P. 34.

Nordhoff, Charles. Whaling and Fishing. Cincinnati, 1856.

Oelen, J. A. van. De seldsaame en noit gehoorde Walvischvangst, voorgevallen bij St Anna-Land, in tjaar 1682, den 7 October, mitsgaders eene pertinente beschryvinge van de geheele Groenlandse vaart, verhandeld in prose en versen. Nevens verscheïde saaken tot die materie dienende, door P.P. van S., met schoone kopere prentverbeeldinge versierd. Leyden, 1684.

OLMSTEAD, F. A. Incidents of a Whaling Voyage. New York, 1841.

PAZ GRAELLS, M. DE LA. Las Ballenas en las costas de Espana. R. Acad. de Ciencas. Tom. 13. Madrid, 1889.

PELLHAM, EDWARD. Gods power and providence shewed in the miraculous preservation and deliverance of eight Englishmen, left by mischance in Greenland Anno 1630, nine monthes and twelve days. London, 1631.

PITKIN, TIMOTHY. A statistical view of the Commerce of the United States of America, its connection with agriculture and manufactures, and an account of the Public Debt revenues and expenditure of the United States. Hartford, 1816.

POSSELT, K. F. Ueber den Grönländischen Walfischfang aus mündlichen Nachrichten Föhringer Seeleute gesamlet. Kiel, 1796.

PROWSE, D. W. A History of Newfoundland. 2nd. edn. London, 1896.

RAU, C. Prehistoric Fishing. Smithsonian Contribution to Knowledge. Vol. XXV. Washington, 1885.

RAVEN, DIRK ALBERTSZ. Journael ofte Beschrijvinge van de reyse ghedaen bij den Commandeur Dirk Albertsz. Raven, nae Spitsberghen, in den jare 1639, ten dienste vande E. Heeren Bewindt-hebbers van de Groenlandtsche Compagnie tot Hoorn. Waer in verhaelt wordt sijn droevighe Schipbreucke, syn ellende op t'wrack, en syn blijde verlossinge. Met noch eenighe ghedenckweerdige Historien. Alles waerdigh om te lesen. Hoorn, 1646.

REGUART, SANEZ. Diccionario historico de los artes de la pesca nacional. Madrid, 1791-5. 5 vols. 4to.

Report of the Departmental Committee on Whaling and Whale Curing in the North of Scotland. Vols. I. and II. Edinburgh, 1904.

Report of the Committee appointed by the Fishery Board

BIBLIOGRAPHY

for Scotland to inquire into the Scottish Whaling Industry. Edinburgh, 1920.

Report of the Interdepartmental Committee on Research and Development in the Dependencies of the Falkland Islands. Cmd. 657. 1920. London. H.M. Stationery Office.

RESTE, BERNARD DE. Histoire des Pêches, des decouvertes et des établissements des Hollandois dans les mers du Nord. Paris, 1801. (A translation of De Jong's Nieuwe Beschryving.)

RICHARDERIE, BOUCHER DE LA. Bibliothèque universelle des voyages. 6 vols. Paris, 1808.

RISTING, S. Hvalfangsten i 1912. Bergen, 1913. (Tillaeg til Norsk Fiskeritidendes Januarhefte 1913).

RONCIERE, CHARLES DE LA. Histoire de la marine française. 5 vols. (to 1920). Paris.

S. P. P. VON. See under Oelen.

SAINT-MAUR, FRANCOIS. Quelques mots sur la pêche de la baleine. Pau, n.d.

SALVESEN, T. E. The Whaling Industry of to-day. Journal Roy. Soc. of Arts. London. No. 3097. Vol. LX. March 29, 1912.

The Whale Fisheries of the Falkland Islands and Dependencies. Scott. Nat. Antarctic Expedn. Edinburgh, 1914.

SANTE, G. VAN. Alphabetische Naamlyst van alle de gronlandische en straat Davissche Commandeurs die zedert 1700 op Gronland en zedert 1719, etc. Haarlem, 1770.

SCAMMON, C. M. Marine Mammals of the North-western Coast of North America, with an account of the American Whale Fishery. 1874.

SCHERZER, K. VON. Das wirtschaftliche Leben der Völker. Ein handbuch über Production und Consum. Leipzig, 1885.

SCHNEIDER, J. G. Sammlung vermischter Abhandlungen zur Aufklarung der Zoologie und der Handelsgeschichte. Berlin, 1784. 8vo.

SCORESBY, W., JUN. An Account of the Arctic Regions, with a history and description of the Northern Whale Fishery. 2 vols. Edinburgh, 1820.

    Journal of a Voyage to the Northern Whale Fishery, including researches and discoveries on the eastern coast of West Greenland. Edinburgh, 1823.

SCOTT, W. R. The Constitution and Finance of English, Scottish and Irish Joint-stock Companies to 1720. Vol. II. Camb. U.P. 1910.

SEGERSZ, JACOB. See under Journael of Dagh-Register gehouden by Seven Matrosen.

Selden Society. Select Charters of Trading Companies. 1530-1707. Edited by C. T. Carr. Vol. XXVIII. 1913.

SMITHERS, HENRY. Liverpool, its Commerce, Statistics, etc. Liverpool, 1825.

SORALUCE Y ZUBIZARETTA, NICOLAS DE. Introduccion, capitulo i y ortas descriptiones de la memoria acerca del origen y curso de la pescas y pesquerias de ballenas y de bacalaos asi que sobre el descubriments de los bancos i isla de Terranova. Vitoria, 1878. 52 p. 8vo.

SPEARS, J. R. The Story of the New England Whalers. 1908.

STRADAVITS. Reyse ter walvis-vangst, rijmsgewijze beschreven door J. A. S. Chirurgijn op het schip Zaandijker Hoop. Antwerp, 1769.

TOWER, W. S. A History of the American Whale Fishery. Publications of the University of Pennsylvania. Series in Political Economy and Public Law. No. 20. Philadelphia, 1907.

UFFENBACH, C. VON. Merkwürdige Reisen durch Niedersachsen, Holland und England. 3 vols. Frankfurt und Leipzig, 1753.

United States, Foreign relations of, 1902. Whaling and sealing claims against Russia. Herbert H. D. Pierce. Counsel for the U.S.A. Washington, 1903.

VERRILL, A. H. The Real Story of the Whaler. New York, 1916.
VOS, MARCUS. Seine beschwerliche Reise nach Grönland. Lübeck, 1778.
WHITE, ADAM. A Collection of Documents on Spitsbergen. Hakluyt Society. London, 1855. (Contains a translation of Martens Spitzbergische Reisebeschreibung, 1675.)
WILKINSON, D. Whaling in Many Seas. 1905.
WITT, JAN DE. The true interest and political maxims of the Republic of Holland and West Friesland. London, 1702.
ZESEN, FILIPS VON. Beschriebung der stadt Amsterdam, darinnen von derselben ersten ursprunge bis auf gegenwartigen Zustand, ihr unterschiedlicher anwachs, herliche vorrechte, und in mehr als 70 Kupferstukken entworfene fuhrnemhste Gebeue, zusamt ihrem Stahtswesen Kaufhandel und ansehnlicher macht zur See, wie auch was sich in mit derselben markwurdiges zugetragen vor augen gestellt werden. Amsterdam, 1664.
ZORGDRAGER. Bloyende opkomst der Aloude en Hedendaagsche Groenlandsche Visschery waar in met eene geoffende ervaarenheit de geheele omflag deezer Visscherye beschreeven, en wat daar in deint waargenomen naaukeurig verhandelt wordt. Amsterdam, 1720. Another edition, s'Gravenhage, 1727. A third edition, Amsterdam, 1728.
Alte und neue Groenlandische Fischerei und Walfischfang. Leipzig, 1723. (A translation of the above.) Another German edition, Nürnberg, 1750.

INDEX

ADMIRAL, 95, 170
Adventure, whaler, 187
Alborough, 98
Ambergris, 42
American whale fishery, 223-55
Anderson, description of whaling, 147-50
Andrews, R. C., 30
Annula, whaler, 95, 98
Antarctic, whaler, 272-3
Arctic Right Whale, 16-17
Arctic, whaler, 9, 259-61
Aurora, whaler, 196, 326
Azores, whaling at, 250

BACSTROM, 192
Balæna antipodarum, 16
—— *australis*, 16, 29, 295
—— *biscayensis*, 16, 17, 26-28, 88
—— *japonica*, 16
—— *mysticetus*, 16, 24-26
—— *novæ-zealandiæ*, 16
Balænoptera borealis, 19, 45, 275, 293
—— *musculus*, 14, 45, 268, 275, 293
—— *rostrata*, 18
—— *sibbaldi*, 14, 19, 45, 293
" Baleinier," 62
Barents, 77-8
Barron, W., 257-8
Basques, 59-64, 66-7
Beale, 210, 215-20
Bearded Whale, 83
Beluga, 22
Bennett, 220-1
Blubber, 39, 43
Blue Whale, 14, 19
Bottlenose Whale, 20, 21, 269
Bounty system, 177-206, 231
Bowhead whale, 17, 24, 236
Brinner, L., 5
Bristol, 67, 75-6, 186-7, 315-6
Brown, 24

Browne, J. R., 250-1
Bullen, C., 202
Bunaveneader, 280-1
Burfield, S. T., 42

CACHALOT, 20
Ca'ing Whale, 21
Canadian Whaling Act, 55
Canning of whale meat, 252-3
Clayrac, 62, 64
Clio borealis, 24
Colnett, 210-15
Combine of whalers, 294, 300
Convoys, 170
Conway, 138-9

DAVIS STRAIT FISHERY, 168, 308
Delphinapterus leucas, 22, 49
Delphinidæ, 21
Departmental Committee on whaling in Scotland, 277-80
Desire, whaler, 95
Diana, whaler, 93
Ducéré, E., 60

Eclipse, WHALER, 269
Economics of whaling, 39-58
Edge's description of the fishery, 116-7
Elizabeth, whaler, 79-82, 88-93
Elking, 163-4
Ellingsen, J., 300
Empress of India, whaler, 257
Eschels, 175

FALKLAND ISLAND WHALING, 50-1, 285, 296-9
Faroes, 286-7
Fecundity of whales, 13
Finmark, 54, 267-8
Fin Whale, 14
Fischer, P., 61
Fitting out whalers, 72-3, 158-9
Flensing the whale, 43

INDEX

Flenslock, 161
Food, human, whales as, 252-53
Food of whales, 14, 24, 30, 31, 33, 270
Fortune, whaler, 109
Fotherby, R., 99, 102, 104
Four Brothers, whaler, 163
Foyn, S., 264
Frankendaal, whaler, 172
Frau Elizabeth, whaler, 172
French whaling, 133-5, 174, 221-2
Frisians, 173-6
Fritters, 153

Gamaliel, WHALER, 94, 98
German whalers, 172-6
Grace, whaler, 75-6
Grace-de-Dieu, whaler, 133
Grampus, 14
Grand Bay Whale, 64
Gray, description of whaling, 150-5
Greenland Company, 141, 144
Greenland Right Whale, 16, 24-26, 270-1.
Greenland, whaler, 200
Grey Whale, 15, 29-30, 243
Grindhval, 21, 268
Guldberg, 23

HARPOON GUN, 264-5
Harisse, H., 66
Hebrides, whaling at, 275-81
Herlofson, 42
Herring fishery and the whalers, 275-80
Hjort, J., 31
Hopewell, whaler, 90-93
Hull, 90-93, 145-6, 186, 193-6, 312, 317
Humpback Whale, 17, 30-37
Hvalfangerforening, 294, 300
Hyperoodon rostratus, 21

ICELAND, 135, 267, 287, 313
Interlopers, 93, 139, 142
Ireland, whaling in, 280-1

Jacques, whaler, 96, 133
James I. and the Dutch, 111-2
James, whaler, 188
Jan Mayen, 157, 161, 193
Jansen, 119
Jansen, M., 172

Janssen, J., 172, 202
Japan, whaling, 215-6, 242-3, 272, 285
John and Francis, whaler, 95, 98
Jonas im Walfisch, whaler, 156

KAT, H. D., 172
Kent, whaler, 215-20
Kerguelen, 289, 292, 313
Killer Whale, 14
Köhler, 199-205
Kokujira, 30
Kuhn, J. M., 172

Lady Forbes, WHALER, 188
Lagoda, whaler, 236-7
Lagoon whaling, 240
Laing, J., 191
Laspeyres, 171
Lays, in whaling, 251
Leems, 87-8
Lion, whaler, 188
Liverpool, 187-8
London, 93, 145, 192

MAAS BARTEN, 161
Making-off, 192
Manby, G. W., 188, 205
Marsden, R. G., 115
Martens, 155-7, 202
Maria, whaler, 236
Markham, 258-9
Mary Margaret, whaler, 79-82, 88-93
Matthew, whaler, 94
McCulloch, 208
Mediator, whaler, 213
Megaptera boops, 17, 30-37, 293, 295
"Mehavn Riots," 274
Migrations of whales, 22-38, 269
Mooi, M., 171
Morinière, N. de la, 59
Morses, 78
Müller, F., 5, 128, 316
Munroe, 312
Muscovy Company, 71, 79, 93, 131, 141, 143
Mystacoceti, 15

NANTUCKET, 224-31, 233-4, 237
Narwhal, 21, 270
Natal, 294

INDEX

Neobalæna marginata, 15
New Bedford, 228, 233-4, 236-7
Noah's Arke, whaler, 106
Noordsche Company, 126, 139
Nordcaper, 16, 26-28
Nordhoff, 250, 252
Norwegian whaling, 264-300, 313

ODONTOCETI, 15, 19
Olmstead, 250-1
Olsen, O., 34, 36
Oranje Boom, whaler, 130
Orca gladiator, 14
Otta Sotta, 85

PACIFIC WHALING, 211-21
Paré, A., 62
Pay, rates of, 159, 189
Physeteridæ, 20
Physeter macrocephalus, 20, 45, 208, 281, 309
Pilot Whale, 21, 268
Plans of whaling steamer, 265-6
Pleasure, whaler, 109
Port Books, 316-7
Portuguese colonies, 296
Posselt, 172-3

QUALITY OF WHALE OIL, 44
Quantity of whale oil from different whales, 45
Quatre - fils - Aymon, whaler, 133

Rattler, WHALER, 212-5
Rape seed, 68-9, 146
Raven, D. A., 130
Reguart, S., 211
Regulation of whaling, 51-8, 274-85, 295-6
Rhachianectes glaucus, 15, 29-30
Richard and Barnard, whaler, 95
Right Whales, 16
Ris, C., 170
Rising Sun, whaler, 192
Risting, 34
Rorquals, 18, 19
Rousseau, whaler, 236
Rudolphi's Rorqual, 19

Saint Andrew, WHALER, 187
Saint Peter, whaler, 109-11

Salamander, whaler, 109
Sarah and Elizabeth, whaler, 219
Sarda, 64, 65, 83
Scammon, 246
Schiemann, 159, 175, 260
Scoresby, 39, 69, 191, 209
Sea Horse, whaler, 93, 192
Sedeva, 85
Sedeva negro, 86
Segersz, J., 118
Sei Whale, 19
"Sewria," 22, 86
Shetlands, whaling at, 275-80
Sibbald's Whale, 18-19
"Skeljungr," 31
Slupsteven, 160
Smeerenburg, 126, 128, 129, 130, 192
Southern Right Whale, 17
Southern whale fishery, 207-22
South Sea Company, 180-3
Spermaceti, 40
Sperm Whale, 20, 208
Spitsbergen fishery, 70-176
Statistics, American, 238, 248
———, British, 209, 306, 307
———, Dutch, 197, 308
———, Falkland Island, 51, 297
———, Hull, 312
———, Ireland, 281
———, Norwegian, 268
———, Scotland, 271, 309-11
Swan, J. G., 253

Thomasine, WHALER, 102
Thorsvig, whaling station at, 300
Tigre, whaler, 94, 98
Toothed whales, 15
Traan, 39
Train oil, 39
Triton, whaler, 236
Troil, Von, 86-7
Truelove, whaler, 194-6, 258
Trumpa, 83
Tuscan, whaler, 220-1

UFFENBACH, 139
United States whale fisheries, 223-55
Untermaas barten, 161

VAL, 160
Value of whales, 268, 270
Vanhöffen, 22

INDEX

Vice-Admiral, 94-5
Vliéland, 78
Volunteer, whaler, 188
" Voorganger," 160
Vrolicq, 134-5

WALRUS, 78
" Whalebone," 40
Whalebone Whales, 15
Whale, whaler, 93
Whaling steamer plans, 265-6
Whitby, 186, 188-91

White Whale, 22, 49, 267, 270-1
Witt, J. de, 164
Witte Paard, whaler, 172

YARMOUTH, 141, 145
Yield of oil from whales, 45, 293
York, 141, 145
York, whaler, 193

ZESEN, F. VON, 138
Zorgdrager, 127, 157-61, 308